SERIOUSLY
DELISH

SERIOUSLY DELISH

• 150 RECIPES FOR PEOPLE WHO TOTALLY LOVE FOOD •

JESSICA MERCHANT

HOUGHTON MIFFLIN HARCOURT

BOSTON • NEW YORK • 2014

Library of Congress Cataloging-in-Publication Data available upon request.

ISBN 978-0-544-17649-2 (cloth); 978-0-544-17653-9 (ebk)

Printed in China

C&C 10 9 8 7 6 5 4 3 2 1

For my mom,

who taught me about bacon.
And therefore, taught me about life.

contents

acknowledgments

To my invisible internet friends, the readers on my blog, the eyeballs on that little corner I've created on the web. You are my friends, my community, my soul mates, and my muse. You make every day better and inspire me to grow as a person, a cook, and a writer. My life would be unchanged had you not entered it. I LOVE YOU.

To Eddie, *the love of my life.* Thank you for eating the meals I make night after night, when I know that you'd much prefer some "regular" food like spaghetti and meatballs or cheeseburgers without all the fancy stuff. Without you, I'd be a lot more irrational and a lot less loved. You complete me, Jerry Maguire style.

To Lacy, *the taster of many foods,* the deliverer of many iced coffees, and the listener of many meltdowns. You teach me how to be a friend, but most importantly, where all the best restaurants are. You're the best faux sister there is. P.S. Thanks for letting me jack your chicken pita recipe for the book.

To my family and friends. I apologize for forcing all of my leftovers on you every single day of your lives. Thank you for always eating every last crumb and telling me when things "totally suck" or "are the best ever." And of course, for your constant love and support. Always.

To Stacey Glick, *my agent and friend.* Thank you for helping me put my thoughts into words, my ideas into stories, and my dreams into a manuscript. And for introducing me to the pretzel croissant at City Bakery. OMG.

To my editor, Justin, *and the entire team at Houghton Mifflin Harcourt.* Thank you for believing in my vision for this book, supporting my occasionally nonsensical made up words, and helping my foodie dreams come true in book form.

To my grandmothers, Lois and Virginia, *two hugely influential women in my life* who now look down on me from heaven. I hope to carry your legacy throughout the rest of my life. You showed me the true meaning of strength and elegance.

introduction

So hi.
I put things in a book for you!
. . . where should we start?

. . . .

For as long as I can remember, my world has revolved around good food.

I grew up in a house where my mom cooked dinner nearly every single night. Every.single.night. Super lucky, I know. These days, the mere thought of making dinner for a family of five or more makes me shudder, and I don't even have children yet.

Heck, I don't even have a pet to feed.

The apple didn't fall far from the tree, though. My mom grew up in a house where ***homemade dinners*** were on the table every evening. Her mom, whom my dad (lovingly, of course) nicknamed Mother Lovett, wasn't so much of a cook as she was a baker. The woman didn't touch an onion until the 1980s and used tons of packaged goods, even forgoing real whipped cream for her beloved boxed Dream Whip. For some households, like the ones where 80-year-old Italian grandmas spent the entire day making meatballs, sauce, and even noodles from scratch, this was practically considered a sin.

Her food was still delicious. But I think that's a requirement of grandmas or something, right? ***Years of love*** are poured into a recipe. She was always cooking for someone—her siblings, my mom, my aunt, her husbands. Yes, plural. She married brothers—at separate times, of course. Like, she married one, became a widow, and then married the other . . . but that's another story for another day.

That's kind of where it all began. It's the basis for how I ended up talking about my favorite treats on the World Wide Web to a bunch of my invisible Internet friends. It wasn't my only influence, however. I was quite possibly one of the luckiest people on earth, being able to share more than 25 of my years with TWO incredible grandmothers. My dad's mom, my Grandma Lois, was the absolute epitome of class. When it came to entertaining and hosting guests, she did so with an elegant simplicity that I have never seen anywhere else. She was known for having the perfect spread of snacks set out the minute you arrived—a few crackers and cheese, a bowl of pretzels and nuts, white wine and cocktails already chilled. There was never too much— never enough to get full on before dinner. It was just the right amount.

Her table was always impeccably set. There were place cards where our names were scribbled with her unmistakable penmanship. We used her wedding crystal to drink ice water, and she had multiple mini salt and pepper shakers scattered on the table. After dinner, chocolate mints were always served from a ***local (and fabulous)*** chocolatier here in Pittsburgh—Sarris Candies—and to accompany dessert we had demitasse served in flowered china cups that she collected over the years and displayed on a shelf in her dining room. If it sounds pretentious, I promise you it was anything but. It wasn't even overly fancy, but it made you feel special. Seriously, that woman's picture should be in the dictionary under the word *lady*. When Grandma Lois passed away suddenly in 2009, it felt like my heart was being ripped from my chest. I still had so many things to learn from her! And that's when I decided that she had already taught me many of the important things. I wanted to be exactly like her and ***carry on her traditions.*** I wanted to make others feel extraordinary while sharing a meal.

But backing up for a minute, if there is one important thing to know about me, it's this: I always really liked the taste of food.

That sounds ridiculous. I know. It's so true, though. I loved how food tasted, with the exception of some vegetables, but I chock that up to my mom being raised in the whole packaged-food-era thing and mostly passing on what she knew. I've kinda grown to enjoy the green stuff, but , , , meh. Not sure if I will ever have the vegetable adoration now that I would have had I been introduced to farm-fresh spinach or broccoli as a tween.

So, the food?

It just always tasted delicious. I realize those are two poorly described clichés right there and that you are probably thinking, "Man, somebody please get this chick a thesaurus." But it's the best way I can describe it from the heart.

The Food. It Tastes Good.

Like many of you lucky ones, for me food was associated with warm loving memories—nostalgic holiday family gatherings, Sunday afternoons post-church, Monday night tacos, and even the occasional **Happy Meal** or drugstore hot dog that my dad treated us to on Friday night when my mom went out with her card club. Who still get together, by the way. They haven't played cards in nearly 30 years, though, probably after realizing that cocktails and dessert were just as fun. If not better.

See? It all comes down to sharing a meal.

Regardless of what I was eating in those early years, whether it was watermelon or mac and cheese from a blue box, I loved it. I adored going to the grocery store with my mom, walking up and down those aisles and just seeing all of the . . . possibilities. We would be there for hours. I mean really hours on end. I wasn't into stuffed animals or **Barbie dolls or trolls** (okay, maybe trolls) or whatever else was trendy in the '80s. I distinctly remember going to the zoo when I was eight or nine years old with a friend from elementary school. Her older sisters drove us and afterward, as we shopped around in the zoo gift store with the few dollars our moms had given us, she walked out with a puffy lion of some sorts and I walked out with one of those brightly colored, twisted lollipops that is nearly a foot long. The sisters just rolled their eyes.

I don't think that was a compliment by any means, but it was disturbingly fitting, given how I'd spend the little money I had throughout the next 15 years.

Mother Lovett was the first to really instill in me a love for being in the kitchen. I find that loving food and loving to cook are two separate things—things that may be brought together by necessity but, if you're lucky, are more so brought together by intense passion. I don't think we ever cooked a savory meal together. I watched her make chicken soup from a box and seasoning packet a few times and then was even more astonished when she **BUTTERED HER RITZ CRACKERS** (I'm pretty sure my father-in-law butters his crackers as well, and now . . . I find it incredibly endearing) and dipped them in the broth, but our time together was mainly spent baking.

Early on I thought I was a baker, but the truth was that I just happen to have the sweetest teeth ever. We call it the "Green gene," Mother Lovett's maiden name and, from what we know, a curse placed upon multiple generations of women for loving their sugar. Seriously, it's quite possible that I could survive on a diet of high-quality chocolate for breakfast, cheesecake for lunch, and **brownies** for dinner, and freaking love it. Maybe some chocolate-covered potato chips in there to get my salt fix? It's in the genes, people.

The long baking days with Mother Lovett happened around the holidays, as it stereotypically went. I'd spend an entire day with her baking chocolate chip cookies, peanut butter blossoms, food-coloring-tinted coconut thumbprints, and glazed orange cookies—my mom's favorite. She'd make chocolate fudge, often putting walnuts in a batch and then layering butterscotch fudge in another batch, even though we always told her that only 75-year-olds and up enjoyed walnuts and **butterscotch**, and couldn't she just do something with peanut butter?

She didn't care.

As the years dwindled down, our bake fests turned more into me having to convince her that yes, the timer did go off and no, you didn't hear it because you are legally deaf and yes, these cookies are done—well, OVERdone—and no, you can't tell because you're also legally blind. Trust me, Gram.

She never did. (She also didn't believe us the morning we picked her up for church and informed her that she had penciled in her eyebrows with a mauve **lip liner** instead of her brow pencil, but eh. Whatever. Memories!)

I find it morbidly fitting that at 88 years old, Mother Lovett had a heart attack while hand-mixing the batter for her coconut-orange cake. She was alone at the time, and while it didn't kill her, it was the beginning of the end, and she never made it back into her own kitchen after that. Frankly, I can't get over that she was baking a cake when it happened and that's actually quite . . . comforting. It was so HER.

Let's Hang On to What We've Got

When I first started seeing my husband, Eddie, he was the first boy I dated who didn't live at home with his parents. Before that I had dabbled in cooking a few dishes, once making shrimp scampi for my dad and brothers and obviously killing it in the grilled cheese and quesadilla arenas, but since I lived at home, I didn't always have full rein in my **parents' kitchen.** I handled the baking, but not the cooking. It wasn't until I realized what this new guy was eating— plain egg whites tossed with whole wheat pasta (no seasoning, no olive oil, no Parmesan, no nothing) and dried-out turkey burgers (again, completely plain???) made on a countertop grill—that I knew there was nooooo way I was living like that if things progressed. We weren't cohabitating, but even if I was going to spend some time at his place after work? I certainly wasn't eating anything like that. Call me high maintenance, but nothing gets in the way of my meals and me. I gotta love them.

And that's the thing: I've always had to eat what I love. Always. There is rarely an exception to that rule of mine, and I just wasn't down with what he ate every night.

The good news? Neither was he. He didn't want to eat those boring meals, but they were born out of necessity, a heavy workload, and, well . . . bachelorism. Is that a thing? It is now. He was quite possibly the biggest bachelor I've ever met—not in the way you are thinking, besides the life-size poster of Christina Aguilera in her "Dirrty" costume (hey, it was the early 2000s) plastered on his fridge—and his culinary choices showed it.

I dived right in. The first few meals I made for us were chicken saltimbocca, homemade BBQ sauce and pulled pork piled high on nachos, chicken enchiladas, and **whole wheat pizza.** Giada and Ina were my new best friends. We were tight.

(I definitely also bought this gorgeous flank steak and, left to my own devices, used that countertop grill—and charred the daylights out of it. Blackened steak, my dear? He still ate it.)

Spoiler alert! We got hitched.

I was cooking all the time! It was great! Lots of exclamation points needed. Friends and family jokingly (but not so much) warned me that if I started cooking from the get-go, he'd always expect it, **blab blab blab.** I didn't care. The thing about cooking for me was that I yearned to share it with those I loved. It's all I wanted. I used his limited palate as my muse, trying to see how far I could push the boundaries on weeknight recipes. I was ambitious. Freakishly so.

But.

I had a full-time job and soon enough, cooking every single night actually proved to be **. . . tiring.** I was finding myself getting burnt out on my absolute favorite hobby. I felt old.

Enter my own personal necessity: quick and easy meals. Quick and easy meals that were sometimes healthy and sometimes not. Quick and easy meals that occasionally tasted as if they had been cooking all day. Quick and easy meals that were fresh, quick and easy meals that were comforting and warm and not straight from a box or a freezer. "Quick and easy" became my mantra.

By the time late 2009 rolled around, I had somewhat of a system down. I knew enough about cooking to throw together my own dishes (some obviously terrible) and learned through **trial and error** and long flip-out sessions with my mom. I was stuck in a job that I always dreaded, and cooking was one of the only parts of my day that I truly enjoyed. I had found a way to have my cake and eat it too.

Sort of literally. Sort of not.

And it was there, one day at that job, where I stumbled upon this thing called a blog. I was so removed from the idea of blogs or personal Web sites, ignorantly assuming since high school that they were basically online diaries that emo girls wrote their feelings in to get attention. I had previously regarded them as weird and maybe even nerdy. I knew nothing about them.

And so I started my own.

Oddly enough, I never intended for my own blog to be strictly about food. Food was such a large part of my life, but it was just . . . there. I loved it so much that it just WAS. It existed. I don't even know if I had an active camera at the time—it was really a tiny piece of junk I'd bought at **Target** one day after dropping (read: smashing) my camera on the dance floor when I drank one too many mojitos at a wedding. And I totally had a little bit of distraught emo girl inside of me, so I figured I would just write about life and my love for James Taylor and spending summers in northern Michigan and maybe, maaaaaybe some food? I really wasn't sure.

But as it turns out, my life was ***incredibly boring.*** I sat at a desk from eight to five, something that from the early age of eight I swore I'd never do, and my husband worked long hours. Apparently reading about someone sitting at work all day is not that exciting, nor is writing about it. So I started talking about dinners I'd made the night before, banana bread I'd bake on the weekends, and some of the workouts I would do. Years prior I had been a certified personal trainer, but the thing was that I still loved all food. And I mean ALL food.

People didn't get it. They still don't. I don't know how else to explain it: I like to exercise, I always have. But I love food. All of it. The more flavor, the better. The more calories, the better! Okay. Not always. Just kidding. Sort of.

But that's that. It is what it is, and I love both. I can't live a life surrounded by only salads and steamed vegetables with a bit of seasoning and egg white omelets and no carbs but sweet potatoes. I would legitimately die (drama). And just because I love to work out and sweat every day, I'm not wired to stop eating all-purpose flour and butter and the occasional dollop of Cool Whip at my parents' house.

"Cooking Well Doesn't Mean Cooking Fancy." —JULIA CHILD

It is annoyingly cliché but true: **Moderation is my life.**

This Web site thing turned into something I didn't expect. I was obsessed with the community that we—myself and those visiting—created on my site. To say it saved my life probably wouldn't be an exaggeration, but if you haven't noticed, I am quite dramatic, soooo yeah. I wanted it to be personal. To be authentic. To just be me. It was my outlet and my hobby and eventually, my job.

The fact is that sometimes your twenties can, for lack of a better word, suck. Even when things are really good. Friends change, and you feel like you should be *"finding yourself"* but you have no idea how to do so. Nothing terrible or out of the ordinary happened in my twenties, except for a wide variety of growing pains that I hope inflicted some sort of wisdom that will blossom in another 30 years. And while my twenties were sucking, I developed this group of invisible Internet friends that I could talk to every single day, this group that got me through it. After blogging for a few months, I determined that I wanted my site to be a place where I could talk about whatever I wanted—the kinds of food I liked, the recipes I made—and just be myself. I wanted to make what I wanted to make and luckily, as it turned out, most people wanted what I wanted.

I finally felt like **I fit in somewhere** and that I had "friends" who understood me. I was discovering who I was and, more important, who I wanted to be.

If we are fortunate enough, some of us grow up in a home where we learn that real, fresh food, cooked by you or me or him or her, is best. And while I learned that lesson growing up, like most lessons, it comes down to experience before you actually grasp such a thing. My twenties were incredibly life-changing when it came to this topic. Yes, when I was 16 and got my driver's license, I was amazed that I could go through a Wendy's drive-thru and get a cheeseburger without having to ask my mom and be rewarded with a big, fat NO. But regardless of what I did in those days—those wonderful metabolism days when eating fast food at 4PM before an actual meal at night was no big deal—I almost always ended up at home that evening for dinner. At home for a warm, freshly made meal that didn't come wrapped in paper or a **Happy Meal box.**

My twenties were a different story, though. For the first time, I realized that I could eat a sleeve of Oreos or a bag of pretzels for dinner and no one would stop me. No one would even see me, and actually . . . no one might even care. In fact, some (I'm looking at you, Kelly) may even encourage it—like my friends in college who also wanted to grab Easy Mac and Twizzlers for dinner because lying in bed watching *Dawson's Creek* was a million times more important than making a meal and having to clean it up. It was one of many moments in my life, but perhaps the first, where I had to learn real discipline. Where I had to be, ugh, a grown-up.

And the thing was that eating that stuff? Made me feel like garbage when I really thought about it. But it was EASY. It was simple, less time-consuming, and played right into my lazy collegiate soul.

But something had to give. While I knew how to make a large handful of dishes thanks to my family, I wanted something new. Something different. I would try some boring, "healthy" standbys that I would find in magazines, and while they got the job done, they never wowed me.

There is no exact science as to how I began cooking my own recipes—but that's just it: I started. If you want to learn how to cook and how to put your own spins on dishes, like anything else you just have to START.

After marriage and a full-time job came into play, something else had to give. If I wanted to maintain any **semblance of sanity,** meals HAD to be easy. But they had to taste good, too.

These simple and easy meals became serious lifesavers. Even if you love to spend time in the kitchen, chances are that after work, on those long weekdays when everyone is exhausted, you have to do grown-up chores and maybe even run the kids to soccer or dance practice, and there just isn't any time. Or there is a little time, but it's precious. And the drive-thru is a hard habit to break.

Making meals at home is important to me for a number of reasons. Nutrition plays a large role. You can make and eat things that make you feel good. You can even make that cheeseburger at home instead of grabbing fast food. At least you know what goes into it and you can use sustainable and maybe even *local ingredients.* Because of this, it often makes it easier to make healthy decisions afterward. As someone who has definitely fallen prisoner to the "I just ate pizza, may as well wash it down with some ice cream!" philosophy, eating a balanced dinner helps squash that.

Another huge thing for me? Variety. It's the key to staving off boredom. Don't you eventually just feel like all fast foods or meals out taste the same? I know I do. Finally, sitting down and eating a meal together is something that is so taken for granted. I want to do whatever I can to make that happen, and preparing a quick meal is often the answer.

This is the reason that many of the recipes I've included here can be made in *20 to 45 minutes,* maybe less. Definitely less if you're an experienced cook or can prep ahead of time. And as annoying as it feels on Sunday afternoon, a few minutes of prepping some stuff for breakfast or dinner each week is a huge time-saver. You will never regret doing it. Get in the habit, make the time. Like most people, I don't love to spend hours and hours in the kitchen on dinner, but I sort of want it to taste like I did.

You may also find a handful of dishes that take a bit longer to cook, but they are completely worth it. I promise.

Oh oh oh, I've also included a chapter dedicated to some of my favorite meals that are meant to be eaten with friends or shared on special occasions. You know. *Celebrations.* Like maybe a random Wednesday night? Live it up.

What's a Food Philosophy?

When it comes to my take on food, I like to think "the more the better." No, not necessarily quantity . . . but variety.

I eat everything.
Absolutely everything.

Okay, with the exception of fennel seeds. Really not a fan.

In the past 15 years, I have experienced numerous ways of eating. I am completely grateful for this because it has allowed me to *nourish my relationship with food.*

For years, I worked around individuals who condoned cutting out entire food groups—just for normal, everyday people. In my teens and early twenties, I fell victim to all sorts of ways of eating, mostly ones trumpeted in the media. Five years ago, I participated in a fitness competition that required 10 to 12 weeks of rotating carbohydrates and didn't allow foods such as apples and yogurt. It was completely bananas. Pun intended. I respect it for others, but so not for me.

I was lucky to grow up in a household with an incredibly healthy mindset that created the base for my food beliefs. My dad has always been super-active: *exercising daily* and inspiring me to start in my teens. While my mom thinks that whole wheat anything tastes horrible and eagerly slathers softened butter on her white bread when making a sandwich, she has the healthiest mindset I know. She is a woman who can bake a batch of brownies and let them sit on the counter for two weeks, enjoying only one per day and savoring every bite. It's ridiculously motivating and encouraging.

As we must, I grew up. I became increasingly aware of what I was putting in my body in my twenties and, for the first time, really determined the kinds of foods that made me feel good. I started experimenting with different flavors and forcing myself to eat vegetables, because after 25 years of loathing them, there was just no other way. Gotta be an adult.

As I approached my thirties and came more into my own, I realized that I could never successfully cut something out of my diet and be happy. And

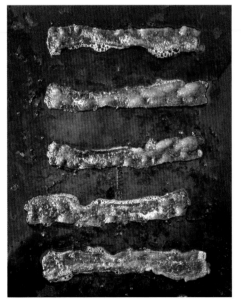

that's what I believe: the good old ***"absolutely everything in moderation."***
It is the reason that you will see butter, all-purpose flour, and granulated sugar in my recipes. But it is also the reason that you will find plenty of organic coconut oil, whole wheat flours, honey, and ground flaxseed. I don't discriminate. Unless again, your name begins with an "f" and ends with "ennel seed."

This is what works for me and is one of the keys to my personal happiness. When you love food as much as I do—when you are passionate about flavors to the point of insanity—you find a way to make everything work. For me, that means if I crave a burger twice in one week? Maybe one of those days I will (perhaps begrudgingly) swap the ***fries for a salad*** and keep the bacon off my burger. But you can bet that the other burger will be loaded and I may even dip a few fries in my milk shake. Maybe have a green juice for breakfast the next day or a peanut butter and banana smoothie? I'll do what I have to do. This is also why you will find a chapter of **slightly lightened-up** desserts here in this little book. Obviously, I am not going to give you a recipe for an apple sliced with cinnamon. But a whole wheat blueberry cake or a crumble made with oats and coconut oil? That I can do.

While eating this way may not work for you personally, that's the beauty in **learning to cook**. You put your own spin on meals. You make them work for you. You make you happy first. I hope you can take some of the recipes here and do what you need to do: Use them to your advantage. Make them your own. Let them inspire you.

Why I Can't Live Without Bacon

(Wait. Is this seriously a question?)

My Must-Haves

Or, things in my pantry that you might think are weird.

This list is by no means conclusive, but it contains some seemingly untraditional items that I use frequently. I believe they should be in everyone's pantry or fridge. Love 'em.

ALMOND MILK: Never being a huge fan of milk growing up, I was elated to find unsweetened vanilla almond milk a few years ago. I do not avoid dairy, but when it comes to using milk in cereal or shakes, I love almond milk and coconut milk the most. I also have success replacing cow's milk with almond milk in most baked goods.

CANNED COCONUT MILK: Both light and full-fat versions are weekly staples for me. I use them in smoothies, in coffee, in cereal, in baking, and almost anywhere else that calls for milk. Again, if you are a coconut hater, you really cannot taste much coconut flavor here—especially in baked goods. You will find that many of my recipes call for coconut milk. If you do not have it readily available, whole milk, half-and-half, or heavy cream is usually the best substitute.

COCONUT OIL (EXTRA-VIRGIN, REFINED): This is such a multitasking ingredient that it's impossible NOT to have it. Not only do I constantly cook and bake with it, but I also even use it as moisturizer. Yes. Like on my skin. Makes you want to lick your arm. As a note, using it to sauté fish or chicken, or baking with it, does not flavor your food with coconut. Fabulous.

GRAPESEED OIL: Roasting veggies is a surefire way for me to get my veg on, and I like to roast at high temps. Mostly because I am the most impatient person in the world. I find that grapeseed oil works a little better than olive oil when it comes to roasting above 425°F. I also occasionally use it in baking.

OTHER RANDOM OILS: I also keep olive oil, canola or vegetable oil, and toasted sesame oil on hand at all times.

SMOKED PAPRIKA: By far my favorite spice. So versatile.

WHOLE FLAXSEED: I love using ground flaxseed as a healthful addition to baked goods, in smoothies, or sprinkled on cereal and yogurt. Freshly ground flaxseed provides the most nutritional value, so I suggest purchasing a spice grinder if you can. If you buy already ground flaxseed, be sure to store it in the fridge after it's opened.

WHOLE WHEAT PASTRY FLOUR: Nearly all of my favorite baked goods are baked with whole wheat pastry flour these days. It is one of my most used ingredients. You should be able to find it in your local grocery store in the organic or health food section. My favorite brand is Bob's Red Mill.

WHOLE WHEAT FLOUR: I use this for "sturdier" baked goods, such as pizza crusts or bread recipes. I don't love it in cookies or muffins—I feel like it is a bit too dry and grainy.

OTHER RANDOM FLOURS: While I know hoarding flour can be nearly impossible unless you have a giant kitchen, I find that having white whole wheat flour and cake flour on hand is a good idea. I also occasionally use oat flour; however, you can create your own by grinding old-fashioned rolled oats in a food processor.

UNSWEETENED FLAKED COCONUT: If the squeaky-teeth texture of coconut has always freaked you out, but you enjoy the flavor, try to find a flaked unsweetened version. It may do the trick!

THREE FAVORITE BEVS INSIDE MY FRIDGE: I clearly talk about food a lot and enjoy creating cocktails, but as for what I love to drink with my favorite dishes other than boozy concoctions?

Coconut water: It's certainly a love-or-hate beverage, and I will admit that at first taste, coconut water was not my cup of tea. It just tasted . . . wet. However, I find that it is an acquired taste, similar to coffee or wine, and now I love it. My favorite is a raw version (the "hard" stuff, in coconut water language), and I enjoy drinking it straight or adding it to smoothies. And the occasional cocktail. Oops.

Kombucha: This is a fermented type of tea and, again, is an acquired taste. Since I enjoy very tart, briny things like vinegars, olives, and pickles, I am all over kombucha. I love the fruit-infused versions the most.

Fruit-infused still or sparkling water: On rare days when I feel slightly bored with regular water or want to try and impress my friends, I love infusing it with a bit of fruit. Try doing this the night before and sticking a pitcher in the fridge. It's gorgeous too. Some of my favorite combos?

- sliced cucumbers and strawberries
- blueberries and fresh mint
- watermelon, lime, and fresh basil
- orange slices and raspberries

Quick & Dirty Tips That Make Life Taste Better

This is how I do stuff, and yes, it might be wrong.

Browning Butter

You just need to know now: I am thoroughly obsessed with brown butter. I am a brown butter freak. You are going to see a bajillion plus one (or, maybe like 10) recipes in this book with brown butter. If you're not a brown butter fan (WHAT?), then you can simply leave it out of the recipe (if it calls for a drizzle) or just use regular, non-browned butter!

To brown butter, all you do is add it to a saucepan over medium-low to medium heat. I have used room temperature butter and cold butter—both work fine. Once the butter melts, continuously whisk it until little brown bits appear on the bottom of the pan. For ease, it is useful to brown butter in a stainless-steel skillet or something that allows you to see the brown bits easily. The minute those brown bits appear, remove the skillet from the heat. Continue to stir for about 30 seconds, then do with it what you may.

You can also store it in the fridge to use at a later date.

Reduce Your Balsamic

Thick and syrupy balsamic vinegar takes sweet and savory dishes to the next level. Have you had it on strawberries? How about fresh mozzarella? How about on ice cream? Don't look at me that way.

To make your own, heat 2 cups of high-quality balsamic vinegar in a saucepan over low to medium heat. Cook until the mixture reduces by half, then remove it from the heat and allow it to cool completely. As it cools, it will thicken even more. To make a slightly sweeter glaze, whisk in 2 tablespoons honey or brown sugar before reducing. Tip: Don't sniff the vinegar as it reduces. Yikes.

Toasting Nuts

There is no quicker way to add some delicious flavor to a salad or side dish than with a little garnish of toasted almonds or pecans. I like to toast nuts quickly on the stovetop since I am one of little patience. I simply add the nuts (whole, sliced, or chopped) to a skillet and heat over low to medium heat. Shake the pan or toss the nuts with a heatproof spatula for 5 to 8 minutes, until golden and fragrant. Remove them quickly so they don't burn.

Toasting Coconut

Toasting that little flake is like heaven to me, a coconut fiend. Add sweetened or unsweetened flaked or shredded coconut to a skillet and heat over low heat. Stir constantly for 5 to 6 minutes, until the coconut is evenly golden and fragrant. Use as you wish.

I have successfully stored toasted coconut in a sealed container in my pantry and fridge for up to 2 weeks. You don't want to know how long Mother Lovett kept it in her fridge. . . .

Freeze Bananas to Make Your Life Easier

Okay, for as much as I have a distaste for vegetables? I am the complete opposite with fruit. It's like all my love for produce was taken up by berries and apples and oranges, oh my. And there just wasn't enough love to go around for the green stuff. Frozen bananas are one of my staples when it comes to having weekly snacks and desserts on hand.

Simply remove the peel and slice the bananas into ½-inch rounds. Place them in a resealable plastic freezer bag, making sure to push all the air out. Freeze until frozen . . . duh.

Frozen bananas can be used in smoothies (like my Banana Macaroon Smoothie on page 52) for some sweetness and milk shake–like texture. You can also whip frozen bananas in your food processor for a little banana "ice cream." And as far as I know, you can thaw frozen bananas and use them in breads and cakes just as you would with regular ripe bananas.

Make Your Own Panko

Panko bread crumbs have changed the way I cook many things. The crunch! Oh the crunch. It's just so good. Panko gives so much more texture than the more commonly known fine bread crumbs, and if you use whole wheat bread? Super health food.

To make your own, preheat your oven to 300°F. Take a few slices of bread and cut them into strips. Fit your food processor with the shredder attachment and feed the bread into the processor. It will come out thicker and flakier than

regular crumbs. Spread the panko out on a nonstick baking sheet and bake for 6 to 8 minutes, tossing every 2 minutes or so. You don't want the crumbs to brown; you just want them crispy. Add in a few shakes of dried basil, thyme, and oregano and before you know it: seasoned panko!

Cook Your Own Beans

I KNOW. Canned beans are so easy to grab, and if you can find organic versions? Even better. But there is nothing like cooking your own beans. It's simple—it just takes a little time.

To make your own, choose your favorite variety and pick over them for hidden stones or debris. Place them in a large bowl and cover them with water and soak the beans overnight. The next day, add them to a large stockpot along with fresh water and extra flavors you enjoy, like diced onion or garlic. Simmer the beans for 30 to 60 minutes, depending on the variety. Make sure to test a couple of beans before determining their doneness. For all intents and purposes, in recipes I list "canned beans" in the ingredient list. Feel free to use your own or use them from a can—just make sure they are thoroughly rinsed and drained.

Roast That Garlic

Roasting garlic turns those little cloves into a sweet, spreadable butter. Many of my recipes call for roasted garlic, and I always like to have a little on hand—pretty much because I want to add it to EVERYTHING.

To roast garlic, preheat your oven to 350°F. Slice the top of the garlic head off so that the cloves are exposed and gently rub your fingers back and forth over the sides to remove as much of the paper as you can. Drizzle the cloves with olive oil and then wrap the head tightly in a sheet of aluminum foil. Roast the garlic until the cloves are caramel in color, about 45 minutes. Let the garlic cool a bit before squeezing the cloves out—otherwise you will burn the heck out of your fingers. The roasted garlic cloves stay good in the fridge for about 1 week.

And Those Peppers Too!

Over the past few years I've fallen madly in love with roasted red peppers. They are to.die.for. I'm not against buying the jarred versions here and there—whether they are packed in water or garlic and oil, it's always a win. But sometimes I have an overabundance of peppers or want to roast other kinds, ones that aren't so easy to find in the store.

I roast peppers by heating the broiler on my oven to its highest setting and placing the oven rack directly underneath. I stick the peppers on a baking sheet, then set it under the broiler and char the skin until it's black. Then I rotate the peppers and repeat, until the entire things are roasted. Next, I remove the peppers from the sheet and stick them in a resealable plastic bag. The bag will get steamy and puff up—keep 'em in there for 30 minutes. After 30 minutes, remove the peppers and rub the charred skin off, then remove the stem and the seeds. And there you go!

Bake Yo' Bacon

I am a huge believer in frying your pork in a cast-iron skillet, then pouring the grease out into a mason jar and storing it in your fridge. Judge not.

BUT. In the case that you are making some sort of feast—like maybe three of the four burners on your stovetop are in use—or maybe you just don't feel like getting splattered with hot grease, bake it, baby.

Preheat your oven to 375ºF. If you choose to place aluminum foil or parchment paper on your baking sheet, make sure it covers all four edges and rides up a bit. Place the bacon slices on the sheet about ½ inch apart and bake for 20 to 25 minutes. The time will depend on the thickness of your pork, but you get the gist. Check it after 20 minutes and determine its finish time just like you would if you were frying it on the stovetop. Once it's finished, remove each piece using kitchen tongs and allow to drain and slightly cool on a paper towel. PS: Make extra.

Then, Yes, Save Your Grease

I'm serious. I grew up with a jar of bacon grease in the fridge, and while its appearance frightened the hell out of me, once I learned about its many uses, I was sold. You can do this regardless of how you cook your bacon. Allow the bacon grease to slightly cool (but not solidify), then pour it into a jar, seal it, and store it in the fridge. Use like butter when you cook. YES.

Use Unsalted Butter

It's just a habit I've gotten into—I do 99.9 percent of my baking and cooking with it. That way, I can control the amount of salt that goes into a recipe and after so many years of cooking can usually judge pretty well how much salt something may need. If you only have salted butter on hand, that is completely fine—you may just want to taste your dish (if possible) before salting or use half the recommended amount of salt. For reference, all of my recipes call for unsalted butter unless otherwise noted.

How I Measure Coconut Oil

If you are familiar with coconut oil, then you know that at room temperature it is in a solid form. Anytime I call for coconut oil in a recipe, I measure it out in its solid form first, then melt it from there.

Full-Fat, Low-Fat & Fat-Free Dairy: What I Use

MILKS: I never use skim milk in my cooking or baking. Occasionally I will use 2 percent, but I find that most recipes that call for milk work better with the full-fat stuff. Buy organic and local if you can.

CHEESE: Fat-free cheese has never made an appearance in this house, surprise surprise. I am a firm believer that a little cheese goes a loooong way, so I prefer to use the full-fat versions. If I am melting cheese on top of a pizza or casserole, I always opt for full-fat—it melts much better than low-fat cheese. However, I do not discriminate when it comes to eating a few chunks of low-fat cheese for a snack. And for goodness sakes, please freshly grate your own cheese for melting. It's 150 times better than the bagged stuff.

GREEK YOGURT: As you will see, tons of my recipes call for Greek yogurt, and it's clearly one of my favorite ingredients due to its versatility. Unless otherwise noted, full-fat yogurt is going to yield the best results; however, I've indicated in a few places where low-fat yogurt is doable. I can't always get behind the fat-free stuff. Once you go full-fat, you never go back.

Two Things I Prep Ahead of Time to Make My Life Healthier

CHICKEN: Whether I roast a whole chicken or throw a few breasts into the slow cooker, I always find it helpful to have some already cooked and shredded chicken in my fridge. I use it every week in an assortment of recipes—soups, pizza, salads, tacos. The list is endless.

QUINOA: And lots of it. I do just about everything with quinoa . . . except for the most common way of eating it as a plain side dish. I like to cook a batch in coconut milk and store it in the fridge—it goes in breakfast bowls, cookies, granola, or parfaits. I will also cook a batch in low-sodium chicken or veggie stock—perfect to have on hand to make veggie burgers or add a healthy punch to meatballs or salads.

How I Write Recipes

When it comes to my recipes, the last thing I want is for you to be confused. Here is an example of a commonly asked question:

If a recipe calls for ½ cup of pecans, chopped, that means to measure out ½ cup of pecans, THEN chop them.

If a recipe calls for ½ cup of chopped pecans, that means to measure out ½ cup of already chopped pecans.

We good?

These Are a Few (or Seven) of My Favorite Things

We all have the kitchen tools and appliances that we don't think we could live without. These are mine.

A GARLIC PRESS IS YOUR BEST FRIEND: I don't know if it's my lack of formal training, my laziness, or my stubby fingers, but I loathe chopping or mincing garlic. I always use my garlic press and actually have two of them, just in case. Easily my most used kitchen tool. Sort of a pain to clean, but again . . . saves my life.

I SPEND QUALITY TIME WITH MY FOOD PROCESSOR: I use it for EVERYTHING. It works for doughs, batters, salsas, salads, nut butters—all things. It is wonderful and I would die without it. I recommend getting the largest one that can fit in your kitchen. Go big or go home.

A CAST-IRON SKILLET: Yeah, it's heavy as heck, but it produces some delicious food. And if you're a single lady, you can use it as a weapon. Just kidding. Sorta. PS: My mom uses one that is more than 100 years old. Talk about seasoned. I'm so jealous.

I'M THE QUEEN OF CUTTING BOARDS: In my mind, you can never have enough. I have tons. You definitely want at least four or five—that way you can simultaneously use one for produce and one for meat without having to scrub in between. Ah . . . how the Internet has increased my laziness. I suggest a mix of bamboo and plastic.

LIVE FOR A BROILER PAN: If I am not grilling, I am broiling. A broiler pan makes all the difference when it comes to poultry, fish, or meat. Go get it.

MY STAND MIXER IS MY LIFE: My KitchenAid stand mixer truly does everything. It even shreds pork and chicken. I love it. They are gorgeous, too, so don't worry about leaving it out on your counter.

YOU CAN NEVER HAVE ENOUGH BAKING SHEETS: It's the truth.

1
breakfast
(. . . for dinner?)

Now that we're friends I can tell you that I was never one to **skip breakfast.** (Or if you've picked up: **any meal . . .** ever.)

As a kid, I always made sure to eat something before I left the house for school on weekdays, most likely learning this fact of life from my dad. He would chow down on a bowl of cereal with bananas and milk, golden wheat toast with a peanut butter smear, or half a grapefruit and an English muffin. It's unknown whether mine was a learned healthy habit or simply because at the ripe old age of nine I was already in lust with food.

My mom survived on the coffee-until-noon diet but would make sure to stuff the pantry and fridge with a variety of cereals that turned your milk into creamy chocolate; fruit for cereal garnish; Pop-Tarts with the crackled frosting atop; freezer waffles and pastries that my brothers would dominate, and cinnamon-raisin bread that I'd toast to perfection, butter until no dry spots remained, then give a good two or three (or ten) shakes of cinnamon sugar. That was easily one of the best things I learned from my Grandma Lois. Cinnamon sugar toast . . . *get in my mouth.*

Despite having so many popular processed foods floating around each morning, I quickly learned that those only tasted good every once in a while, and that Lucky Charms that have been sitting in the pantry, bag half-opened for two months, does not a delicious breakfast make. Those marshmallows just don't hold their crunch! (Note the present tense.)

Weekends were an entirely different story. On Saturdays, as he still often does, my dad would make us all "short stacks"—blueberry pancakes for himself and me; plain ones for my mom and brothers—a tradition passed down from his great-grandmother and albeit unknown to us, a rather healthier portion than what you can get at IHOP. We'd butter each 'cake and squeeze way too much maple syrup on top, which one of us would inevitably end up finishing off before the others even got their first serving. On *special occasions,* we'd squirt whipped cream on top, too, and to this day my mom has three or four cans of whipped cream that always hang in her fridge for when my brother Andy unexpectedly pops in and sprays it directly into his mouth.

After church on Sundays, my mom would do the cooking—a feast of eggs, scrambled or dippy; buttered wheat and white toast triangles; sausage links; thick-sliced bacon crisped just right; and a big bowl of fruit. This brunch was often so ridiculously large and filling that we wouldn't feel the need to eat again until dinner, and almost every single one of us would fall into a food coma for the next few hours, scattered about the floors and couches with football blasting on TV.

These days, I have a huge issue: I essentially turn almost anything into a breakfast food. I can justify chocolate, beef, beer, or coconut in some sort of breakfast food. No, not together. At least not yet.

It's kind of the best thing ever, though.

By far, I'd have to say that breakfast is my favorite meal. But that's where the area gets a bit gray. I love breakfast for breakfast, but **I REALLY love breakfast for dinner.** In fact, I think breakfast foods taste fabulous at all times of the day. Eggs are the one single food that I will make work anywhere, in anything. And the best part is that as much as I love eggs or any sort of savory breakfast, I equally enjoy sweet breakfasts, too.

Can't help it. It's the sweet teeth.

Occasionally I eat breakfast foods all day long and don't even realize it—granola with fruit and yogurt in the morning, eggs with toast and avocado for lunch, multigrain pancakes with bacon for dinner. It happens, and it's wonderful. Perhaps it's because breakfast gives off such nostalgic, intoxicating scents—toast and sausage and eggs and bacon wafting through the house? Sign me the heck up.

Perhaps it's because bacon love really originates there when you're a kid. I'm sure I had it in some mac and cheese or a good old **BLT,** but breakfast is where it really begins, right?

Perhaps it's because adding an egg in some form to anything does make it better—rice, burgers, pizza, salads—and this needs to be a more commonly known thing. Can we do that?

I think it's because the vast variety allows you to never get bored. I've shared some of my favorite daily staples here that are pretty simple to make, but also a few extras that get loud cheers at brunch. Oh, and don't forget the whole wheat cinnamon rolls—and you know "whole wheat" is just code for "eat as many as you want." Duh.

I've always wanted to be trendy. I always want to like the latest stuff, the cool things, the things that everyone is talking about. It has to be the firstborn-child nature in me, the need to be a people-pleaser and fit right in.

One of those bandwagons that I jumped right on was juicing. No, I'm not talking about one of those juice cleanses. I accidentally thought it would be a good idea to try one of those last year, a few days after I'd had a fortunate run-in with a breakfast taco, a Five Guys burger, and a Primanti Brother's sandwich. On the same day.

Which, by the way, if you're unfamiliar, a Primanti's sandwich is a Pittsburgh tradition: Everything is on the sandwich. I mean everything. The fries, the coleslaw—it's all on the sandwich. All stuffed in between two thick, glorious slabs of white bread and meat and cheese. It is, in a word, fantastic.

The juice cleanse, however? The three days that I went with only juice and no solid food? Nightmare. Not for me. I didn't experience any of the wonderful side effects others have mentioned: clearer minds, vibrant dreams, energized wake-ups. Instead, I just experienced a whole lot of hunger. Missed chewing on stuff.

Years before I had ever considered doing such a thing, I bought my own juicer. Not only does it make it simpler to produce pitcher-perfect orange juice for brunch, but it also makes it exceptionally easy to get in some veggies and use up all the produce in your fridge. Like the stuff that is dying in the crisper drawer. Story of my life.

I will occasionally frequent a green juice, usually made with some spinach or kale, apples, cucumbers, lemon, and the like, but shockingly (not really) it isn't my favorite. I much prefer the crazy concocted fruit juice flavors—the ones that come from mixing your favorite fruits, ones you never get to see in a store. This pineapple-strawberry juice is my all-time favorite, not only because it's a knockout (so gorgeous, right?) but also because it's spiked with a touch of fresh mint and ridiculously delicious. Pretty things are fun to drink.

strawberry sunshine *juice*

SERVES 2 • TIME: 10 minutes

2 cups cubed fresh pineapple

1 pound fresh strawberries, hulled

1 large handful fresh mint

1 Add all of the ingredients to a juicer in the order listed. Pour the juice into a pretty glass.

It should come as no surprise by now, but this breakfast would be considered anything but traditional in the home I grew up in. Luckily, in my current house? It's a staple. I have an unnatural adoration for corn, so working it into my favorite meals is something I make happen often. Perhaps my favorite part about these corn cakes is that they can serve as a base for whatever flavors you'd like to add. Like, say, if someone you live with (ahem . . .) doesn't really enjoy avocado.

I know. Whyyyyy?

In that unfortunate situation, a little freshly grated cheese instead goes a long way. Their loss.

bacon, egg & avocado corn cakes

MAKES 12 cakes • TIME: 30 minutes

1 cup whole wheat pastry flour

1 cup finely ground cornmeal

1 teaspoon baking soda

$^1/_2$ teaspoon salt

$^1/_2$ teaspoon freshly ground black pepper

$1^1/_2$ cups fresh or thawed frozen corn kernels

1 shallot, diced

2 garlic cloves, minced

2 large eggs

1 cup low-fat milk

2 tablespoons olive or canola oil

4 large eggs, for serving

1 avocado, pitted, peeled, and sliced into 12 slices

1 pint grape tomatoes, quartered

 In a large bowl, whisk together the flour, cornmeal, baking soda, salt, and pepper. Add the corn, shallots, and garlic to the dry ingredients and mix until combined.

 In a small bowl or measuring cup, whisk together the 2 eggs and milk. Add the wet ingredients to the dry and mix with a spoon until just combined.

3 Heat a large skillet over medium heat and add the oil. Use a $^1/_3$-cup measure and scoop the corn cake batter into the skillet, leaving about an inch in between each corn cake. Cook until the cakes begin to set and bubble on the top, 3 to 4 minutes. Gently flip and cook for another 1 to 2 minutes. Remove the corn cakes with a spatula and place on a plate or baking sheet. Repeat with the remaining batter.

4 Cook the 4 eggs to your liking: sunny side up, over easy, poached, scrambled, or your preferred style.

5 To assemble the corn cakes, add the avocado slices and tomatoes over the top. Top each with a cooked egg.

NOTE: I first became brave enough to poach my own eggs after reading one of the tutorials by Deb Perelman on the Smitten Kitchen blog. In my last few years of poaching, I've learned that it really does work best if your eggs are fresh, your water is not boiling at all, and you are patient. These days, I can poach an egg with success almost every time. It just takes lots of practice. Hope you're hungry.

lemon–
chia
seed
waffles

. . . .

SERVES 2 to 4 • TIME: 30 minutes

. . . .

1½ cups whole wheat pastry flour

2 tablespoons cornstarch

2 tablespoons granulated sugar

2 teaspoons baking powder

½ teaspoon baking soda

¼ teaspoon salt

1½ cups buttermilk

⅓ cup coconut oil, melted and
slightly cooled

Zest of 4 lemons

1 large egg, lightly beaten

¼ teaspoon lemon extract

1 teaspoon vanilla extract

2 tablespoons chia seeds

Maple syrup, for serving

Ch-ch-ch-chia?

I'm completely ripping off the favorite lemon–poppy seed flavor, but it's with good reason. Healthful reason!

These little waffles have all the lemon flavor with a little chia crunch. I adore chia seeds because they are so simple to work with. Throw them on some peanut butter toast, into a smoothie, on top of yogurt—you don't even know they are there, and you're getting a healthy dose of . . . good stuff. Yes. Good stuff.

This is all good stuff.

1 Preheat your waffle maker to the desired setting.

2 In a large bowl, whisk together the flour, cornstarch, sugar, baking powder, baking soda, and salt. In a small bowl, whisk together the buttermilk, coconut oil, lemon zest, egg, lemon extract, and vanilla extract. Add the wet ingredients to the dry and stir until the batter comes together. Stir in 1½ tablespoons of the chia seeds.

3 Pour the batter into your waffle maker and cook according to the manufacturer's directions. Once finished, top the waffles with maple syrup and a sprinkle of the remaining chia seeds.

Green smoothies have been all the rage in the past few years, but I tried my first nearly ten years ago when I was working in a gym. Let's just say that I could not get behind it. At all.

Thankfully, things have changed. Or shall I say: I made them change.

Green shakes have become imperative to my weekly menus—mostly making appearances for breakfast or the occasional snack—because when you don't really love vegetables? You gotta find a way to get that greenery in. I'm long past the age where I can ignore what benefits spinach and kale will provide me in the long run, and man, I want to live long.

So this is my green shake. My fave. Adding the frozen avocado is similar to adding frozen bananas, but if it's possible makes the drink even creamier! Gah. Can you even imagine?

The key to making a kickass green shake that doesn't leave you gagging (that is, that doesn't have spinach chunks floating around in it) is to blend, blend, blend. Sure, one of those crazy high-powered blenders that costs an arm and a leg will probably be your best bet, but I would rather buy shoes. Instead, any higher-end blender (I got mine at Target for $99) with a crazy blade will do. After all of the ingredients are in, blend that baby up for close to 5 minutes. It will ensure that no chewy vegetable bits remain and that you get that thick smoothie texture.

If I can do it? You definitely can.

how sweet is this green shake?

SERVES 1 • TIME: 10 minutes

6 ice cubes

2 cups fresh spinach

$^1/_2$ cup frozen mango

1 frozen banana

$^1/_2$ avocado, pitted and peeled

1 tablespoon natural peanut butter

$1^1/_2$ cups unsweetened vanilla-flavored almond milk

1 teaspoon vanilla extract

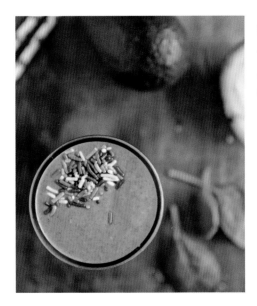

1 Combine all of the ingredients in a blender in the order they are listed and puree until smooth and creamy.

whipped *goat cheese* with warm *vanilla berries* on toast

SERVES 4 · TIME: 20 minutes

6 ounces goat cheese, at room temperature

2 tablespoons half-and-half

1½ cups fresh strawberries, hulled and quartered

1 cup fresh blueberries

2 tablespoons water

1 tablespoon honey

1 vanilla bean, split and the seeds scraped out

Pinch of salt

4 thick slices whole-grain bread, toasted

Fresh mint leaves, for garnish

This is only the first installment in what I shall refer to as my infatuation with foods on toasts. Seriously. There's almost an entire chapter dedicated to this. I'm not sure what it is, but a thick, grainy slice of bread, toasted until crusty on the outside and then covered in something I love, just makes me lose my mind. I suppose we can be normal and refer to these as open-face sandwiches, but to me that just sounds like a bunch of veggies or something.

Growing up, I had many of the common foods on toasts that you probably did too. Peanut butter and jam, peanut butter and banana, cream cheese and strawberries, chicken salad, and your traditional "dippy egg"—known as sunny side up or over easy for those of you who didn't grow up in Pittsburgh.

This is just the adult version of one of those. As much as I hate growing up, this is easily one of the best parts. Obviously.

1 Add the goat cheese to the bowl of a food processor and pulse until crumbly. Scrape down the sides of the processor with a spatula and blend constantly for 1 minute. With the processor on, stream in the half-and-half. Blend for another 1 to 2 minutes, stopping to scrape down the sides again if necessary. Puree until creamy and no large crumbles remain, 2 to 3 minutes.

2 Add the strawberries, blueberries, water, honey, the seeds scraped from the vanilla bean, the actual vanilla bean, and salt to a small saucepan. Heat over low heat until the mixture is simmering, stirring occasionally. Continue to cook over low heat until the berries soften and become a bit syrupy, 2 to 3 minutes. Turn off the heat and discard the scraped vanilla bean.

3 Spread 2 to 3 tablespoons of the whipped goat cheese on each slice of toasted bread. Spoon the warm berries over the top. Garnish with fresh mint leaves.

NOTE: If you aren't a fan of goat cheese, swap the spread for a traditional or whipped cream cheese. No big deal.

Can you milk an almond?!

We're gonna try.

I've already professed my undying love for almond milk and want to share a quick coconutty (of course) version with you. True coconut milk comes from the meat of a fresh coconut, but since such delicacies aren't always readily available to me, I settle for this easier coconut-flavored almond milk.

It's my delicious solution.

coconut-
almond
milk

MAKES about 4 cups
TIME: 24 to 48 hours

1 pound raw almonds

2 cups unsweetened flaked coconut

4 cups water

1 teaspoon vanilla extract

2 tablespoons honey (optional)

1 Place the almonds and coconut in a large bowl and add enough water to cover. Soak the mixture for 24 to 48 hours on the counter. The longer you soak, the better.

2 After soaking, drain the almonds and coconut. Add them to a blender with the 4 cups water and blend until the mixture is completely pureed.

3 Assemble a large piece of cheesecloth or a very fine-mesh strainer over a large bowl. Pour the almond milk through the cloth or sieve, pressing all of the liquid out of the pulp with a spoon. Sometimes I do this process twice.

4 Stir the vanilla extract into the milk. Taste the milk and, if desired, add the honey or another sweetener. Store sealed in the fridge for up to 5 days.

baked black raspberry oatmeal with a brown butter drizzle

SERVES 2 • TIME: 35 minutes

1½ cups old-fashioned rolled oats

½ cup loosely packed light brown sugar

1 teaspoon baking powder

½ teaspoon ground cinnamon

¼ teaspoon salt

½ cup canned light coconut milk, plus extra for drizzling

¼ cup applesauce

1 tablespoon unsalted butter, melted

1 large egg, lightly beaten

1 teaspoon vanilla extract

⅔ cup fresh raspberries

2 tablespoons unsalted butter, browned (see page 26)

One of my deepest, darkest secrets is my insane love for Quaker instant oatmeal packets. You know the ones? Peaches and cream, strawberries and cream, apples and cinnamon, maple and brown sugar?

Ugh. I love those things, even to this day.

The instant oatmeal packets were actually my breakfast of choice all the way through high school. I could never do plain oatmeal—even just some simple brown sugar wouldn't cut it for me, probably because I was spoiled with the fabulousness of the artificial flavors I had consumed since I was a kid. I mean, fresh peaches and milk in my homemade old-fashioned rolled oats just DIDN'T taste the same.

So unfair.

These days, I still longingly gaze at those instant oatmeal boxes in the grocery store, willing one to accidentally-on-purpose fall into my shopping cart. Every now and then I will buy one—and savor a packet once a week, usually on Saturday mornings after yoga. I'm sure it's the whole "tasting like my childhood" thing, but um . . . those things are good. Ain't any other way to say it.

In order to squash my instant oat habit and also cure my craving for a warm bowl of, well, something first thing in the morning, I've come to enjoy baked oatmeal more than I ever thought I could. I think it's the texture that gets me. Can we almost describe it as a kind of oatmeal cake-like thing?

Yes. I think we can.

1 Preheat the oven to 350°F. Spray a small baking dish (such as a square or oval baker that serves 2 to 4) with nonstick spray. Set aside.

2 In a large bowl, whisk together the oats, brown sugar, baking powder, cinnamon, and salt. In a smaller bowl, whisk together the coconut milk, applesauce, melted butter, egg, and vanilla extract. Add the wet ingredients to the dry and mix until the oatmeal is combined and wet. Gently stir in the raspberries with a spatula or large spoon.

3 Bake for 25 minutes, or until the top of the oatmeal is set and golden brown. Remove the dish from the oven and let cool for 1 to 2 minutes, then serve with a drizzle of brown butter and coconut milk.

NOTES: Alternate fruits based on the seasons—blueberries are particularly delicious, since they burst and explode inside the creamy oats. You can also add a mashed banana to the oatmeal batter before baking for an additional hint of flavor. And on top of the brown butter? Add some toasted coconut (see page 27) or sliced almonds or an extra drizzle of milk. So fancy.

sweet potato hash, scrambled egg & herb goat cheese freezer breakfast burritos

MAKES 8 burritos • TIME: 45 minutes

Nothing is simpler than an already prepared, ready-to-go, just-waiting-for-you breakfast that isn't a granola bar or a banana.

Being able to eat a savory, warm breakfast that took just seconds to make on a busy weekday morning is the best feeling ever. It's like you got to eat a REAL breakfast. A weekend breakfast. A pampering breakfast.

These breakfast burritos take a little prep work beforehand, but oh my gosh, they are so worth it. You won't ever want to grab a frozen breakfast sandwich again. And they are totally customizable. Put whatever you want inside. Does it get any better?

Uh, no.

(Okay, maybe if you can add a mimosa.)

For the hash, heat a large skillet over medium heat and add the olive oil. Add the onion and cook until slightly softened, 2 to 3 minutes. Add the garlic, potatoes, salt, pepper, and paprika and stir. Cover and cook until the sweet potato is tender, stirring occasionally, 6 to 8 minutes. Set the skillet aside to cool.

 For the eggs, whisk together the eggs, salt, and pepper in a large bowl. Heat another skillet over medium heat and add the olive oil. Once hot, add the eggs to the skillet and stir constantly with a heatproof spatula until the eggs are just cooked. Set aside.

 For the goat cheese, in a small bowl, mix together the goat cheese, basil, parsley, rosemary, and thyme.

4 Spread about a tablespoon of the goat cheese in the center of each tortilla. Add a scoop of the potatoes and the eggs, equally divvying them between the 8 tortillas.

5 Lay a square of plastic wrap on the counter and place a tortilla in the center. Fold in 2 sides of the tortilla and then roll it up tightly to create a burrito, and wrap it tightly in the plastic wrap. Repeat with the remaining tortillas and lay them all on a baking sheet. Freeze for 30 minutes.

6 Remove the baking sheet from the freezer and store the burritos however it is most convenient—in a large resealable bag or in the door of the freezer.

7 To serve the burritos, remove from the freezer and microwave until warm, 30 to 60 seconds.

SWEET POTATO HASH

1 tablespoon extra-virgin olive oil

1/2 sweet yellow onion, diced

2 garlic cloves, minced

2 cups 1/2-inch cubed peeled sweet potato

1/4 teaspoon salt

1/4 teaspoon freshly ground black pepper

1/4 teaspoon smoked paprika

SCRAMBLED EGGS

8 large eggs

1/4 teaspoon salt

1/4 teaspoon freshly ground black pepper

1 1/2 teaspoons extra-virgin olive oil

HERB GOAT CHEESE

4 ounces goat cheese, at room temperature

1/2 teaspoon dried basil

1/2 teaspoon dried parsley

1/4 teaspoon dried rosemary

1/4 teaspoon dried thyme

FOR SERVING

8 (8-inch) multigrain flour tortillas

brown sugar– bacon biscuits

MAKES 10 to 12 biscuits
TIME: 30 minutes

1 cup all-purpose flour, plus extra for dusting

1 cup whole wheat pastry flour

1/3 cup loosely packed light brown sugar

3 teaspoons baking powder

1 teaspoon baking soda

1/4 teaspoon salt

4 tablespoons (1/2 stick) cold unsalted butter, cut into pieces

4 slices thick-cut bacon, cooked and crumbled

1 cup low-fat buttermilk

There are two very distinct groups of people in this world: those who enjoy bacon in their baked goods and those who don't. Which are you?

I'm sure it goes without saying which side I lean toward. Bacon FTW.

My mom is on the other end of the spectrum. I can't even tell you how much it kills me, because this is the woman who instilled the love of bacon within me. Heck, she is the woman who told me about her favorite "delicacy"—French fries topped with gravy—something she ate in college constantly. She fries her bacon the old-school way, she keeps that jar of grease in the fridge, and she would eagerly add bacon to ANYTHING.

Well, almost anything. Just not her cookies.

I don't discriminate when it comes to my favorite cut of pork. I've been known to put it on top of cupcakes, inside cupcakes, inside cookies, as a garnish on frosting, mixed into ice cream, and now, inside biscuits.

The good news is that these biscuits are a perfect way to bridge the gap. They aren't super sweet, so the whole no-bacon-in-my-baked-goods argument kind of goes out the window. They still get slightly sky-high even with the incorporation of whole wheat pastry flour, so you can make an incredible sandwich with them. They serve as a great base for a sausage gravy or an accompaniment to your fried eggs with a drizzle of honey. If you're feeling like going the dinner route, they create an awesome hearty soup or stew dipper.

The bad news is . . . you may get addicted. Not a bad problem to have, eh?

1 Preheat the oven to 425°F.

2 In a large bowl, whisk together the flours, brown sugar, baking powder, baking soda, and salt. Add the butter pieces to the dry ingredients and use your hands, a fork, or a pastry blender to incorporate the butter into the flour until you have coarse crumbs. I prefer to use my hands, and this takes 1 to 2 minutes. Once the butter is incorporated, add the crumbled bacon and stir to evenly disperse it throughout the flour. Pour in the buttermilk and stir the mixture with a large spoon until the dough begins to come together, using your hands if necessary.

Remove the dough from the bowl and place on a floured work space. Knead the dough a few times, adding more flour if it is too sticky, then pat it into a 1-inch-thick circle. Use a 2-inch biscuit cutter and cut out rounds of dough, then place them on a nonstick baking sheet about 2 inches apart. Bake for 10 to 12 minutes, or until the biscuits are golden brown.

④ Remove the baking sheet from the oven and let the biscuits cool for 1 to 2 minutes before serving.

NOTE: Make mini biscuits! Everything is more fun when it's tiny, right? Use a tool much smaller than your traditional biscuit cutter, such as a soda pop cap or even the lid to one of your spices (clean it first . . .). Follow the directions and use your smaller round to make mini biscuits, baking them for 6 to 8 minutes or until golden. You may want to crumble your bacon into extra-teeny crumbles, just so every little biscuit gets some love.

baked breakfast *risotto*

SERVES 4 • TIME: 1 hour

4 cups low-sodium chicken stock

1½ cups Arborio rice

½ sweet yellow onion, diced

2 garlic cloves, minced

¼ teaspoon salt

¼ teaspoon freshly ground black pepper

½ pound hot Italian sausage, removed from casing

2 slices thick-cut bacon

4 large eggs

Pinch of salt and freshly ground black pepper

2 scallions, sliced

2 tablespoons chopped fresh chives

People constantly ask me where I find my inspiration. The truth is, I get it everywhere. Weird places too. Like I might be driving to the mall and see a billboard with an orange on it. I start thinking about oranges and then decide I want to make a Creamsicle soda float. How good does that sound right now?

I know.

But then I continue to talk to myself out loud (fellow drivers surely think I'm a wacko) and determine that maybe, just maybe, orange is a little boring? A little too predictable? So then I throw a few ideas around and come up with pomegranate. Yes, pomegranate cream soda floats. Let's do it.

That's just one example, but a good one for the crazy things that evolve from my recipe brain. However, many times I get my inspiration from local restaurants around Pittsburgh. We have fabulous ones—so many, in fact, that I don't think my husband and I have eaten at a chain restaurant other than Five Guys in almost two years. Not because we are being annoying snobs, but because the local food is just so darn delicious.

This breakfast risotto was born after I had a similar variety at brunch one morning with my cousin Lacy. Lacy and I are brunch fanatics—if it were up to us, we'd probably eat brunch every Saturday and Sunday of our lives. Brunch has three requirements, though: friends, food, and cocktails.

All are a must for brunch. Otherwise it's just . . . late breakfast.

This risotto is a bit time-consuming but works for any meal of the day. And it also reheats well. Yessss.

1 Preheat the oven to 400°F.

2 Add the stock, rice, onion, garlic, salt, and pepper to a 9x13-inch baking dish and stir. Bake until the rice is plumped and the liquid is absorbed, 25 to 30 minutes.

3 While the rice is baking, heat a large nonstick skillet over medium heat. Add the sausage and break it apart with a spoon. Cook until browned, stirring occasionally, 5 to 6 minutes. Remove the sausage with a large slotted spoon and place it on a paper towel to drain. Remove or wipe away any oil or grease left in the skillet and reduce the heat to medium-low.

Cut the bacon into pieces and add it to the hot skillet. Cook the bacon until it's crispy and the fat is rendered, 4 to 5 minutes. Remove the bacon with a slotted spoon and place it on a paper towel—you can add it to the same plate as the sausage.

 Right before the rice is finished baking, heat the same skillet over low to medium heat. Cook the eggs as desired—over easy or sunny side up—and sprinkle each with a pinch of salt and pepper.

 Remove the rice from the oven and stir in the sausage, bacon, and scallions. Serve it topped with the eggs and sprinkled with the chives.

banana macaroon smoothie

. . . .

SERVES 2 · TIME: 10 minutes

. . . .

3 frozen bananas

1 1/2 cups canned light coconut milk

1 1/2 cups coconut water

1 cup plain full- or low-fat Greek yogurt

1/4 cup unsweetened flaked coconut, toasted (see page 27)

2 teaspoons vanilla extract

Honey, for the glass

If I've said it once, I've said it a million times: I would so much rather eat my calories than drink them. With that being said, I do love a good smoothie when it's especially hot outside or when I'm in a crazy rush and have to make breakfast happen on the go.

Because if I don't make it happen, I will surely want to swing by Dunkin' Donuts, and let's be honest: One doughnut is rarely enough.

My go-to smoothie ingredient is always, always, always a frozen banana or two. I just can't get over the creamy, thick consistency it contributes to the drink. It is so much like a milk shake that with a few of my other favorite flavors, even I, the dessert queen, can almost be tricked.

Almost.

1 Combine the bananas, coconut milk, coconut water, yogurt, 2 tablespoons of the toasted coconut, and the vanilla extract in a blender and puree until smooth and creamy.

2 To rim glasses with coconut, put a drop of honey on your finger and rub it along the glass rim. Add the remaining 2 tablespoons of toasted coconut to a plate and turn the glass upside down onto the plate. Gently press the honey-coated rim into the coconut and push the coconut gently to adhere. Pour the smoothies into the coconut-rimmed glasses.

NOTE: One of those coconut haters? If you just dislike the texture, simply leave out the flaked coconut so you can still enjoy the tropical flavor. If you don't want any coconut in your smoothie at all, I absolutely suggest adding some additional frozen fruit, some peanut butter (or chocolate peanut butter!), and even some plain frozen yogurt to give you your fix.

oatmeal cookie *granola*

MAKES about 4 cups
TIME: 1 hour (includes cooling time)

2¼ cups old-fashioned rolled oats

1 cup sliced almonds

½ cup ground flaxseed

1 tablespoon light brown sugar

1 teaspoon ground cinnamon

¼ teaspoon salt

½ cup honey

2 tablespoons unsalted butter, browned (see page 26)

2 tablespoons coconut oil

2 teaspoons vanilla extract

½ cup miniature chocolate chips

I think we can all agree: Granola is a dangerous thing.

You swing by your local Whole Foods, fill a bag full from the bulk bin, and before you know it, you're pulling into your driveway with an empty plastic bag for a passenger and crumbs covering your legs. Where did it all go? What just happened? Am I granola wasted?

Granola is one of those munchies that seem impossible to stop eating once you've started. And the worst part is the suggested serving size? How unfair. It's, like, ridiculously small to the point of embarrassment. I need at least three times as much to satisfy my crunch craving and, well, you know I want even MORE than that.

This is a super-basic granola but one of my favorites. It tastes like a giant oatmeal cookie and due to its simplicity is just begging for you to add something extra that you may want. Dried mango slices? Peanut butter morsels? Vanilla beans or even salty pecans?
I'm so overwhelmed.

 Preheat the oven to 325°F and line a baking sheet with parchment paper.

 In a large bowl, whisk together the oats, almonds, flaxseed, brown sugar, cinnamon, and salt.

3 Heat a small saucepan over low heat and add the honey, brown butter, coconut oil, and vanilla extract. Stir until the liquid is warm and the ingredients have melted together. Remove the pan from the heat and pour the mixture over the oats. Stir it with a large spoon to coat and bring the mixture together. Spread it evenly over the parchment-covered baking sheet.

4 Bake for 10 minutes, then use a spatula to toss the granola. Bake for 10 minutes more and then toss again. Bake for an additional 10 minutes, tossing twice during the cooking time. Remove the pan from the oven and let cool for 5 minutes. Sprinkle the chocolate chips over the granola and lightly toss. Let the granola cool completely on the baking sheet.

NOTES: Allowing the granola to cool before storing it is the key to getting granola "clumps." To help the clumping process, you can squeeze together handfuls of the granola once or twice during the cooling process. Store in a sealed bag or container for up to 1 week.

honey–whole wheat–yogurt short stacks with blueberries

MAKES 10 to 12 cakes · TIME: 20 minutes

1 cup whole wheat pastry flour

2 teaspoons baking powder

1 teaspoon baking soda

¼ teaspoon ground cinnamon

¼ teaspoon salt

¾ cup almond milk or low-fat cow's milk

½ cup plain full- or low-fat Greek yogurt

1 large egg, lightly beaten

3 tablespoons honey

2 teaspoons vanilla extract

¾ cup fresh blueberries

We've already covered the fact that my dad makes some pretty awesome pancakes. What we have yet to discuss, though, is that my husband has become equally as pancake-obsessed in the past five years and tries to compete.

That is one battle that I am not going to participate in, thank you very much.

I mentioned that my dad makes pancakes every weekend, but there is one week out of the year when he makes them every single day. And that's when we are on vacation in northern Michigan. It's where the whole pancake thing began—with his great-grandmother making the short stacks and, in his words, he ate them faster than she made them.

I've never been down with the competitive breakfast game; I'd much rather choose to walk out of my bedroom, plop down at the kitchen table, and within minutes be greeted with a steaming-hot stack of breakfast cakes and a side of butter and syrup. It wasn't until this recipe came along that I was even capable of entering the pancake game. It wasn't until both my dad and Eddie tasted these ones that they got nervous about having a competitor.

It's hard to believe that these pancakes are made with both yogurt and whole wheat flour. They are so fluffy that it's like Hungry Jack made them himself. The flavors are up to you, and while blueberries are solidified as pancake dogma in my house, strawberries or peaches work too. Even some mashed banana! Get on this flavor train.

1 In a large bowl, whisk together the flour, baking powder, baking soda, cinnamon, and salt. In a smaller bowl, whisk together the milk, yogurt, egg, honey, and vanilla extract. Slowly add the wet ingredients to the dry and mix them with a large spoon until a batter forms. A few small lumps may remain.

2 Heat a nonstick skillet or electric griddle over medium-low heat. Once hot, use a ¼-cup measure or a medium-size ice cream scoop and add the batter to the hot surface, leaving about 2 inches between each pancake. Drop a few blueberries into the batter of each pancake. Let the pancakes cook until bubbles begin to form on top, 3 to 4 minutes. Gently flip each pancake and cook them until golden and fluffy, an additional 1 to 2 minutes.

Top the pancakes with the softened butter, maple syrup, and even some freshly whipped cream, if you'd like.

NOTES: If cooking pancakes in large batches, I like to preheat my oven to 200°F and place the cooked pancakes on a foil-lined baking sheet until the batch is complete and ready to serve.

I don't do it every weekend, but cooking your pancakes in a little bit of butter? So fabulous. Try it.

Unsalted butter, at room temperature, for serving

Maple syrup, for topping

Freshly whipped cream, for serving (optional)

greens & fontina baked eggs with garlic butter bread crumbs

SERVES 4 • TIME: 45 minutes

6 ounces fresh spinach

8 ounces Fontina cheese, freshly grated

8 large eggs

1/2 teaspoon salt

1/2 teaspoon freshly ground black pepper

2 tablespoons half-and-half

2 tablespoons unsalted butter

1 garlic clove, minced

Behold: my favorite breakfast.

Okay—one of my favorites. One of many?

I've never been good with favorites. It's a chore to attempt to choose my favorite song, movie, restaurant—heck, even my favorite color is inconclusive based on the day.

But I can say with certainty that when I think about current favorite breakfasts, breakfasts I find perfect for brunch parties and the breakfast I want to eat right this instant as I'm writing, Fontina baked eggs comes to mind.

First off, baked eggs are another fantabulous way to incorporate some veggies into your life. And forgive me if I'm wrong, but don't they say that if you consume some veg at your first meal of the day, it sets you on the right track and you're more likely to consume more veg throughout the day? I think they say that.

I wish "they" would say something beneficial about having cheesecake for the first meal of the day. But whatever.

Second, baked eggs are another one of those meals where there happen to be some seriously incredible options and variations. Some of my favorites include roasted red peppers and feta or garlic mushrooms and Gruyère. Please tell me you're craving that now.

In my opinion, baked eggs aren't complete without some sort of dipper—some kind of toasty bread or baguette that allows for dunking or layering or just any old way to get that egg out of the dish. These garlic butter breadcrumbs intensify the flavor of the baked eggs and truly make for the perfect breakfast. Or brunch. Or brinner.

You know! Breakfast for dinner? Brinner. Uh-huh.

1 Preheat the oven to 400°F. Spray a 9x13-inch baking dish with nonstick spray.

2 Take the fresh spinach and layer it evenly on the bottom of the baking dish. Add half of the Fontina cheese and then randomly place the eggs over the top. It helps if you crack each egg into a bowl first, then gently dump it from the bowl onto the spinach. Don't worry if the eggs fall through the cracks in the spinach or shift around. Sprinkle the eggs with the salt and pepper and then drizzle the half-and-half over the top. Cover the mixture evenly with the remaining cheese.

3 Place the baking dish in the oven and bake for 20 to 25 minutes, checking on the eggs in the last 5 minutes to see if they are cooked to your liking. If you want the yolks completely cooked, the dish might need an additional 5 to 10 minutes in the oven. If you'd like to make the cheese bubbly and golden, you can turn on the broiler and broil the dish for 1 to 2 minutes; however, this will also cook the eggs a bit more.

4 While the eggs are baking, add the butter to a small saucepan over medium heat. Whisk the butter constantly until it bubbles, and the minute the brown bits appear on the bottom of the pan, remove it from the heat and whisk for an additional 30 seconds. Let the butter stand for 1 minute. Add the garlic and stir for another minute. Stir in the bread crumbs and toss well to coat and combine.

5 Once the eggs are finished, remove the dish from the oven and cover it in the bread crumbs and fresh herbs. Serve with the toasted bread.

⅓ cup panko bread crumbs

1 tablespoon chopped fresh basil

1 tablespoon chopped fresh cilantro

1 tablespoon chopped fresh parsley

1 small loaf ciabatta bread, sliced and toasted

I'm all about taking quinoa to the next level.

The super-trendy grain that's really a seed usually plays its biggest role as a rice-like side dish or in some sort of salad, but I like cooking it with some coconut milk and eating it for breakfast.

The texture is what really gets me when it comes to quinoa. It has its own little snap, crackle, pop—it's a little chewy and can take on most flavors that you pair it with. I love adding some of my favorite fruit, perhaps a little flaked coconut, some chopped almonds, and an extra drizzle of milk. This meal keeps me full forever and ever. Err . . . or for a few hours.

It's also pretty bomb with a sprinkle of chocolate chips. And my longtime favorite: roasted cherries.

And yes, I just said bomb. Is this the '90s? I wish.

1 Preheat the oven to 400°F. Place the cherries on a baking sheet and roast for 20 minutes, tossing once during the cooking time.

2 While the cherries are roasting, place the quinoa in a fine-mesh strainer and rinse. Add the coconut milk, quinoa, water, vanilla extract, salt, and nutmeg to a small saucepan set over medium heat. Bring the mixture to a boil, then immediately reduce the heat to a simmer, cover, and cook for 15 minutes.

3 Remove the quinoa from the heat and fluff it with a fork. Stir half of the roasted cherries into the quinoa and spoon it into bowls. Top the quinoa with the remaining cherries, a drizzle of coconut milk, a sprinkle of toasted coconut, and the almonds.

roasted cherry, coconut & quinoa breakfast bowls

SERVES 2 • TIME: 35 minutes

1½ cups fresh Bing cherries, pitted and stemmed

½ cup quinoa

¾ cup canned light coconut milk, plus extra for drizzling

⅓ cup water

2 teaspoons vanilla extract

¼ teaspoon salt

Pinch of ground nutmeg

2 tablespoons unsweetened flaked coconut, toasted (see page 27)

2 tablespoons sliced almonds

whole wheat double-chocolate muffins

MAKES 12 muffins • **TIME: 30 minutes**

2 cups whole wheat pastry flour

1/2 cup unsweetened cocoa powder

1/3 cup granulated sugar

2 teaspoons baking powder

1/2 teaspoon salt

1 cup low-fat milk

2 large eggs, lightly beaten

3 tablespoons plain low-fat Greek yogurt

2 tablespoons unsalted butter, melted and slightly cooled

2 teaspoons vanilla extract

5 ounces high-quality dark chocolate, chopped

Let's get real. Muffins are just another excuse to eat cupcakes for breakfast. I've always said that muffins are really just cupcakes without a cute little hat and, well, if you add a glaze on top, you basically have dessert.

And seriously. Who doesn't want dessert for breakfast?

Muffins are extremely versatile in the breakfast arena. In my opinion, it's pretty darn rare that you can just eat ONE muffin and be satisfied, unless maybe it's accompanied by a large latte with cream. But when paired with some peanut butter, a handful of almonds, a side of fruit, or even crumbled into some Greek yogurt, it makes all the difference. It's like you are actually eating some cake in your yogurt.

It's downright legit.

Since we have these little cake-like muffins, leave it to me to make a double-chocolate version that could equally work for dessert if you're in a pickle. These muffins are super-fudgy and will cure those early morning chocolate cravings in just a few bites.

What? Doesn't everybody wake up craving chocolate?

1 Preheat the oven to 350°F. Line a muffin tin with liners and set aside.

2 In a large bowl, whisk together the flour, cocoa powder, sugar, baking powder, and salt. In a smaller bowl, whisk together the milk, eggs, yogurt, butter, and vanilla extract. Add the wet ingredients to the dry and mix them until just combined. Gently stir in the chopped chocolate until it is evenly dispersed. Be sure to not over-mix.

3 Use a 1/4-cup measure to scoop the batter evenly into the muffin liners. Bake the muffins for 15 to 17 minutes. Remove from the oven and let cool slightly.

For all you crazy kids who don't love chocolate first thing after you wake from slumber (I don't even get how that is possible), these bran muffins are totally for you.

They are not boring in the slightest and not what you think. They are like an updated, modern, contemporary bran muffin.

They are the hipster version of muffins.

They knew they were cool before you did.

1 Preheat the oven to 350°F. Line a muffin tin with liners and set aside.

2 Place the wheat bran on a baking sheet in a thin layer. Bake for 8 to 10 minutes to toast the bran, shaking the pan once or twice during baking. Remove the pan from the oven and add the bran to a bowl. Pour the milk over the top of it and let it sit for 5 minutes.

3 In a large bowl, whisk together the flour, brown sugar, flaxseed, baking soda, baking powder, cinnamon, ginger, nutmeg, and salt. In another bowl, stir together the zucchini pumpkin puree, coconut oil, egg, and vanilla extract. Add the wet wheat bran to the pumpkin mixture and stir it to combine.

4 Add the wet ingredients to the dry and stir until just combined. Do not over-mix! Fill each muffin liner almost full. Bake the muffins until the tops are set, 20 to 22 minutes. Remove the pan from the oven and let cool slightly.

not-so-boring *bran* muffins

MAKES 12 muffins • TIME: 40 minutes

1 cup oat bran

1 cup whole milk

1 cup whole wheat pastry flour

$2/3$ cup loosely packed light brown sugar

$1/4$ cup ground flaxseed

$1 1/2$ teaspoons baking soda

1 teaspoon baking powder

1 teaspoon ground cinnamon

$1/4$ teaspoon ground ginger

$1/4$ teaspoon ground nutmeg

$1/2$ teaspoon salt

1 cup freshly grated zucchini

$3/4$ cup pumpkin puree

$1/3$ cup coconut oil, melted

1 large egg

2 teaspoons vanilla extract

strawberry coffee cake scones

MAKES 8 scones • TIME: 30 minutes

- 1 cup all-purpose flour, plus extra for dusting
- 1 cup whole wheat flour
- 2 tablespoons granulated sugar
- 1½ teaspoons baking powder
- ½ teaspoon baking soda
- ¼ teaspoon salt
- 1 cup hulled and chopped fresh strawberries
- 3 tablespoons cold mascarpone cheese
- 2 tablespoons cold, unsalted butter
- 1 cup low-fat buttermilk

I must preface this with a disclaimer: I used to be a scone hater. Yes, I did.

The only memory I really have regarding scones is from elementary school. A student's mom brought in scones during one of those "tell-me-about-your-background" days (which was great fun for me, since I had to explain how Mother Lovett married two brothers at the ripe old age of 10), and only one word came to mind: dry. Like can't-speak dry. Like need-some-water-before-I-choke dry.

Well, okay, two words: dry and . . . raisins. I did not like raisins back then. Did anyone? And paired with a drier-than-dirt pastry that didn't have much flavor? It was such a disappointment. It kept me away from scones for at least 15 years. I was very distraught after that experience.

Fast forward to my early twenties, when a friend's sister came forth bearing a batch of freshly baked scones. I wasn't intrigued one bit and actually easily turned down a bite, but after a bunch of encouraging peer pressure, I bit the bullet. Or the scone.

Whoa. My life was changed. They really were the best scones I had ever tasted: They didn't have one hint of dryness, and they were almost slightly cake-like in texture. And even better yet: There were no raisins.

Over the years, I have thrown every single flavor imaginable into this scone recipe. It is extremely forgiving, and as long as you stick to the basic flour/butter/liquid ratio, you will be good to go. This version reminds me of one of my favorite ice cream flavors—strawberry cheesecake—and also indulges my infatuation with mascarpone cheese. And coffee cake.

I know. Is there any food that I'm not infatuated with?

1 Preheat the oven to 425°F.

2 In a large bowl, whisk together the flours, granulated sugar, baking powder, baking soda, and salt. Add the strawberries and stir. Add the cold mascarpone and butter and use a fork to combine the mixture and break the cheese into small bits. Stir well. Pour in the buttermilk and stir the mixture until a dough forms, using your hands to bring it together if necessary.

3 Place the dough on a floured surface and knead it 3 or 4 times, adding a little more flour if it's super-sticky. Pat the dough into a circle that is about 1 inch thick and place on a baking sheet.

4 For the streusel, combine the flour, brown sugar, cinnamon, and butter in a bowl and mash it together with a fork or your fingers until the mixture is crumbly. Sprinkle it all over the top of the dough. Slice the dough round into 8 triangles. Bake the scones until set and golden in color, 10 to 12 minutes.

NOTES: For a savory change of pace, remove the fruit from your scones and add some freshly grated cheddar cheese and chives. Or try a few spoonfuls of pesto and Parmesan cheese. Dip them in soup or replace your traditional dinner rolls with a little something extra.

STREUSEL

$\frac{1}{3}$ **cup all-purpose flour**

3 **tablespoons light brown sugar**

$\frac{1}{2}$ **teaspoon ground cinnamon**

3 **tablespoons unsalted butter, at room temperature**

breakfast cookies

MAKES 20 cookies • TIME: 45 minutes

1½ cups old-fashioned rolled oats

⅔ cup whole wheat pastry flour

⅓ cup ground flaxseed

2 tablespoons light brown sugar

½ teaspoon baking powder

½ teaspoon baking soda

½ teaspoon ground cinnamon

¼ teaspoon salt

2 very ripe bananas, mashed

1 large egg, lightly beaten

2 tablespoons coconut oil, melted

2 tablespoons peanut butter, melted

2 teaspoons vanilla extract

1 cup chopped dried figs

¼ cup chopped dark chocolate

For years, my husband has been asking me to make "healthy" cookies. He is a self-proclaimed cookie snob. Traditional chocolate chips are his favorite, and he loves to stand over the sink and eat two or three with a Diet Coke in hand. Why a Diet Coke? I have no idea. We've all got our vices.

The funny thing is that I HAVE made him some so-called "healthy" cookies before and he's turned his nose up. I don't blame him—it's a rough day when you're craving a cookie and you are handed something that doesn't quite resemble the chewy dough ball you've been desiring.

My solution to healthy cookies has been this: breakfast cookies. They may not taste cookie-ish enough to happily be considered an indulgent dessert after dinner, but they taste pretty darn delicious for breakfast. And they're filled with fiber and health too.

Because you know, chocolate has antioxidants. And well, that just seals the deal for me.

1 Preheat the oven to 350°F.

2 In a large bowl, whisk together the oats, flour, flaxseed, brown sugar, baking powder, baking soda, cinnamon, and salt. In a smaller bowl, mix together the mashed bananas, egg, coconut oil, peanut butter, and vanilla extract. Add the wet ingredients to the dry and mix them until just combined. Stir in the dried figs and the chocolate until evenly dispersed.

3 Scoop out the dough 2 tablespoons at a time and place on nonstick baking sheets, keeping the cookies 2 inches apart from each other. Bake until cookies are set and slightly golden, for 12 minutes, then remove the sheet from the oven and let the cookies cool on the baking sheet. These cookies are best when eaten the first or second day but can be stored in a sealed bag or container for up to 5 days.

whole wheat cinnamon rolls

MAKES one 8x8-inch pan • **TIME:** 2 hours

. . . .

½ cup 2% milk

½ cup water

3 teaspoons active dry yeast

1 tablespoon honey

2 cups all-purpose flour, plus extra for dusting

1½ cups whole wheat flour

1 large egg

1 teaspoon vanilla extract

½ teaspoon salt

½ teaspoon ground cinnamon

Confession time: I grew up eating cinnamon rolls out of a can.

You know the ones. You bake them in a little round cake pan and, when they are still hot, you pour the glaze that comes in a little squeeze pack over the top? Yeah. Those. My mom still makes them.

I ate my fair share of them as a kid, but I ate even more of the orange roll version. Now those were tasty. My brothers and I fought over 'em like cats and dogs. For a hungry family of five, one batch was never enough.

It wasn't until I got married that I tasted my first batch of real, homemade cinnamon rolls. Bona fide cinnamon rolls. Cinnamon rolls that mattered. I thought Eddie was going to lose his mind. He was in absolute heaven.

Now, I am not one for changing the true identity of foods. I didn't want to destroy the integrity of the cinnamon roll—it needs to remain doughy, warm, gooey, and soft. I kneel at the altar of butter and flour when it comes to a baked good's authenticity.

But I also like to make a few tiny changes if changes can be made. Makes things a little more tolerable on the waistline, if you will. These cinnamon rolls may never be considered a health food—if I ever see a healthy cinnamon roll, well, I may run for the hills—but they are made with a good bit of whole wheat flour that can make you feel a little better about yourself.

Because we all know that, just like doughnuts, one cinnamon roll doesn't cut it.

1 Add the milk and water to a small saucepan and heat over low heat until the liquid reaches 100° to 105°F. Once warm, add the liquid to the bowl of your electric stand mixer that is fitted with a beater attachment. Stir in the yeast and honey with a spoon. Let the mixture sit until foamy, 10 to 15 minutes.

2 Add 1½ cups of the all-purpose flour, all of the whole wheat flour, the egg, vanilla extract, salt, and cinnamon to the yeast and turn the mixer on low speed. Beat the ingredients until the dough begins to come together (it will still be sticky). Switch attachments on the mixer, fitting it with the dough hook.

3 Turn the mixer on to medium speed and knead the dough for 8 to 10 minutes, gradually sprinkling in the remaining ½ cup all-purpose flour as it kneads. Remove the dough from the mixer and knead it by hand a few times before placing it in an oiled bowl. Cover the bowl with a towel and let it sit in a warm place to rise for 1 to 1½ hours.

After the dough has risen, sprinkle the counter with flour and place the dough on the counter. Roll the dough into a 6x12-inch rectangle.

 For the filling, brush the melted coconut oil all over the dough. In a small bowl, mix together the brown sugar and cinnamon. Sprinkle it evenly over the coconut oil. Beginning at one of the long ends, tightly roll the dough up and pinch the ends. Slice the dough into 12 equal rounds.

 Spray an 8x8-inch pan with nonstick spray. Place the rounds in the pan. Cover it and let the pan sit in a warm place to rise again for 30 minutes. Meanwhile, preheat the oven to 350°F.

 Bake the rolls until golden brown, 25 to 30 minutes. For the glaze, in a small bowl, whisk together the powdered sugar, milk, and vanilla extract until smooth.

8 Remove the pan from the oven and immediately pour the glaze over the rolls. Let cool for 1 to 2 minutes before serving.

FILLING

3 tablespoons coconut oil, melted

$1/3$ cup loosely packed light brown sugar

$1/2$ teaspoon ground cinnamon

GLAZE

$3/4$ cup powdered sugar

$1^1/2$ tablespoons milk

$1/4$ teaspoon vanilla extract

2
snack time
(because i said so!)

Always being a fairly big **proponent** of the **three-meals-a-day** rule, I often come across a problem: *I really like snacks.*

See, the issue arises because I like to feel full. I enjoy having three large meals instead of five or six small ones; it's what works for me; it keeps me happy and satisfied. But I also love snacky foods, and I love having a bunch of snacky foods made into a full meal.

That's kind of my solution: Make enough snacks to get full. I like variety.

A few years into our marriage, I selfishly became brave enough to plan a snack-like dinner one Saturday night for Eddie. We are talking about a true meat-and-potatoes man. A guy who needs his serving (or four) of protein plus two (preferably warm) side dishes and maybe even a salad beforehand. One heck of a good-old-fashioned meal.

Don't worry: I came prepared with loads and loads of wine.

He was surprisingly receptive to the idea. There were a few nervous glances as I piled various cheeses, breads, chutneys, nuts, and cured meats on to a large cutting board, but the diverse spread saved me. I think.

I knew he would be able to get "full," which is some odd fear in his mind. Like if he can't get full, he may ***spontaneously combust*** or something? The world will end? There will never be another meal?

And he was. Full, that is. Eddie loved the dinner that night, but I think he loved it so much due to the spontaneity. Had I planned a few days in advance and let him know about all this snackage that would take the place of our traditional meal, it may not have been the case. Still, it was the perfect example of one of my favorite ways to eat—snacks all around.

I believe there are three specific ***snacking strategies.*** There is snacking in place of a meal, like the dinner I just described. Then there is snacking in between meals, like maybe after lunch or dinner when you're in need of a salty-sweet fix or just some afternoon energy. Then there are entertaining snacks: book club parties, football games, and so on . . . and those may be my favorite kind.

I come from a long line of on-a-whim entertainers. Meaning that my family has no rules when it comes to visiting their siblings, parents, or relatives without calling first. A simple knock—or walk in—is all it takes, and boom, you have a house full of guests for the next six hours. Those are my absolute favorite nights.

Due to my high-maintenance snacking demands, I have an assortment of snacks that I'm hoping you'll love just as much as I do. I've broken it into two categories: some snacks here that are geared more toward some daily, ***prep-ahead-because-you-know-you'll-be-hungry*** dishes and some extra finger foods that will make you an entertaining queen. Or king.

Of course, you don't have to follow the rules and can make whatever you want, whenever you want. I'm secretly hoping you'll do that. We're so much alike.

BBQ roasted chickpeas

MAKES 1½ cups • TIME: 45 minutes

1 tablespoon smoked paprika

1 tablespoon onion powder

1½ teaspoons light brown sugar

1½ teaspoons garlic salt

½ teaspoon chili powder

½ teaspoon freshly ground black pepper

1½ cups canned chickpeas, rinsed and drained

1 tablespoon extra-virgin olive oil

NOTE: Try the sour cream and onion mix for the homemade popcorn on page 88. Simply roast the chickpeas with a little salt and pepper and, once they are finished, toss them in a bit of the seasoning.

I feel a little hypocritical talking about snacks here because if I'm being honest, more often than not, these chickpeas end up in my main meal. Don't get me wrong—they are fabulous for snacking. You know the whole once-you-pop-you-can't-stop thing? Like Pringles in the '90s?

These are just like that. Super addicting but a million times healthier. Loaded with fiber, loaded with flavor. And incredibly satisfying with the crunch, crunch, crunch.

It's true: A bowl of roasted chickpeas (it better be a big one) will go a long way when it comes to snacking. But they also make a great addition to salads and even warm rice pilafs when added at the very end. If I'm feeling lazy and have a bowl on hand, sometimes I add them as a simple side dish to whatever I'm having for lunch.

They are such big-time people-pleasers. It doesn't seem like you're eating a bean, a legume that's packed with nutrients that are good for you. It's like you're eating a funner snack like a chip or a pretzel. (I'm still waiting to find FUNNER in the dictionary.)

What's your favorite flavor? I bet we can turn it into a roasted chickpea. I almost promise you.

1 Preheat the oven to 425°F.

2 In a small bowl, whisk together the paprika, onion powder, brown sugar, garlic salt, chili powder, and pepper.

3 Pat the chickpeas completely dry with a towel and remove any of the skins that become loose. Add the chickpeas to a bowl and toss them with the olive oil and three-quarters of the spice mixture. Mix well to coat the chickpeas and spread them out on a nonstick baking sheet. Bake the chickpeas for 20 minutes, toss them with a spatula, and bake for 15 minutes more. Remove the pan from the oven and let the chickpeas cool on the baking sheet.

4 Taste the chickpeas and season them with the additional spice mix if needed. If you don't need it, simply place it in a sealed plastic bag and save it for the next batch.

5 Roasted chickpeas are best the day they are made—after a few hours they can start to lose their crunch. However, you can store them in a container with a sheet of plastic wrap lightly covering the top for 2 to 3 days.

I've trashed up my fair share of banana breads. I've added bacon, topped them with coconut streusel, poured peanut butter into the batter, and made every variation of chocolate banana bread that exists. And while I completely adore all things banana bread, nothing beats the classic.

This is like the classic plus. It's a total whole wheat bread but with the addition of brown butter. Which I believe gives everything a special little kick.

If I could cover my entire life in brown butter, I would. Heck, I think I already kinda do.

1 Preheat the oven to 325°F. Spray a 5x9-inch loaf pan with nonstick spray.

2 In a large bowl, whisk together the browned butter and brown sugar. Once it is combined, stir in the coconut milk, bananas, eggs, and vanilla extract. In a small bowl, whisk together the flour, baking soda, salt, and cinnamon.

3 Add the dry ingredients to the wet and mix them with a large spoon until just combined. Pour the batter into the greased loaf pan. Bake the bread for 60 to 65 minutes, rotating the pan once during the cooking time. Remove the bread from the oven and let cool in the loaf pan for 20 minutes. Gently remove the bread and place on a cutting board or counter lined with parchment paper. Let cool completely before cutting.

brown butter **banana** bread

MAKES one 5x9-inch loaf
TIME: 1½ hours

8 tablespoons (1 stick) unsalted butter, browned (see page 26)

½ cup loosely packed light brown sugar

½ cup canned light coconut milk

4 very ripe bananas, mashed (about 1¼ cups)

2 large eggs

2 teaspoons vanilla extract

1⅔ cups whole wheat pastry flour

1 teaspoon baking soda

½ teaspoon salt

¼ teaspoon ground cinnamon

chocolate
& toasted coconut
quinoa
parfaits

SERVES 2 • TIME: 25 minutes

½ cup quinoa

½ cup canned light coconut milk

½ cup water

¼ teaspoon salt

1½ cups plain full-fat or low-fat Greek yogurt

⅓ cup unsweetened flaked coconut, toasted (see page 27)

4 ounces high-quality dark chocolate, chopped

Quinoa-yogurt parfaits are one of those treats that I discovered through food blogging. I surprisingly wasn't ever hesitant because I'm always looking for another way to use the trendy seed, and yes, I'm calling it a treat because when chocolate and coconut are involved, you don't even care about the quinoa.

Actually wait, you DO care about the quinoa—because you use it to justify some extra goodies in your parfait. Quinoa and chocolate? It's a health food! Complete protein and complex carbohydrates and extra antioxidants.

All that's missing is some wine.

1 Add the quinoa to a fine-mesh strainer and rinse it well. Place the quinoa, coconut milk, water, and salt in a small saucepan over medium heat. Bring the mixture to a boil and immediately reduce the heat to low. Cover the pan and cook until the liquid is absorbed, 15 minutes. When the quinoa is finished, scoop it into a bowl and allow it to cool. You can even stick it in the fridge to speed up the process.

2 To assemble the parfaits, use a pretty glass or jar and layer a few tablespoons of the quinoa, a few tablespoons of yogurt, and a sprinkling of coconut and chocolate together. Repeat the process 2 or 3 more times to create the parfait.

NOTES: I also like to make a big batch of quinoa at the beginning of the week to use for breakfast bowls and parfaits. Just scoop it right out of the fridge. The parfaits can also be made about an hour ahead of time and stored in the fridge if you'd like to serve them at a brunch or a party.

The more commonly known parfait is usually stuffed with fruit, and there need be no exception to the rule here. Try stuffing some strawberries and kiwis between your quinoa and yogurt layers, or even some super-fresh peaches and brown sugar in the summer. Come autumn, mix a few spoonfuls of pureed pumpkin and pumpkin pie spice right into the yogurt, then sprinkle in some toasted pecans and almonds.

easy dark chocolate peanut butter

• • • • • • • • • • • • • • • • • • • •

MAKES 1½ cups • TIME: 20 minutes

• • • • • • • • • • • • • • • • • • • •

3 cups dry-roasted unsalted peanuts

2½ ounces high-quality dark chocolate, chopped

⅛ teaspoon salt

I'm just gonna put it out there: I grew up in a Jif household. Surprisingly enough, I was burnt out on peanut butter and jelly by first grade—180 straight days of kindergarten lunches may do that to you. Plus, I was really only a fan of strawberry jam, and my brothers always fought hard to throw grape in the grocery cart. Two against one: They win.

I got my peanut butter fix in other ways. My favorite snack was something my mom made for us after school: a banana boat. It was a slice of bread slathered with peanut butter. A banana was placed right on top, the sides of the bread folded up, and then stuck through the center were some of those mini pretzel sticks to hold the whole mess together.

It was wonderful.

I also was a big fan of peanut butter–blanketed English muffins each morning, topped off with a little drizzle of honey. I ate those for a good four or five years.

This was all back in the day when strolling down the peanut butter aisle wasn't similar to having to choose a name for your firstborn. How can you possibly choose today? The variety is incredible—and not just in flavor, but also in nuts. Cashew, walnut, almond, pistachio, macadamia—you name it, it's there.

(As a side note, I used to beg my mom, probably to the point of tears, to buy me that jar of peanut butter and jelly that was swirled together. Remember that? She continuously reminded me that I didn't love grape jelly, but I didn't care. I needed that swirled peanut butter jar. Never got it. Moms know best.)

The one way that I always took my peanut butter was straight up with chocolate. I cannot remember a time when I wasn't completely infatuated with the combination, which I'm sure began with a few peanut butter cups on Halloween or after I raided Mother Lovett's stash of candy in the cupboard below her bar.

Even at the age of 17, when I went through a breakup that I thought was the end of my life (another spoiler alert: It wasn't.), I survived on handfuls of Cheez-Its and spoonfuls of peanut butter covered in chocolate chips for a week. To this day, it's still one of my favorite snacks. And it doesn't even remind me of the guy.

1 Add the peanuts to the bowl of your food processor and blend to combine. Blend continuously until the peanuts begin to turn creamy, 3 to 4 minutes. Turn off the food processor and scrape down the sides at any time if needed. Continue to puree until you see peanut butter forming.

2 While the peanuts are doing their thing, add the chocolate to a bowl. Microwave it on medium power for 30 seconds, then stir and microwave again on medium power for 30 seconds. Stir until all of the chocolate melts. If it needs more heat, continue to microwave in 15-second increments, but be careful to not burn the chocolate.

3 Add the melted chocolate and the salt to the creamy peanut butter and turn the food processor back on until it's combined. Store the peanut butter in a sealed container or jar. It will keep for up to 2 weeks at room temperature. Otherwise, store it in the fridge and it will keep for a month or two.

NOTE: Switch up the nuts! Swap some unsalted almonds for the peanuts, or even try adding hazelnuts instead.

chewy granola bars

Ab, granola bars. You're like granola's sneaky sister: just as addicting but proportionally packaged so we eat only as much as we should. Which rarely happens.

I've searched far and wide for a homemade chewy granola bar that compares to the ones stuffed in my lunch box as a kid. It's tough searching high and low for a real food version when the packaged classics contain tons of preservatives to give you the chew. How depressing. . . .

This is as close as I've come to chewy homemade granola bars. They are equally as addicting and perhaps more dangerous—after all, you must make them yourself and then cut them into squares and exercise self-control. Evidently two more than you expect will end up right in your mouth but, well, that's okay. They're homemade!

These are perfect for a Saturday morning bike ride or a road trip when the drive-thru is tempting you.

These are perfect as an afternoon snack, or a little post-dinner dessert, or crumbled on top of some ice cream or fro yo.

These are perfect for doing whatever the heck you want with them.

MAKES 9 to 12 bars • TIME: 40 minutes

2 cups old-fashioned rolled oats
½ cup ground flaxseed
⅓ cup walnuts, coarsely chopped
3 tablespoons sunflower seeds
2 tablespoons light brown sugar
2 tablespoons chia seeds
½ teaspoon salt
½ teaspoon ground cinnamon
½ cup coconut oil
½ cup creamy almond butter
⅓ cup honey
1 teaspoon vanilla extract

1 Preheat the oven to 350°F. Line an 8x8-inch baking dish with parchment or waxed paper, leaving extra paper hanging over the edges. Spray the paper with nonstick spray.

2 In a large bowl, whisk together the oats, flaxseed, walnuts, sunflower seeds, brown sugar, chia seeds, salt, and cinnamon. Set aside.

3 In a small saucepan over low heat, combine the coconut oil, almond butter, honey, and vanilla extract. Stir the mixture until the oil and almond butter melt. Remove the pan from the heat and pour into the oat mixture. Stir the mixture until all of the ingredients are wet and the granola begins comes together. Press the mixture into the lined dish, smoothing out the top and corners with a spoon.

4 Bake the bars until slightly brown on top, 25 to 30 minutes. Remove from the oven and let the bars cool in the pan completely. When you're ready to cut the bars, lift the parchment paper from the pan so it comes out in one square. Cut the square into 9 or 12 bars and wrap each in plastic wrap to store. These will stay fresh for 2 to 3 days at room temperature or a bit longer in the fridge.

broiled grapefruit with ricotta & crushed amaretti cookies

SERVES 2 · TIME: 15 minutes

1/3 cup full-fat ricotta cheese

1 grapefruit, halved

2 tablespoons light brown sugar

1/4 teaspoon salt

1 tablespoon honey

2 amaretti cookies, crushed

Fresh mint, for garnish

Grapefruit is another one of those things that often makes an appearance at breakfast, but my favorite way to eat this broiled version is for a late afternoon snack. Citrus fruits are widely rumored to be a bit of an appetite suppressant, so when the grapefruit is warm and golden, then topped with a bit of whipped ricotta, it's the perfect keep-me-full-until-dinner snack.

And make-me-feel-kind-of-healthy snack.

You know, so you're not reaching your hand way down far into the cereal box (for the third time) while you're searing the chicken or stirring the soup? No? Only me?

To give this snack a little extra flavor—and, well, if we're being honest, to satisfy my sweet teeth that beg for sugar every day around 3 PM—I crush a few amaretti cookies on top. They add the perfect texture (I always need the crunch!) and amount of candied sweetness. Some grocery stores carry amaretti cookies in the bakery, but you can rest assured that if you have an Italian market near you, they will have boatloads of them. They may become your new favorite thing.

1 Preheat the broiler in your oven to the highest setting and place an oven rack directly underneath.

2 Add the ricotta cheese to a food processor and blend until creamy.

3 Cover each grapefruit half with the brown sugar and a sprinkle of salt. Place the grapefruit halves on a baking sheet, cut side up. Broil the fruit until the sugar has melted and it is bubbly, 2 to 3 minutes. Remove the sheet from the oven and let the fruit cool slightly.

4 Cover the grapefruit halves with some of the whipped ricotta, a drizzle of honey, and crushed amaretti cookies. Top with a sprig of mint.

It's true: I am obsessed with everything.

No, not everything everything, like everything in the world. But the everything seasoning that I believe originated on bagels and now can be found on flatbreads and crackers and even hummus. Everything is everywhere. So original.

An extra-toasty everything bagel with cream cheese is my drug of choice. That flavor. Ugh. The flavor! I can't even take it.

These chips are a little different and heavily seasoned, so I don't suggest dipping them in salsa—unless you really love salsa. I prefer them as a dipper for hummus or even your traditional potato chip dip. Like French onion or horseradish-bacon or anything else like what I used to pull out of Mother Lovett's fridge. I would go.to.town.

These chips also make an excellent bed for a perfectly sliced wedge of cheese and maybe a dollop of grainy mustard. One caveat: They are messy, as are all things with multiple seeds. Prepare to find seeds in every crevice of your life for weeks after baking these.

Totally worth it, though.

1 Preheat the oven to 350°F. Combine the minced onion, sesame seeds, poppy seeds, minced garlic, salt, and pepper in a bowl.

2 Brush the tortillas with the olive oil on both sides. Sprinkle one side with a tablespoon or two of the seasoning. Use a sharp knife or pizza cutter to slice each tortilla into 6 triangles. Place the triangles on a nonstick baking sheet. Bake the tortillas until golden and crisp, 8 to 10 minutes. I love to eat these with hummus!

everything baked tortilla chips

SERVES 4 · TIME: 20 minutes

2 tablespoons dried minced onion

2 tablespoons sesame seeds, toasted (see page 27)

1 tablespoon poppy seeds

1 tablespoon dried minced garlic

1 teaspoon flaked sea salt

1/4 teaspoon freshly ground black pepper

8 (4-inch) flour tortillas

1/4 cup extra-virgin olive oil

"sour cream & onion" popcorn

SERVES 2 to 4 • TIME: 15 minutes

6 cups freshly popped air-popped popcorn

2 tablespoons extra-virgin olive oil

3 tablespoons chopped fresh dill

3 tablespoons freshly grated Parmesan cheese

3 tablespoons powdered buttermilk

1½ tablespoons onion powder

1 teaspoon garlic powder

1 teaspoon salt

½ teaspoon freshly ground black pepper

By now you've probably figured out what a nostalgic person I am and more so, how foods play a role in my nostalgia almost every day. If there is any flavor that is more throwback than sour cream and onion? I have no idea what it could be.

Sour cream and onion flavors tempted me like crazy as a kid. I remember being utterly terrified to try such a thing because, yuck, I didn't like onions and why would I want my potato chips to taste like one? It didn't take long, but as expected, I was hooked, kinda like everyone else in the '80s and '90s.

These days, I'm amazed by the potato chip flavors out there. Buffalo wing, cheddar BBQ, sweet Thai chile, and all sorts of things similar. It this real life?

While there are times when I think nothing makes a better partner to my lunchtime sandwich than some crunchy potato chips (actually, I'd rather put the chips directly on my sandwich, but that's a whole other subject), I refrain from snacking on them because they don't fill me up. Additionally, I've barely blinked and reached the bottom and then I'm like . . . uh, what? I just ate 500 calories worth of crunchy air and now I need a snack.

Enter popcorn, please. My dad made popcorn on the stovetop at least three times a week back in the good old days. In fact, he still does—he pops it with a bit of oil, no butter, no salt. As much as I love buttery flavor on my popcorn, sometimes a small handful of the plain stuff transports me right back to being 13 again.

This popcorn is for those nights—maybe those late nights—when you really want a snack but you just don't think plain popcorn is going to cut it. You want something more flavorful, saltier, crunchy, and crave-worthy. While we're not adding any extra crunch, the homemade sour cream and onion seasoning satisfies the salt monster.

It's, like, almost 1988 again up in here.

1 Drizzle the popcorn with the olive oil and toss it well to coat. In a small bowl, whisk together the dill, cheese, buttermilk, onion powder, garlic powder, salt, and pepper. Pour it over the popcorn and toss the popcorn to evenly coat it in the mixture. Taste the popcorn and season it additionally if needed.

NOTE: You should be able to find powdered buttermilk in the baking aisle of your local grocery store. If you can't find buttermilk, powdered milk can work in a pinch.

Here are my thoughts on nuts: They typically belong in a pretty little candy dish that sits on your coffee table.

For me? They just don't belong in cookies. Or brownies. Or any baked goods, for that matter.

While I'm not above throwing out some raw almonds or store-bought spiced walnuts on a whim, I love creating my own special spice toss or flavored seasoning for nuts. It just gives them a little something extra when set out at a party.

These cashews are the dear recipients of my outrageous coconut obsession. Not only do we get a bit of the curry flavor, but the coconut and coconut oil also add some sweetness that is sort of reminiscent of candied nuts. Just a little. Oh—like those ones they have at the mall during the holidays or in the theater during intermissions? Ha. Trying to eat just a few of those things is an absolute joke. Talk about addicting.

Luckily, you can make addictive foods at home and overeat them with privacy.

① Heat a large skillet over medium-high heat and add the coconut oil. Add the cashews and toss to coat them in the oil. Toast the nuts for 2 to 3 minutes, stirring with a heatproof spoon while toasting to ensure that they don't burn. Add the coconut, curry powder, salt, and pepper and continue to stir and toss to coat. Cook for another 2 to 3 minutes while stirring, until the coconut is toasted and the curry is fragrant. Remove the cashews from the heat and spread them out on a baking sheet. Allow the nuts to cool completely and dry before eating.

toasted coconut– *curry* cashews

MAKES about 2 cups • **TIME:** 1 hour

1$\frac{1}{2}$ tablespoons coconut oil

12 ounces raw unsalted cashews

2$\frac{1}{2}$ tablespoons unsweetened flaked coconut

2 teaspoons curry powder

$\frac{1}{2}$ teaspoon salt

$\frac{1}{2}$ teaspoon freshly ground black pepper

doing a *cheese* **board** like whoa

When it comes to preparing appetizers or snacks, a cheese board is almost always my go-to. I love making a massive selection that will please almost anyone . . . and on the rare occasion, tricking Eddie into thinking this is dinner.

Because it totally can be.

The great thing about cheese boards is that you can easily determine the serving size based on what you want to add to your board. If you're serving a crowd and want to get all mathematical, it's best to have around 2 ounces of cheese per person. I'm a bit wacky though and love to have a selection—so even if it is just four of us? I might still put out multiple (read: five or six) cheese wedges.

This isn't so much of a recipe as it is a suggestion and vision board for your cheese. Make it your own and include whatever YOU like to eat with cheese. (In my case, that would normally be, um, everything. In the universe.)

Cheeses

I aim to have five different cheeses on my board—one from each category below. If it's a huge party? I might pick two cheeses from a few categories.

This is how I roll:

- BLUE CHEESE: My preference tends to be Gorgonzola or a rich smoked blue.
- SOFT OR SEMI-SOFT CHEESE: Brie or Camembert is the most common.
- HARD CHEESE: My favorite is a brick of Asiago or Parmigiano-Reggiano.
- AGED CHEESE: A killer aged cheddar or Gouda works wonders here.
- GOAT OR CHÈVRE: My number one choice? Humboldt Fog cheese.
- Of course, you can also add in a WINE-SOAKED CHEESE or a fresh mozzarella too.

Bready Things

Cheese and bread go hand in hand, right? Make sure to offer a mild, plain version as well as a variety of seedy picks. I will usually choose at least three of the following:

- Seedy, grainy bread
- Hard sesame breadsticks
- Toasted crostini
- Water crackers
- Multigrain crackers
- Bagel or pita chips
- Flatbreads

Jams & Chutneys

Spreads are ideal because you not only add them on crackers and bread—but also directly on the cheese. My choices for sweet spreads include fig preserves, quince paste, apple and berry chutneys, and plain old honey—perfect for drizzling. I also like to throw in some savory versions and serve a hot pepper jelly or bacon marmalade. For over 20 years, my family has been using preserves from American Spoon in northern Michigan. They are by far my favorite. I also find great ones on the displays near the cheese counter at Whole Foods.

Fruits & Nuts

I prefer fruits that don't brown easily when sliced, so my ideals include grapes, cherries, dates, dried figs, and apricots. Occasionally I will set out a few ripe pears with a paring knife for slicing.

Many people can be very picky about nuts, but I find that having an unsalted, roasted version (like peanuts or pistachios) is best, along with one or two more choices. I love Marcona almonds, smoked almonds, and candied pecans.

Charcuterie

Depending on if you're partying with meat lovers, you may want to add anywhere from one to three options of your favorite deli selections here. I often choose good old pepperoni, salami (the varieties are endless these days: black truffle, spicy Italian, or smoked), and paper-thin sliced prosciutto.

Tart & Briny Snacks

As a lover of all things vinegar-based, this is the most significant part of my board. I love to include:

- Olives—any and all varieties
- Marinated artichoke hearts
- Cornichons
- Roasted red peppers
- Balsamic glaze
- Sweet peppadew peppers
- Pickled jalapeño peppers
- Sweet Dijon mustard
- Spicy grainy mustard

how sweet
house guac

MAKES 3 cups • TIME: 10 minutes

4 very ripe avocados, halved and pitted

Juice of 2 limes

1 large tomato, chopped

½ red onion, diced

1 jalapeño chile pepper, diced

⅓ cup chopped fresh cilantro

½ teaspoon salt

½ teaspoon freshly ground black pepper

I have been known to eat an entire bowl of guacamole by myself in one sitting. To say that I am in love would be a severe understatement. It would probably even be offensive.

Over the years there has been a lot of guac to cross my path. I've determined what I love and don't love, and this is it. My number-one preference is for the dip to remain completely authentic in flavor—so I don't want any sour cream or yogurt mixed in. I am happiest when my red onion and jalapeño are finely diced and when my tomato is mostly seeded. Lots of salt and pepper are a must.

And the limes—well, they are the key. Oh, and so are the margaritas.

1 Scoop the avocado flesh into a large bowl. Add the lime juice, tomato, onion, jalapeño, cilantro, salt, and pepper. Mash the avocados with a potato masher or a fork—you can leave it as chunky as desired. Taste and season additionally if desired.

NOTES: For all of you cilantro haters out there who claim your guac tastes like soap, simply leave it out. No biggie. And if you want to trash up your guac (aka, one of my favorite things to do), feel free to add some juicy mango chunks or crispy bacon. I've done it, my friends. It's fab.

super-creamy **white** bean dip

SERVES 4 to 6 • **TIME: 15 minutes**

3 cups canned cannellini beans, drained and rinsed

1 head roasted garlic, cloves squeezed out (see page 29)

6 tablespoons extra-virgin olive oil

1/2 teaspoon salt

1/2 teaspoon freshly ground black pepper

I'm a bit boring in my hummus choices. Here's the proof. While I've been tempted in the past by roasted red pepper and garlic, and I've even made some of my own crazy flavors, such as sweet corn and jalapeño or coconut milk and citrus, there is just something about creamy traditional hummus with a good glug of olive oil.

True, this is slightly off track from traditional—I prefer white beans because they are so super creamy it's like they almost melt in the food processor. They also don't require any peeling of the shells, which if you want finely smooth hummus is pretty much a requirement of garbanzos. Make sure to be generous with the salt and pepper for flavor—and then spread this on anything your little heart desires.

1 Combine the beans and garlic cloves in a food processor and blend until combined. With the processor on, stream in the olive oil. Continue to blend until the dip is creamy. Add the salt and pepper and blend once more. Taste the dip and season it additionally if desired. Add a few roasted garlic cloves on top for garnish.

Sometimes when you're at a party, don't you just want to scream "Give me the Brie and nobody will get hurt!" and then run like a maniac with a box of crackers?

Me too.

Baked Brie cheese will never be an outdated appetizer in my mind. I mean, how can warm, bubbly, melted cheese ever get old? It can't. It just can't.

I don't care if it's so 1995. Whatever. This is a staple.

This Brie is a little higher in the maintenance department than some of the traditional recipes because it requires roasting the blueberries for a few minutes before adding them on top of the Brie. Fruit and basil is one of my favorite combinations, and when it's warm and syrupy atop a round of cheesy goodness, I really only need a spoon.

Or 25,000 crackers.

1 Preheat the oven to 400°F. Place the blueberries on a nonstick baking sheet. Roast the berries for 15 minutes, then remove from the oven.

2 Place the wheel of Brie in the center of a pie plate or circular baker. Spoon the roasted blueberries on top. Place the dish in the oven and bake the Brie just until the cheese begins to bubble out of the rind, 10 to 12 minutes. Remove the dish from the oven and cover it with the fresh basil. Eat immediately, while the cheese is hot and gooey.

roasted
blueberry–basil
brie

SERVES 4 · TIME: 30 minutes

½ pint fresh blueberries
1 (8-ounce) wheel Brie cheese
3 tablespoons chopped fresh basil

grilled
scallion, corn & shrimp
quesadillas

• • • • • • • • • • • • • • • • • •

SERVES 4 • TIME: 20 minutes

• • • • • • • • • • • • • • • • • •

6 scallions, cleaned

1 tablespoon extra-virgin olive oil

1/2 pound peeled and cooked shrimp

Zest and juice of 1 lime

1/2 teaspoon chili powder

1/2 teaspoon smoked paprika

1/4 teaspoon salt

1/4 teaspoon freshly ground black
   pepper

4 (8-inch) whole wheat flour tortillas

6 ounces Monterey Jack cheese,
   freshly grated

2 ears grilled corn (see page 158),
   kernels cut from cob

If you're looking for a way to get me to eat vegetables, look no further than your cheese drawer.

Isn't this what moms have to do for toddlers?

Anyway, a surefire way to guarantee I will down my veggies includes two things: roasting the vegetables and combining them with some sort of cheese. Even better is grilling the vegetables, because nothing is better than the taste of anything grilled. It's like a summer party in your mouth.

Quesadillas have been a go-to snack my entire life. No, really—my whole life. Granted, it was the two-tortillas-and-bagged-cheese-in-the-microwave kind of quesadilla, but it instilled in me a pure love for stuffing food in between tortillas.

The other great thing? Quesadillas are a huge people-pleaser and on top of that: insanely easy. All of these ingredients (including the veg!) can be prepped beforehand, allowing you to assemble them at the last minute for grilling. And my suggestion is to make a few extra. A couple more than you think you need. In my experience, cooled quesadillas can be wrapped in aluminum foil and then stuck in the fridge for a few days, making it super easy to grab a quick snack or lunch. Sort of like leftover pizza.

And who doesn't love that?

1 Preheat the grill to the highest heat setting. Brush the scallions with the olive oil and place them directly on the grates, cooking them until grill marks appear on all sides, 5 to 6 minutes. Remove the scallions from the grill and let cool slightly.

2 Place the shrimp in a bowl and add the lime zest and juice, chili powder, paprika, salt, and pepper, tossing to combine. Slice the scallions, discarding the ends.

3 Assemble the quesadillas on a cutting board or large plate. Lay one tortilla down and add a handful of the cheese, then half of the shrimp and half of the corn. Sprinkle with half of the grilled scallions and add another handful of cheese. Top with the other tortilla. Repeat with the remaining ingredients to make a second quesadilla.

4 Add the quesadillas carefully to the grill with a large spatula, being careful not to lose the contents. Cook them until the cheese melts and grill marks appear on the tortillas. Once the cheese is melted and the quesadillas are holding together, gently flip them and grill the other sides until char marks appear. Remove the quesadillas from the grill and let sit for 2 to 3 minutes before slicing them into triangles.

spiced *autumn* crostini

SERVES 6 · TIME: 30 minutes

1 whole-grain baguette, sliced into rounds

4 ounces mascarpone cheese

2 tablespoons pumpkin puree

¼ teaspoon salt

½ teaspoon freshly ground black pepper

¼ teaspoon ground nutmeg

¼ cup hazelnuts

1 tablespoon unsalted butter

10 fresh sage leaves

Due to my now highly discussed and evidently apparent infatuation with things on toast, crostini is an entertaining must in my book. One baguette and a few different ingredients can make for a variety of appetizers and boom—you're done.

The thing is that these days, you can slap anything on some toasted baguette and call it a crostini. That may be cringe-worthy to a food purist, but to me? I'm so on board. And speaking of boards, it's because I GET bored.

I firmly believe that variety helps us maintain healthy eating habits, but the truth is that I also get bored, bored, bored with the same food choices over and over again. It's amazing, because Eddie can go six months eating the exact same lunch every day. He is a creature of habit. It makes me a little batty because I'm all "don't you even REALIZE how many delicious flavors you are missing every day?!"

Nope. He doesn't.

While I am fanatical about variety and different foods, I often try to keep my flavors centered on something warm and comforting, something possibly nostalgic (surprise, surprise), and something that I find most everyone will enjoy. Pumpkin can be a shaky flavor—not everyone likes it, but the people who do love it tend to be obsessive. This crostini has hints of fall and autumn in every bite and enough texture to please all senses. It's reminiscent of pumpkin pie, but the mascarpone and fried sage keep it savory. And the hazelnuts give it the typical crunch I crave.

Here's a hint: It can easily be made on a few large pieces of toast for an October lunch. Winning. . . .

1 Preheat the oven to 350°F. Place the sliced baguette rounds on a baking sheet. Bake the bread for 10 minutes, then flip the toasts over and bake for 5 minutes more. Remove the sheet from the oven.

2 While the bread is toasting, combine the mascarpone, pumpkin, salt, pepper, and nutmeg in a bowl and stir together until smooth.

3 Add the hazelnuts to a small skillet and heat them over medium-low heat. Toast the hazelnuts until golden and fragrant, 3 to 5 minutes, occasionally shaking the pan or stirring the nuts so they don't burn. Remove the pan from the heat immediately and place the nuts in a bowl. Once the hazelnuts have cooled, coarsely chop them.

4 Wipe out the same skillet with a paper towel and heat it over medium-low heat. Add the butter and, once it's melted, add the sage leaves. Cook the sage leaves until golden and crispy, flipping after 30 seconds. Transfer the leaves to a paper towel to cool slightly.

5 To assemble the crostini, spread the pumpkin-mascarpone mixture over the toasts. Cover each toast with a sprinkling of the chopped hazelnuts. Crumble the fried sage between your fingers and sprinkle it over the toasts.

NOTE: If you have some guests who aren't pumpkin lovers, swap it for butternut squash. Simply combine it the same way with the mascarpone and swap the seasoning for some cinnamon and nutmeg only (no salt and pepper), and you're set.

roasted **whiskey** chicken wings

Chicken wings and I have a rocky relationship. They are one of those foods that require a good bit of work for a little result—and do I want to participate in some manual labor to only get a few bites of food? And to have about a third of it end up on my face?

However, there is nothing like biting into some sticky barbecue chicken wings with a glass of beer on a Monday night while watching the Steelers play. It's one of those classic tastes—almost like spaghetti and meatballs with red wine or chips and salsa with margaritas. Something that may not happen very often, but something that can't be passed up. It's like a passage of life or something.

Like many guys, Eddie is a big wing person. He's not a big whiskey person, but I am, and well . . . I know that if I want to do some convincing, it must be done through food.

I am hooked on whiskey glazes, often using them on pork chops or broiled salmon. The flavor is fabulous and pleases all. These wings are also awesome when grilled. For real.

SERVES 2 to 4 • TIME: 1½ hours

- 2 pounds chicken wings
- 3 tablespoons extra-virgin olive oil
- 1 teaspoon salt
- 1 teaspoon freshly ground black pepper
- ¾ cup whiskey
- ½ cup loosely packed light brown sugar
- 1 garlic clove, minced
- 1 tablespoon honey
- 1 tablespoon Worcestershire sauce
- 1 teaspoon apple cider vinegar
- ½ teaspoon ground mustard

1 Preheat the oven to 450°F. Place the chicken wings on a nonstick baking sheet and brush them all over with the olive oil. Season the chicken with the salt and pepper. Place the sheet in the oven and roast the chicken for 45 minutes. Remove the sheet from the oven and let the chicken cool on the baking sheet.

2 Meanwhile, while the chicken is roasting, add the whiskey, brown sugar, garlic, honey, Worcestershire sauce, vinegar, and ground mustard to a small saucepan and whisk it together. Heat the liquid over high heat and allow the mixture to come to a boil. Reduce the heat to a simmer and cook until the liquid reduces by half, 8 to 10 minutes. Remove the pan from the heat and pour into a bowl to let cool. It will slightly thicken as it cools.

3 Once the chicken is cool enough to handle, brush it liberally with the whiskey glaze. Serve with extra glaze for brushing.

grilled fruit *salsa*

MAKES about 2 cups • TIME: 25 minutes

1 pineapple, peeled, cored, and sliced into rings

1 mango, peeled, halved, and pitted

6 large fresh strawberries, hulled and halved

1 red onion, sliced into rounds

2 tablespoons extra-virgin olive oil

1 jalapeño chile pepper, seeded and diced

1/3 cup chopped fresh cilantro

Juice of 2 limes

1/2 teaspoon salt

1/4 teaspoon freshly ground black pepper

A very defining food moment in my life was when I discovered fruit salsa. It sounds so trivial, but it became one of those events in life that I remember clearly: fruit salsa at a party with cinnamon pita chips. Stereotypical and delicious.

After that is when I hit the ground running when it came to feeling comfortable developing my own recipes. Again, it's something so simple, but I fell in love with combining one certain fruit with a certain vegetable or your typical salsa ingredient and tossing it all together with some lime juice.

I am now a fruit salsa fiend.

Sure, it comes from my love of fruit, and dipping some chips into salsa is something that will never get old. But my favorite way to use fruit salsa is as a topping on meat or fish, a dip for quesadillas and tacos, or as a garnish on crab cakes. The sweet, fresh, and spicy flavor adds a whole new element to most dishes—one that is unexpected but welcomed.

Grilling fruits and vegetables is nothing out of the ordinary, but grilling fruits and vegetables and then chopping them into tiny pieces and dipping chips in that mess? Yikes. Superb. What I'm trying to say is: Just use this on everything.

1 Preheat the grill to medium-high heat. Brush the pineapple, mango, strawberries, and onion with the olive oil. Once the grill is hot, carefully add the fruit and vegetables directly on the grates. Cook the fruit just until grill marks appear and then remove from the grill.

2 Let the fruit and vegetables cool until you can comfortably work with them. Chop everything into uniformly sized cubes and place in a large bowl. Add the jalapeño, cilantro, lime juice, salt, and pepper. Stir to mix. Taste the salsa and season it additionally if desired. I love this after it sits for a few hours—the flavors really come together.

If you fear Brussels, this is where you begin. Crunchy chips, melty cheese, spicy sausage, and a whole ton of flavor. It's exactly where Brussels sprouts belong.

1 Slice the stems off the Brussels sprouts and remove any of the tough leaves on the outside. Thinly slice each sprout and place in a large bowl.

2 Heat a large skillet over medium heat and add the olive oil. Add the shallots and garlic, stirring occasionally and cooking until softened, about 5 minutes. Add the sliced Brussels with the salt and the pepper and stir. Cook the sprouts, stirring occasionally, until they are softened and brighter in color, 5 to 6 minutes. Add the balsamic vinegar and stir to coat. Remove the sprouts from the skillet and place them back in the bowl.

3 Keep the same skillet over medium heat and add the chorizo. Use a large wooden spoon or heatproof spatula to break it into small pieces. Cook until the fat is rendered and the sausage is browned, 5 to 6 minutes. Place a paper towel on top of a plate and scoop the chorizo onto the plate to drain a bit.

4 Preheat the broiler on your oven to high heat and place an oven rack directly underneath. Evenly spread the chips out on a baking sheet. Add a handful of grated cheese to the chips, then cover them with the Brussels sprouts. Spoon the sausage on top. Add the remaining cheese. Pop the baking sheet into the oven and broil just until the cheese melts and begins to turn golden and bubbly, 2 to 3 minutes. Top with the cilantro and serve immediately.

chorizo & balsamic **brussels** nachos

SERVES 2 to 4 · TIME: 30 minutes

1 pound Brussels sprouts

2 tablespoons extra-virgin olive oil

2 shallots, diced

2 garlic cloves, minced

1/4 teaspoon salt

1/4 teaspoon freshly ground black pepper

2 teaspoons balsamic vinegar

1/2 pound fresh chorizo sausage, removed from casing

1 (16-ounce) bag blue corn chips

8 ounces Monterey Jack cheese, freshly grated

1/4 cup torn fresh cilantro leaves

3

sandwiches & stuff on toast

(and when salads aren't enough)

Lunch is a *funny thing* when your job revolves around creating new recipes.

Breakfast and dinner come fairly easily, but lunch falls right smack in the middle of meal development and photography and lots of different types of foods being all up in your face. And sometimes, those dishes alllll include chocolate.

I don't hate it.

But on those days? The ones where I'm making ten recipes or photographing scoops of ice cream or potato chip dips? Lunch may end up being a bite of everything that's going on in my kitchen. Lunch may mean a taste of pizza, a **million handfuls** of granola, and way too many spoonfuls of pie. It totally depends.

Eddie, on the other hand, needs full-blown meals for lunches. I mean, he basically eats an actual dinner for lunch. Then eats another dinner for dinner. His lunch usually involves some sort of poultry or meat, a big honking side dish, and some green beans or the like. And it all must be warm. There is no such thing as a sandwich during his workweek. Wait. Am I really the high-maintenance one?

When I was growing up, lunch was often something like tuna sandwiches or a grilled cheese. As you will learn, my mom was the queen of mayo-based salads. This is probably where my *infatuation* with things on toast began—thank goodness for her—because she never made a sandwich without toasted bread. And now? It's ruined me. I pretty much require that my sandwiches come on toast.

On days I get to go out for lunch, I find it to be such a treat. I truly find lunches out to be one of the biggest indulgences—it's such a great way to pamper yourself. But there is something to be said for inviting friends over for lunch on a Saturday afternoon. You can throw together a beautiful spread, it's a great excuse for some afternoon cocktails, and if you're lucky, the party usually rolls on into the evening. It's just fun. It's unexpected, it's welcoming, it breaks up the week and gives you something to look forward to. It doesn't happen every day and it probably doesn't happen as often as dinner parties, which is why I hold it in such high regard. It can be super casual or it can be dressy. You can even have a tea party, just for the heck of it. Anything goes.

It should come as no surprise that I rarely want a salad at lunch. Or should I say, I rarely ONLY want a salad. I can handle said salad if I get a cup of soup before, some crusty bread with my lettuce leaves, and perhaps a slice of **chocolate cake afterward.** Or I can occasionally handle a salad when done the Pittsburgh way—piled high with French fries, cheese, and bacon. And then you know that light ranch dressing and a diet soda make all the difference. Clearly. But we'll get to salads later.

What I have for you here are some . . . "heartier" lunches, if you will. A few of the options are still light and won't weigh you down or cause you to slip into a food coma 25 minutes after consumption. Then there are others that work on the days when you're a bit hungrier or craving some comfort food midday. When all you want to do is snuggle up and have a taste of home. Those are my favorite days.

If there is one thing you can find in my house five out of seven days, it's avocado toast. It's my go-to breakfast, lunch, snack, or even dinner, depending on my mood, my level of busy-ness, and how much I'm willing to admit that I've eaten it twice a day. That's real life right there.

So yeah yeah, I love things on toast, and this is where my current infatuation began. Mashed avocado. It's perfect.

I have two preferred ways of eating avocado toast: plain and with crumbled goat cheese on top. I, shockingly, don't enjoy most vegetables on it, especially when it comes to onions or peppers, because I start to feel like I'm eating guacamole on toast and that's just not what I'm going for.

But this is another one of those cases where I love something so much that I'm willing to throw in some greenery. And arugula? Well, it was one of the first leaves I became acquainted with, and I enjoy its peppery pop.

What we have going on here is lots of flavor. A little citrus, some salt, a hint of sweetness and the tiniest of spice. It takes avocado toast to a whole new level and makes for a beautiful presentation if you want to serve it to guests. Gorgeous food = fun to eat.

 In a small bowl, combine the avocado, ⅛ teaspoon of the salt, and ⅛ teaspoon of the pepper and mash it together with a fork. In a separate bowl, combine the arugula with the olive oil and lime juice and remaining salt and pepper, then toss to coat.

② Spread the avocado mash over the toast. Distribute the arugula evenly over the avocado and then add a drizzle of honey on top.

fun & fancy avocado toasts

SERVES 2 • TIME: 10 minutes

1 very ripe avocado, pitted, peeled, and mashed

¼ teaspoon salt

¼ teaspoon freshly ground black pepper

1 cup fresh arugula

1 teaspoon olive oil

Juice of 1 lime

2 slices whole-grain bread, toasted

1½ teaspoons honey

hard-boiled egg & hummus chive toasts

SERVES 2 • TIME: 25 minutes

2 slices whole-grain bread, toasted

2/3 cup hummus

2 large hard-boiled eggs

8 grape tomatoes, quartered

Pinch of flaked sea salt

Pinch of freshly ground black pepper

1 tablespoon chopped fresh chives

It's almost embarrassing to claim such a simple snack as a "recipe," but this is one of my ultimate staples. It's filling and satisfying, packed with flavor, good for you, and can be changed daily based on your hummus preference.

I'm sort of a plain hummus girl, by the way. So boring. I know.

This is one of those toasts that I throw together if I have no idea what else to eat, and actually, is one of those things that I'm sort of horrified to even mention. Just because it's that freaking easy.

Using an old-school tip from my mom, on the occasional Sunday that I remember, I will hard-boil half a dozen eggs to use throughout the week. Whether it be on salads, sandwiches, this toast, or whatever, I never regret it. I rarely prepare only enough hard-boiled eggs for me to eat—I always find that making a few extra is a key to standby healthy snacking.

Hope you enjoy my embarrassing toast.

1 Spread each slice of bread with a generous helping of hummus. Place the sliced eggs on top of the hummus and cover with the tomatoes. Season with the salt and the pepper and sprinkle with the chives.

burrata *caprese* toasts

SERVES 2 • TIME: 10 minutes

4 ounces fresh burrata cheese

2 slices whole-grain bread, toasted

2 Roma tomatoes, sliced

Pinch of flaked sea salt

Pinch of freshly ground black pepper

6 fresh basil leaves, chopped

2 tablespoons balsamic glaze
(see page 26)

When I think of perfect foods, a few things come to mind.

Bacon. Organic ripe strawberries. Humboldt Fog cheese. Grilled hot dogs in the summer. Sweet corn.

And burrata. Always burrata.

If you're unfamiliar with this glorious ball of goodness, burrata is fresh mozzarella that is filled with cream. That filling essentially turns it into a slightly spreadable mozz, and when combined with tomatoes, basil, salt, and pepper? Is something I would gladly eat every day.

In fact, last summer I ate this meal for dinner nearly two weeks in row. Fourteen days straight.

Totally unlike me, totally hypocritical of me, and totally delicious.

1 Add half of the burrata to each piece of toast and use the back of a spoon to spread it out. Cover each piece with the sliced tomatoes, salt, pepper, and chopped basil. Add a generous drizzle of balsamic glaze on top.

NOTE: Burrata can be found near the fresh mozzarella in the dairy section, though is often most accessible in larger organic food or specialty stores. It's worth the price. Promise.

Salty-sweet combos are a must for me. Sure, I've discussed my sweet teeth, but even a sugar girl needs her salt every now and then. And I so often crave it with something sweet. Just how life goes.

While I will continue to wax poetic about combining bacon with chocolate (yeah, I know) to get that fix, I love taking a savory snack and adding just a hint of sweetness. So that's where the figs come in.

My fig discoveries happened like so: dried figs, fig jams, then fresh figs. When you live in the ever-so-tropical Pennsylvania, fresh figs are few and far between. And often cost one dollar per fig in the grocery store. ONE DOLLAR. It's ridic.

That's one of the reasons that fig jam is a staple. The other reason is that it's just plain fantastic, and a third reason would be that it truly works with everything. It's fabulous on pizza, in cookies, off a spoon. It works with cheeses and meats, sugar and salt, bread and butter. It's versatile to the point of ludicrosity.

pretty
prosciutto
& fig
toasts

SERVES 2 • TIME: 10 minutes

¼ cup fig preserves

2 tablespoons mascarpone cheese

2 slices whole-grain bread, toasted

¼ pound prosciutto, thinly sliced

1 tablespoon chopped fresh basil

1 In a small bowl, stir together the fig preserves and mascarpone until creamy. Spread the slices of toast with the fig spread and layer slices of the prosciutto on top. Sprinkle each slice with the basil. If you are lucky enough to have fresh figs, go ahead and slice some on top.

I have always been a tuna lover. I'm sure we can agree that there are definitely tuna lovers and tuna haters in the universe and, well . . . I'm lucky to be a lover.

Salads were one of those things that were a staple for summertime lunches, and I'm not talking about the kind with lettuce leaves and tomatoes. We're talking tuna, chicken, or egg salads tossed with a good bit of mayo and some salt and pepper and—if my mom got her way—a whole lot of crunchy celery.

Perhaps the wildest part about my tuna love is that I can eat it plain. I mean, completely plain—no seasoning, no oil, no toast, nothing. Freaky. It's obviously more enjoyable with a little added flavor, but that should give you an idea of the extent to which I adore it. Crazy weird?

When avocado purchases became a constant in my grocery trips, I began searching for other exciting ways to use them. I believe it first started out with a mash of tuna and guacamole, and while guac ranks way up there, I couldn't get down with those two flavors. I think it was the overabundance of lime. But I did love the creaminess of the avocado, so I mashed it up alone and combined the two. Clearly born out of my relationship with avocado but also a healthy alternative to the option loaded with lots and lots of mayo.

I like my tuna-avocado salad as is: with tuna and avocado. However, it is incredibly delicious with a spoonful (or two. or three.) of mayo whipped in, so if you're feeling frisky, go for it. And then . . . you can just stuff it in anything.

Plus, this quick aioli drizzle? Oomph.

1 Mash the avocado in a bowl. Add the tuna and season it with the salt and pepper. Stir to combine the tuna and avocado. Fill the pitas with the tuna and add a few lettuce leaves and slices of tomato.

2 For the quick aioli, combine the mayonnaise, mustard, garlic, and lemon juice in a bowl and whisk it together. Continue whisking the mixture and stream in the olive oil. Stir until the olive oil is combined. Drizzle the aioli on top of the tuna and add it to the pita.

avocado *tuna* salad **pitas** with an **aioli** drizzle

SERVES 2 · TIME: 15 minutes

1 very ripe avocado, pitted and peeled

6 ounces chunk light tuna in water, drained

$1/4$ teaspoon salt

$1/4$ teaspoon freshly ground black pepper

2 whole wheat pitas

1 cup lettuce greens

1 Roma tomato, sliced

QUICK AIOLI DRIZZLE

2 tablespoons mayonnaise

1 tablespoon whole-grain Dijon mustard

1 minced garlic clove

2 teaspoons freshly squeezed lemon juice

1 tablespoon extra-virgin olive oil

thai chicken lettuce wraps

SERVES 4 • TIME: 30 minutes

1 cup sweet chili sauce

½ cup canned light coconut milk

½ cup rice vinegar

6 tablespoons light brown sugar

4 garlic cloves, pressed or finely minced

2 teaspoon-size knobs of fresh ginger, grated

2 tablespoons creamy peanut butter

Juice of 2 limes

1 tablespoon soy sauce

1½ tablespoons extra-virgin olive oil

2 boneless, skinless chicken breasts, cut into 1-inch pieces

½ teaspoon salt

½ teaspoon freshly ground black pepper

12 butter lettuce leaves

2 scallions, sliced

2 tablespoons peanuts, chopped

The first lettuce wraps I tried were the ones at P.F. Chang's. You know, the infamous chicken lettuce wraps that, in my opinion, kind of started a worldwide lettuce wrap trend? And by worldwide, I mean in my town. My bubble is small.

I was so hesitant at first. This was back in the day when I was sincerely afraid of vegetables, even crunchy, near-flavorless iceberg sheets that were water-packed and gave the most refreshing sensation to the spiciness of the chicken. Trust me—I can appreciate it now.

In addition to my lettuce fear, at the time the extent of my Asian cuisine knowledge came from take-out Chinese food. Famous white boxes with no lettuce in sight that always included the same order: lemon chicken. It wasn't until I met my husband that I tried Thai food for the first time, which is quite hilarious considering it may be the only "first" regarding food that he initiated. As someone who ate Thai during work lunches at least once a week, he asked for the highest level of spice possible while I meekly asked for the lowest.

Things haven't changed much.

Thai continues to be one of our favorite date night eats, and if we go anywhere with lettuce wraps on the menu? We usually order them. And now we are slightly spoiled because we also make our own. Or, he's slightly spoiled. Because I make them.

That's okay, though. I kinda like him.

1 Combine the chili sauce, coconut milk, vinegar, brown sugar, garlic, ginger, peanut butter, lime juice, and soy sauce in a saucepan, whisking it to combine. Bring the sauce to a boil, then reduce the heat to a simmer and cook for 3 to 4 minutes, until slightly thickened. Remove the pan from the heat and set aside.

2 Heat a large skillet over medium heat and add the olive oil. Add the chicken, sprinkle it with the salt and pepper, and cook until it is golden brown, 4 to 5 minutes per side. Add ¼ cup of the Thai sauce to the skillet and stir the chicken, cooking for 1 to 2 more minutes. Turn off the heat and transfer the chicken and sauce to a bowl.

3 Assemble the lettuce wraps by spooning the chicken into the lettuce leaves, adding a sprinkle of sliced scallions and chopped peanuts, and rolling them up. Use the extra sauce on the side for dipping.

green grilled cheese

. . . .

SERVES 2 • TIME: 25 minutes

. . . .

2½ tablespoons extra-virgin olive oil

1 leek, cleaned, trimmed, and sliced

1 garlic clove, minced

6 ounces fresh spinach

4 slices whole-grain bread

2 tablespoons pesto (see page 160)

4 ounces Fontina cheese, freshly grated

2 ounces sharp white cheddar cheese, freshly grated

This took a lot of convincing.

Favorite: grilled cheese.

Not a favorite: green vegetables.

How I forced myself to combine the two was . . . well . . . mandatory. There came a point in my life when I realized that to be an actual grown-up, to not eat like a teenage boy, and to be able to not regurgitate green vegetables one day when I am trying to get my future children to feast upon them, then I must consume them.

It was not a good day.

I often get questions, like serious questions, from people who want to know how I am able to eat any vegetables at all after having had such a distaste for them. They want advice. Actual tips. I know how they feel, because I desperately wanted to like vegetables and wanted to enjoy them. Not just because some dishes looked tasty, but because, um, my jeans also really wanted me to like vegetables. Desperately.

So here's what I did: I forced myself. Like every other bad habit in the world, I really believe that you won't quit (or in this case, begin) until you really want to.

I started roasting vegetables first, and I mean charring them to a crisp. I'd cover them with sea salt and Parmesan cheese, add them into kitchen sink pasta dishes, put them in enchiladas, and dip them in things like hummus or caramelized onion and bacon Greek yogurt dip. Sometimes I'd roast a small amount and make myself eat them as a side dish paired along something I really loved, like pizza or pot roast or even a cheeseburger. That made it a lot easier.

There are cases where I believe that life is too short to do something you really dislike, such as running. However, there are other things you can do in place of running that are just as great. There isn't really anything you can do in place of eating vegetables. Unfortunately. Just gotta suck it up.

This is a way to begin, though. Or, if you're a green lover, a delicious way to continue. This combines my freakish love of grilled cheese (truly I will stuff anything in one) with my fairly newfound discipline of trying to be an adult. If I'm going to eat all that melty cheese and crunchy, buttery bread, I may as well get a few extra nutrients, right?

I guess so.

1 Heat a large skillet over medium-low heat. Add 1 tablespoon of the olive oil, then add the leeks and toss to coat. Cook until the leeks are softened, 5 minutes, then stir in the garlic and cook for

30 more seconds. Add the spinach to the skillet and stir. Cook until the spinach is wilted, another 2 to 3 minutes. Remove the greens and leeks from the skillet and place them in a bowl.

2 Keep the same skillet hot over medium-low heat. To assemble the grilled cheese, brush the outside of each bread slice with the remaining 1½ tablespoons olive oil. Spread ½ tablespoon of the pesto on the inside of each bread slice. On the bottom slice of each piece of bread, layer a handful of the cheeses, half of the spinach mixture, and another handful of cheeses. Top each with the other bread slice.

3 Cook the sandwiches until golden brown on each side, 4 to 5 minutes. Taking the time to cook them over medium-low heat ensures that the cheese will melt and the bread won't burn.

NOTE: I find that having cheese on both ends of the grilled cheese is imperative to keeping the sandwich in one piece. It holds it together like glue.

Another page, another grilled cheese. Do I really need to explain my feelings on this?

I didn't think so.

1 Heat a large skillet over low heat and add 1 tablespoon of the oil. Add the onions with the pinch of salt and stir them to coat. Cover the skillet and cook the onions until softened and slightly golden, about 15 minutes, stirring every few minutes. Add the brown sugar and stir to combine, then cover and cook for 5 minutes more. Remove the onions from the skillet and set them aside in a bowl. Add ½ tablespoon of the oil to the skillet and add the mushrooms. Cover the skillet and cook the mushrooms, tossing once or twice, for 8 to 10 minutes. Stir in the garlic and cook for 30 seconds. Remove the mushrooms and garlic from the skillet, placing them on a plate.

2 Keep the same skillet hot over medium-low heat. To assemble the grilled cheese, brush the outside of each bread slice with the remaining 1½ tablespoons olive oil. Liberally spread the BBQ sauce on the inside of each bread slice. Evenly layer the cheese, onions, and mushroom slices on the bottom pieces of bread and top them with another handful of cheese. Add the top slices of bread.

3 Cook the sandwiches until golden brown on each side, 4 to 5 minutes.

BBQ portobello grilled cheese with caramelized onions

SERVES 2 • TIME: 25 minutes

3 tablespoons extra-virgin olive oil

1 red onion, thinly sliced

Pinch of salt

½ teaspoon light brown sugar

2 portobello mushroom caps, thinly sliced

2 garlic cloves, minced

4 slices whole-grain bread

¼ cup BBQ sauce

6 ounces sharp cheddar cheese, freshly grated

oven-toasted artichoke, roasted red pepper & fresh mozzarella sandwiches

SERVES 2 • TIME: 30 minutes

- 2 tablespoons unsalted butter
- 1 tablespoon fresh chopped basil
- 2 whole-grain hoagie buns, sliced
- 4 ounces fresh mozzarella cheese, sliced
- 1 (12-ounce) jar roasted red peppers in water, drained, or make your own (see page 30)
- 1 (6-ounce) jar marinated artichokes, drained
- 2 tablespoons balsamic vinegar

A few years ago, Eddie and I found ourselves walking around Reading Terminal Market in Philadelphia during lunch hour. Like, real lunch hour. Like crazy-busy, it-just-hit-noon, people-are-dying-to-be-out-of-the-office lunch hour.

It was nuts.

And for one of the first times ever, I was hungrier than him. He had finally learned that it benefited everyone when he packed a few snacks, becoming great at carrying bags of trail mix, dried fruit, and apples with him no matter where he was. It curbed his hangry husband syndrome big time and life was so much . . . happier and relaxed.

So on this day, he ate some trail mix while I was shopping . . . and there I was, wildly hungry with a million options at my fingertips. You know the times when you're so hungry you just have no idea what you even want to eat? That was me. Reading Terminal Market is a fabulous place to be at a moment like that, but also a very overwhelming place.

I walked around like a lost puppy for a good 20 minutes until I couldn't take it anymore and stopped dead in my tracks, walked up to a counter, and pointed to something in a deli case. It turned out to be a sandwich with artichokes, roasted red pepper, and mozzarella, which the man behind the counter toasted, and it was so fabulous that I can still taste it. It was just what I needed that day.

It was actually so scrumptious that when we arrived back in Pittsburgh, we immediately went to the store for the ingredients and I made it for dinner that night. This is one of the only meatless sandwiches that my husband truly loves—and sometimes adds chicken to. I don't blame him, as it meshes perfectly flavor-wise. And while it's tasty (and quicker) as a cold sandwich, my heart just can't let go of toasted sandwiches. I don't know what it is.

Well, yes I do.

It's the cheese. Always. So melty,

1. Preheat the oven to 375°F. In a small bowl, stir together butter and basil.

2. Assemble the sandwiches by laying out the buns and spreading each with a tablespoon of basil butter. Layering equal amounts of the fresh mozzarella, roasted red peppers, and artichokes on the bottoms. Drizzle each sandwich with a tablespoon of balsamic vinegar, then close the buns and wrap them tightly in aluminum foil. Bake the sandwiches for 20 minutes, then unwrap them and bake for 5 minutes more.

Do peanut butter and jellys even need an introduction?

It's quite obvious that I never want to grow up, but sometimes I want my food to taste like I did.

Don't be scared.

 Combine the pineapple, bourbon, juice, honey, and salt in a small saucepan over medium-high heat. Bring the mixture to a boil. Reduce the heat to a simmer and cook until it thickens and becomes syrupy, 8 to 10 minutes. Smash the pineapple with a fork or a potato masher as it breaks down while cooking. Remove the pan from the heat and pour the mixture into a bowl. Let cool for 15 minutes.

2 In a bowl, mix the peanut butter with the chipotle peppers and adobo sauce until combined.

3 To assemble the sandwiches, spread the toast with liberal amounts of the pineapple spread and peanut butter.

grown-up
pb & j's
(chipotle peanut butter & bourbon pineapple spread)

SERVES 2 • TIME: 30 minutes

1 cup pineapple cut into small chunks

2 tablespoons bourbon

2 tablespoons pineapple juice

2 tablespoons honey

1/4 teaspoon salt

1/3 cup creamy or chunky peanut butter

1 teaspoon chopped chipotle chile peppers in adobo sauce

1/2 teaspoon adobo sauce from can

4 slices whole-grain bread, toasted

smoked salmon BLTs with herbed mayo

SERVES 2 · TIME: 25 minutes

¼ cup mayonnaise

1 teaspoon chopped fresh basil

1 teaspoon chopped fresh parsley

1 teaspoon chopped fresh oregano

4 slices whole-grain bread, toasted

4 butter lettuce leaves

6 slices bacon, cooked

¼ pound smoked salmon

2 tomatoes, sliced

If we're being totally honest here? You have probably already figured out that I will put anything on a BLT. And I do mean anything. In fact, putting something on a BLT may be a surefire way to get me to eat it. Sort of like the green grilled cheese. I'm like a toddler in that way. Not afraid to admit it.

Putting something fancy like smoked salmon on a BLT just makes me feel good. It makes the day feel special. It makes it feel like a holiday. Like I deserve it. And who doesn't want to feel special on a random Monday afternoon?

Exactly. You deserve it.

 1 In a small bowl, whisk together the mayonnaise with the basil, parsley, and oregano.

2 Spread the mayo on 2 slices of the toast—1 for each sandwich. Layer the lettuce, bacon, smoked salmon, and tomatoes on each sandwich equally. Top each with the second slice of toast.

This is a chicken salad that I thought would break my mom's heart.

See, she is pretty set in her ways. She will always pick a traditional cheeseburger with bacon over something trendier, say, a burger slathered with peanut butter and arugula (what?). She favors traditional, "normal" dishes and doesn't tend to be very adventurous in her meal choices— but just because she loves the classics so much. She was downright offended when I once (very inoffensively, I might add) said that she wasn't a "foodie," which got me thinking: Maybe she is a foodie. A classic foodie. A traditional foodie.

That's why I clearly thought she would lose it when I served her chicken salad that was spiked with smoked paprika and tossed with pineapple chunks when she was so used to her own version with a chopped hard-boiled egg and that darn celery.

I think the tiny bit of mayo was my saving grace.

That wasn't one of the last times I assumed—after all, I make things up in my head way too often—but I was glad that I was wrong. I think it's important that if you have an adventurous palate and an adoration for trying new foods, but you spend a good amount of time with someone who doesn't? That you simply take it slow, have some patience, and try, try again. Take something you know they enjoy and simply swap out one flavor for something else that you know they like.

You may just be pleasantly surprised.

1 In a large bowl, mix together the chicken, salt, pepper, paprika, and cumin until combined. In a small bowl, whisk together the yogurt and mustard. Add the yogurt mixture to the chicken and toss well to combine. Fold in the pineapple chunks, scallions, and almonds and toss to mix. I love to eat this on sandwiches, particularly croissants, or scooped up with crackers.

smoky chicken salad with greek yogurt & pineapple

SERVES 2 to 4 • TIME: 30 minutes

2 boneless, skinless chicken breasts, cooked and shredded

1/2 teaspoon salt

1/2 teaspoon freshly ground black pepper

1/2 teaspoon smoked paprika

1/4 teaspoon ground cumin

2/3 cup plain full-fat or low-fat Greek yogurt

1 1/2 tablespoons Dijon mustard

1 cup fresh pineapple cut into 1/2-inch cubes

4 scallions, sliced

1/4 cup sliced almonds

3-bean
crispy
quinoa
skillet

SERVES 2 • TIME: 20 minutes

2 tablespoons extra-virgin olive oil

1 tablespoon toasted sesame oil

1½ cups cooked quinoa

2 garlic cloves, minced

½ cup canned chickpeas, rinsed and
   drained

½ cup canned pinto beans, rinsed and
   drained

½ cup canned cannellini beans, rinsed
   and drained

4 scallions, sliced

1 tablespoon sesame seeds, toasted
   (see page 27)

This versatile and quick skillet is one of my favorite lunches because you can just do things with it. Yes, things. Lots of things.

You can eat it straight from the skillet, standing-over-the-stove-style.

You can crisp up some tortillas or grab a bag of blue corn chips and scoop it up like so.

You can toss some leftovers (or freshly made contents) on top of a salad as a different mix-in.

You can use it as a filling in some enchiladas with cheese or even—say it with me—a microwaved quesadilla. I think by now we've established that sometimes they are necessary.

It works as a main dish or as a side dish, it's great warm or straight-from-the-fridge cold, and it's tasty enough as is or is perfect to set up a completely different flavor profile based on your preferences and favorite spices.

If you can't tell, I just really like it.

1 Heat a large skillet over medium-high heat and add the olive and sesame oils. Add the cooked quinoa and garlic to the skillet. Toss it quickly and spread it evenly over the bottom of the skillet, then cook until it becomes golden and slightly crispy, 2 to 3 minutes. Stir and toss the quinoa and continue to cook it for 2 to 3 minutes longer, until it becomes crispy.

2 Reduce the heat and add all of the beans to the quinoa. Cook the mixture for another minute or two, just until everything is warm. Top with the scallions and sesame seeds.

4 salads, soups & vegetable-like things

(ugh, if we must)

So, yes. I just spent an entire chapter telling you that more often than not, *salads are not enough* for me.

And now I'm going to try and sell you on why you should eat all the things on the next few pages. Salads, vegetables, soups that are really just an excuse for extra cheese and bread. All the things.

The green stuff may not be my favorite, but I force it upon myself. Plain and simple. ***There is no other choice*** if I want to feel good inside and outside. There is no other choice if I want to live long and prosper! Insert all cliché reasons to consume veggies here.

The truth is, I wanted to include a chapter on mostly salads and vegetables to show you what does work for me. To show what I, as someone who strives to have a healthy lifestyle but does not enjoy vegetables like most people, am willing to eat and actually enjoy eating. Every single one of the salads and vegetable dishes in here? I love. I actually eat. I may not want them every single day—after all, someone wired me wrong. Forced me to be predisposed to wanting cheesecake and pizza for every meal of my life. But by now you know the drill: Gotta grow up.

This is how I do it.

The good news is that not every single thing on the next few pages is a vegetable dish. And that is because I am a severe soup swooner. I adore soup.

Like most of my culinary instincts, it comes from my mom. She loves soup too. It pains me to say, however, that in my house, ***I'm a soup loner.*** Eddie goes wild for chili, but that's where his brothy preferences end. The rest is left up to me. It doesn't stop me from making a gigantic pot, though.

I like to eat soup for lunch and dinner, so when I make a large batch, I'll freeze half and plow through the other half in about a week, maybe less. I also might invite some friends over so I'm not loving on my soup alone. Lots of crusty bread too. Sometimes with melted cheese. See? Swooner.

To mesh the two ideas, I think we can agree that soup and salad often go together. Soup is filling and warm, the salad is fresh. ***It just works.*** And soup is also one of those tricky places where a few unsuspecting vegetables can be slipped in and others are none the wiser. Well, except me. Since I made it.

I just ignore them, though. Put some cheese on top. The world is a better place.

lunchtime

roasted broccoli–swiss soup

SERVES 4 • TIME: 35 minutes

4 cups broccoli florets

2 tablespoons extra-virgin olive oil

2 tablespoons unsalted butter

1/2 sweet yellow onion, diced

2 garlic cloves, minced

2 tablespoons all-purpose flour

3 cups low-sodium vegetable stock

1/2 cup half-and-half

6 ounces Swiss cheese, freshly grated

2 ounces Gruyère cheese, freshly grated

1 1/2 teaspoons prepared horseradish

1/2 teaspoon salt

1/2 teaspoon freshly ground black pepper

Long before I started roasting broccoli and covering it in a shower of Parmesan cheese, I didn't put up a fight when it came to broccoli-cheddar soup. Even though it contained my least favorite vegetables.

Those little trees. Why must they be so . . . tree-like?

Cream soups have always been a big thing on my mom's side of the family, so easily that is where I started out. My grandma, my aunt, and my mom have always been huge fans, often choosing beer cheese or cream of asparagus from the menu as their entrée over anything else.

And can you blame them? Cream-based soups just melt in your mouth. They are heavenly.

My trick for loving this soup is chopping the broccoli into tiny pieces and using the best Swiss with a hint of Gruyère. Like a soup-fondue hybrid. It's wonderful paired with half a panini but also with some simple garlic toast. Or with that darn salad.

But just remember.

Soup without bread is like chocolate without peanut butter. You just don't do it.

1 Preheat oven to 375°F. Add the broccoli and 1 tablespoon olive oil to baking sheet and toss. Roast for 20 minutes, tossing once during bake time.

2 Heat a large pot over medium heat and add the remaining 1 tablespoon olive oil and butter. Add the onion and garlic and stir. Cook until slightly softened, 2 to 3 minutes. Whisk in the flour to create a roux that will thicken the soup. Cook the flour and onion mixture until it turns golden and is fragrant, 1 to 2 minutes. Add the stock and half-and-half and stir constantly until the liquid thickens slightly, 5 minutes. Reduce the heat to low.

3 Add the broccoli and cheese to the soup. Stir constantly until the cheese melts, then cover and cook for 10 minutes. Add the horseradish, salt, and pepper, then taste and add more seasoning if you desire.

Mother Lovett made a mean bean soup. It was one of those soups that you need a ham hock for and that cooks literally all day on the stove. The beans release so much starch that it's almost like you're eating a cream-based soup, and it's the most comforting thing on a cold winter night.

This is not that.

But! It's my sorta makeshift Mother Lovett quick-for-lunch bean soup. It's incredibly filling and fast to whip up. It works in the warmer months too—especially if you're like me and are a weirdo who loves soup in summer—because you don't have to slave over a hot stove for TOO long in 90-degree weather. It also becomes awesome when piled high with tortilla chips.

Wins all around.

1 Heat a large pot over medium heat and add the olive oil. Once hot, add the onions, chile and bell peppers, salt, and pepper and stir. Cook until slightly softened, 5 minutes. Stir in the garlic, paprika, cumin, and chili powder, stirring occasionally and cooking for another 5 minutes. Add the beans, stock, corn, diced tomatoes, and green chiles and stir well. Cover and cook over medium heat for 15 to 20 minutes. Taste the soup and season it additionally if desired.

30-minute southwest black bean soup

SERVES 4 to 6 • TIME: 30 minutes

2 tablespoons extra-virgin olive oil

1 sweet yellow onion, diced

1 fresh poblano chile pepper, diced

1/2 red bell pepper, diced

1/4 teaspoon salt

1/4 teaspoon freshly ground black pepper

3 garlic cloves, minced

1 1/2 teaspoons smoked paprika

1 1/2 teaspoons ground cumin

2 teaspoons chili powder

3 cups canned black beans, rinsed and drained

2 cups low-sodium chicken stock

1 cup fresh or thawed frozen sweet corn kernels

1 (28-ounce) can diced tomatoes

1 (4-ounce) can diced green chiles

amaretto–butternut squash soup with cinnamon toast croutons

In looking for a way to take butternut squash soup up a notch, I heavily weighed my options. I didn't want to add any extra vegetables and change the flavor, but I wanted something new.

Something to add a little kick.

I didn't want a ton of spice. I didn't want beans or something that required chew—after all, creamy pureed butternut soup melts in your mouth like nothing else.

Enter amaretto.

Bourbon was first on the list, but I just thought amaretto was . . . seasonally appropriate, if you will. It's not an overwhelmingly strong flavor as it can sometimes be in foods, and feel free to swap it for the bourbon if that's more your thing. But it's incredibly warming and reaches into the soul. And the crunch on top?! Oh, the crunch on top.

I am so all over it.

SERVES 2 to 4 · TIME: 45 minutes

1 cup whole wheat bread cubes

1 tablespoon extra-virgin olive oil

2 teaspoons granulated sugar

1/2 teaspoon ground cinnamon

2 tablespoons extra-virgin olive oil

2 tablespoons unsalted butter

1 sweet yellow onion, diced

1/4 teaspoon plus a pinch of salt

2 garlic cloves, minced

3 tablespoons amaretto

4 cups peeled and cubed butternut squash

2 cups low-sodium vegetable stock

2 cups water

1/2 cup canned coconut milk, plus extra for drizzling

1/4 teaspoon freshly ground black pepper

2 scallions, sliced

2 tablespoons sunflower seeds

1 Preheat the oven to 400°F. Spread the bread cubes on a baking sheet and toss them with the olive oil, sugar, and cinnamon. Bake the cubes until golden and crunchy, 10 to 12 minutes. Remove the sheet from the oven and let the croutons cool on the sheet.

2 Meanwhile, while the croutons are baking, heat a large pot over medium heat and add the olive oil and butter. Add the onions with the pinch of salt and stir. Cook until softened, 5 minutes. Add the garlic and cook for another minute, then pour in the amaretto and cook for 5 minutes, stirring occasionally.

3 Add the squash cubes, stock, and water to the pot. Cover, reduce the heat to medium-low, and simmer until the squash is soft, 20 minutes. Once the squash is soft, remove the pot from the heat and carefully pour the entire soup mixture into a high-powered blender (you may need to do this in batches). Puree until creamy, about 5 full minutes. Transfer the soup back to the pot and heat it over low heat. Stir in the coconut milk, remaining 1/4 teaspoon salt, and pepper. Taste and season the soup additionally if needed. Ladle the soup into bowls and set the croutons on top. Garnish with the scallions and sunflower seeds. Drizzle extra coconut milk on top, if desired.

Chili is one of those dishes where I never use a recipe. I'm talking never ever ever.

So forgive me for being a hypocrite.

You could hand me an award-winning chili recipe and I'd still probably refuse to measure out my cumin or tomato paste. I just throw stuff in until it tastes good. Lots of spoonfuls into my mouth, another little shake of spice. Easy as that.

The thing is, I live with a gigantic chili lover. Eddie will eat chili until he is blue in the face, and he really enjoys different types of chili. He eats it plain or tops it with cheese, diced red onion, and crushed chips. It's nearly a weekly staple come fall and winter, so I'm always looking for ways to change it up.

This is one of them. Still chili, but with a little different flavor. Shredded chicken. BBQ sauce. Lots of cheddar on top. Done.

 Heat a large pot over medium heat and add the olive oil. Add the onion, jalapeño, and garlic and stir to coat. Cook the mixture until it has softened, 5 minutes. Add the paprika, chili powder, cumin, black pepper, salt, and red pepper flakes. Stir and cook for 5 more minutes.

Add the chicken, red peppers, beans, stock, tomatoes, and BBQ sauce and stir well to combine. Cover the pot and reduce the heat to medium-low. Cook the chili for 20 minutes. Remove the lid and stir. Taste and season additionally with more salt, pepper, or spice if you desire. Cover and cook for 10 more minutes.

Top each serving with cheddar cheese and cilantro.

NOTE: Beware of sweetness in your BBQ sauce. You may need to decrease the amount of sauce or up the spice if you don't want your chili extra sweet.

BBQ chicken chili

SERVES 4 to 6 • TIME: 45 minutes

2 tablespoons extra-virgin olive oil

1 red onion, diced

1 jalapeño chile pepper, seeded and diced

2 garlic cloves, minced

1½ tablespoons smoked paprika

1½ tablespoons chili powder

1 tablespoon ground cumin

1 teaspoon freshly ground black pepper

½ teaspoon salt

Pinch of crushed red pepper flakes

2 boneless, skinless chicken breasts, cooked and shredded

1 (12-ounce) jar roasted red peppers in water, drained and chopped, or make your own (see page 30)

1½ cups canned cannellini beans, rinsed and drained

1½ cups canned light or dark red kidney beans, rinsed and drained

3 cups low-sodium chicken stock

1 (28-ounce) can diced tomatoes

½ cup BBQ sauce

Freshly grated cheddar cheese, for garnish

Torn fresh cilantro, for garnish

creamy slow cooker chicken noodle soup

SERVES 4 to 6 • TIME: 6 to 8 hours

1¹/₂ pounds boneless, skinless chicken breasts, cut into chunks

1 sweet yellow onion, diced

3 carrots, peeled and sliced

2 celery stalks, chopped

¹/₂ teaspoon salt

¹/₂ teaspoon freshly ground black pepper

6 cups low-sodium chicken stock

2¹/₂ cups whole wheat egg noodles

1 cup whole milk

¹/₂ cup all-purpose flour

A creamy (yet light . . . uh-huh) rendition on the original, all thrown into the slow cooker to make your life a million times easier.
Or just a few hours easier.
You know. Same thing.
I love you.

 Add the chicken, onion, carrots, celery, salt, and pepper to a 7-quart slow cooker. Pour in the chicken stock and turn the cooker on to low. Cook the soup for 6 hours.

Add the egg noodles. Return the lid to the pot and cook for 30 minutes more. After 6 hours, take off the lid and add the egg noodles. Return the lid to the pot and cook for 30 minutes more.

Add the milk and flour to a gravy shaker or water bottle to create a slurry and shake until no lumps remain. Pour the slurry into the slow cooker and turn the heat to high. Cook the soup for 1 hour more, stirring once or twice.

This is the salad that made me love beets.

This is the salad that made my husband love beets more than he already did.

One of our favorite local restaurants serves a roasted beet salad with a huge scoop of creamy local goat cheese, a generous drizzle of honey, and a few arugula leaves. No joke, the beets taste like candy. Legit.

I was scared at first too. Beets are so hit or miss—but the salad was too pretty to be a miss.

If you can't find golden beets, using all red ones will work just fine. I love how aesthetically pleasing the multicolored beets are on a plate, and I find that sometimes, beet haters don't even realize they are eating beets when they're golden.

Now that's my kind of trickery.

1 Preheat the oven to 400°F. Rub the beets with 3 tablespoons of the olive oil, then wrap them together in aluminum foil and place on a baking sheet. Roast the beets for 1 hour. Remove the beets from the foil and place them on a plate to cool. You can throw the plate in the fridge if you'd like to speed up the process. This salad can work warm or cold, so as long as the beets are at a comfortable temperature to touch, they're perfect.

2 Once they beets are cool enough to touch, rub the skins until they peel right off. If there are any tough areas, use a vegetable peeler. Chop the beets into 1-inch cubes and season them with ½ teaspoon each of the salt and pepper.

3 Add the watercress to a bowl and use your hands to lightly toss it with the remaining olive oil and salt and pepper.

4 To assemble the salads, add both golden and red beets to each plate (for aesthetic appeal!) along with a handful of the watercress. Add some of the goat cheese on the side and drizzle everything with a tablespoon of honey.

NOTE: You can prep the beets ahead of time if you wish. Simply keep them in the fridge until you're ready to use.

roasted beet salad with honey & goat cheese

SERVES 4 · TIME: 1½ hours

3 golden beets, scrubbed clean with greens removed

3 red beets, scrubbed clean with greens removed

¼ cup extra-virgin olive oil

1 teaspoon salt

1 teaspoon freshly ground black pepper

4 cups watercress

4 ounces goat cheese, sliced into 4 rounds

¼ cup honey

wedge salads with pomegranates, chives & toasted almonds

SERVES 4 · TIME: 20 minutes

1 head iceberg lettuce, cut into
   4 wedges

1/2 teaspoon salt

1/2 teaspoon freshly ground black
   pepper

1/2 cup Greek Yogurt Parmesan Ranch
   Dressing (page 155)

2/3 cup pomegranate arils

1/4 cup sliced almonds, toasted
   (see page 27)

2 tablespoons chopped fresh chives

Everyone always gets up in arms about iceberg lettuce and how plain it is and how nutritionally devoid it is, and yada yada yada, but to be completely transparent? I sorta like it.

It's probably because it doesn't taste like a stinky stalk of kale or something. It's just . . . CLEAN.

I find it to be refreshing. And is there anything more classic than a wedge salad? The traditional blue cheese and bacon version is obviously a win in my book, but if it isn't apparent, I like to play with flavors.

This is my modern wedge salad. Since you can find pomegranate arils in the grocery store year-round these days, it's a great summer meal. But let's be real: Could this be more perfect for the holidays? Just look at all the green and those little red jewels. Adorbs. (I know. I really just said that.)

1 Season the iceberg wedges with the salt and pepper. Add a few tablespoons of the dressing to the lettuce, then cover each wedge with pomegranate arils, sliced almonds, and chives.

greek chicken panzanella with honey-lemon vinaigrette

SERVES 2 • TIME: 1 hour

CHICKEN

2 boneless, skinless chicken breasts,
   cut into 1-inch cubes

2 tablespoons extra-virgin olive oil

Juice of 2 lemons

2 garlic cloves, minced

1 tablespoon chopped fresh dill

½ teaspoon salt

½ teaspoon freshly ground black
   pepper

CROUTONS

2 cups whole wheat bread cubes

2 tablespoons extra-virgin olive oil

¼ teaspoon garlic salt

When I first learned about panzanella, I was all "whoa whoa whoa—I can have bread IN my salad?"

It was a game changer.

And it just so happens that Greek salads are my favorite, because, come on—there are so many delicious things. Artichokes! Olives! Feta! Dill!

It's one of the few salads that when I order one, I don't make any crazy requests or ask for something to be left off or do an exchange in dressing. I'm a server's worst nightmare.

Sticking with the classic Greek theme, this salad is doused in a honey-lemon vinaigrette and tossed to perfection. It's almost reminiscent of a chopped salad (which is another favorite of mine) because there is so much going on other than lettuce, and it's all uniformly sized. Packed to the brim with flavor, this is definitely one of those salads that even the biggest salad hater could call a meal.

Just ask me.

1 Preheat the oven to 375°F. Add the chicken to a baking dish or resealable plastic bag. Whisk together the olive oil, lemon juice, garlic, dill, salt, and pepper. Pour the mixture over the chicken and set the dish or bag in the fridge to marinate for 30 minutes.

2 For the croutons, place the bread cubes on a baking sheet and toss them with the olive oil and garlic salt. Bake the cubes until golden and crunchy, 10 to 12 minutes. Remove the sheet from the oven and let the croutons cool on the baking sheet.

3 Heat a large nonstick skillet over medium heat. Remove the chicken from the dish or bag and add it to the skillet. Cook the chicken until golden on all sides, 10 minutes. Stir and flip the chicken a few times while cooking. Remove the chicken from the heat and set aside until ready to use.

4 To assemble the salad, toss the spring greens and croutons with the salt and pepper and divide evenly among the plates. Add equal amounts of the artichoke heats, cucumber, onion, tomatoes, and olives to the plates. Add the chicken and top the salad with the crumbled feta.

5 For the vinaigrette, whisk together the lemon juice, vinegar, honey, garlic, salt, and pepper in a bowl. Stream in the olive oil while continuing to whisk so the dressing comes together. Drizzle the dressing over the salad and toss.

SALAD

6 cups spring greens

¼ teaspoon salt

¼ teaspoon freshly ground black pepper

1 (6-ounce) jar marinated artichoke hearts, drained

1 cucumber, chopped

½ red onion, sliced

½ pint cherry tomatoes, quartered

½ cup kalamata olives, pitted and sliced

4 ounces feta cheese, crumbled

VINAIGRETTE

3 tablespoons freshly squeezed lemon juice

2 tablespoons red wine vinegar

1½ tablespoons honey

1 garlic clove, minced

¼ teaspoon salt

¼ teaspoon freshly ground black pepper

⅔ cup extra-virgin olive oil

I'm all about a pasta salad that tastes great warm but is even better eaten cold. It saves me when it comes to those omg-I'm-so-starving-I'm-about-to-eat-the-entire-contents-of-my-fridge moments. Just grab the container and a fork. Good to go.

simple asparagus ribbon pasta salad

SERVES 4 • TIME: 30 minutes

1. Hold each asparagus spear at the tip and gently slice strands downward with a vegetable peeler, tossing the ribbons into a large bowl. Heat a skillet over medium heat and add the olive oil. Add the asparagus ribbons and the zucchini halves to the skillet and toss to coat. Cook just until the veggies soften a bit, 2 to 3 minutes. Add the garlic and cook for 30 seconds. Turn off the heat.

2. For the dressing, in a small bowl, whisk together the dressing ingredients.

3. Add the cooked pasta to a large bowl. Add the tomatoes and the asparagus and zucchini mixture. Toss the pasta with the dressing and add the feta. Toss once more. Refrigerate for at least 30 minutes before serving. Before serving, taste and season additionally if desired.

12 asparagus spears

2 tablespoons extra-virgin olive oil

1 zucchini, halved lengthwise and sliced

2 garlic cloves, minced

DRESSING

3 tablespoons extra-virgin olive oil

2 tablespoons red wine vinegar

1 tablespoon chopped fresh basil

1 tablespoon chopped fresh cilantro

1 tablespoon chopped fresh oregano

2 teaspoons honey

$\frac{1}{2}$ teaspoon salt

$\frac{1}{2}$ teaspoon freshly ground black pepper

8 ounces whole wheat linguine or fettuccine, cooked

1 pint grape tomatoes, quartered

4 ounces feta cheese, crumbled

crab cake cobb salad stacks

SERVES 2 to 4 • TIME: 40 minutes

CRAB CAKES

½ pound lump crabmeat

1 tablespoon diced red bell pepper

1 tablespoon diced green bell pepper

1 tablespoon diced red onion

1 garlic clove, minced

4 multigrain crackers, crushed

1 large egg, lightly beaten

1½ teaspoons Dijon mustard

½ tablespoon plain full-fat or low-fat Greek yogurt

¼ teaspoon salt

¼ teaspoon freshly ground black pepper

⅛ teaspoon cayenne pepper

1 tablespoon extra-virgin olive oil

It should come as no surprise that back in the day, when I refused to eat salads? You could convince me with a Cobb. I was never one to turn down a plate full of bacon, blue cheese, and hard-boiled egg, especially when it included avocado and an excellent dressing.

And I'm still not. Come on. You know that by now.

These adorable stacks are just another way I like to get my veggies in a very vegetable-less salad. And make that Cobb your own! Who cares what a traditional Cobb is? Pfff. Whatever you like: Add it.

I think for the Cobb you just need to keep the bacon, so, uh, yeah . . . definitely do that.

Definitely.

1 For the crab cakes, in a large bowl, combine the crabmeat, peppers, onion, garlic, and crackers. Mix well. In a small bowl, whisk together the egg, mustard, and yogurt. Add the egg mixture to the crab and mix well to combine. Stir in the salt, black pepper, and cayenne.

2 Use your hands to form 4 patties out of the crabmeat mixture. Heat a large skillet over medium heat and add the olive oil. Add the crab cakes to the skillet and cook until golden, 5 to 6 minutes per side. Remove the cakes and let drain on a paper towel for 1 to 2 minutes.

③ For the vinaigrette, combine the vinegar, honey, garlic, salt, and pepper in a jar or a bowl, shaking or whisking until smooth. Pour in the olive oil and shake or whisk again for 30 seconds. Set aside.

④ To assemble the stacks, season the tomatoes, eggs, onion, and avocado with the salt and pepper. Lay a lettuce leaf on each plate. Add 1 or 2 crab cakes on top of the lettuce, then add a slice of tomato, a slice of hard-boiled egg, an onion slice, a few pieces of bacon, and a few slices of avocado. Add a bit of blue cheese on top and around the sides of the stack. Drizzle with the vinaigrette.

VINAIGRETTE

$1/3$ cup red wine vinegar

2 teaspoons honey

1 garlic clove, minced

Pinch of salt

Pinch of freshly ground black pepper

$2/3$ cup extra-virgin olive oil

SALAD

4 tomato slices

2 large hard-boiled eggs, sliced

4 red onion slices

$1/2$ avocado, pitted, peeled, and sliced

$1/4$ teaspoon salt

$1/4$ teaspoon freshly ground black pepper

4 romaine lettuce leaves, halved

4 slices bacon, cooked and cut into thirds

4 ounces blue cheese, crumbled

grilled *watermelon* salad with **baby** *kale* & burrata

SERVES 2 · TIME: 20 minutes

4 cups baby kale

2 tablespoons extra-virgin olive oil

2 teaspoons honey

¾ teaspoon salt

¾ teaspoon freshly ground black pepper

4 watermelon wedges, rind removed

2 tablespoons extra-virgin olive oil

4 ounces burrata cheese

There's fruit salad, and then there are salads with fruit. I'm a fan of both.

The latter may even rank higher because when you have a salad with fruit, it can also include other fabulous additions like cheeses and whatnot—you know, things that may not make it into your traditional summer fruit salad that sits on the picnic table on the Fourth of July.

I especially enjoy fruit on salads when kale is involved. Kale can be a tad bitter and difficult for even the longtime veggie fans to learn to enjoy. Adding some sweetness kicks that bitterness to the curb and really just makes the whole thing more . . . interesting. Baby kale is better. So cute and baby-like. Not as bitter.

I really just added the fruit because the kale was begging for something sweet. I have reached the point where I think my food speaks to me. Help.

1 Add the baby kale to a large bowl. Whisk together the olive oil, honey, and ¼ teaspoon each of the salt and pepper, pour over the kale, and toss well to coat. Set aside.

2 Preheat the grill to the highest heat setting. Brush the watermelon on both sides with the olive oil and season it with the remaining salt and pepper. Cook the watermelon directly on the grates until grill marks appear, 2 to 3 minutes per side.

3 Assemble the salads by adding a few handfuls of baby kale to each plate. Add 2 grilled watermelon wedges on top. Cut the burrata in half and place on the side of each plate.

I know. You are probably thinking, "Another salad? But you said my lunch deserves better!"

Yes. Yes, it does. But it's lunchtime and salads have somehow ended up being a thing for lunch and well, I don't exactly think I have the clout to stop that trend. Do I?

Plus, it's just those boring, traditional salads—browning romaine, tomatoes, red onion, stale croutons, and cubed cheese—that I have a hard time holding on to. Crazy things including fruit and wild dressings are acceptable in my book. Who would have thought?

I also really like salads that don't necessarily look like salads. Like the good old tossed salad in a bowl? There is a time and a place for it, but it's not here. Try experimenting with the fruit and veg in your life and piling it into a gorgeous mess on an old and delicate floral plate. Or in a big ol' melon half!

It will make you WANT to eat it. Swear.

1 Heat a nonstick skillet over medium heat and add the prosciutto. Cook and toss with a wooden spoon (or something that won't scratch your skillet) until it is crisped and slightly golden in color, 5 to 6 minutes. Remove the prosciutto and place it on a paper towel until ready to use.

2 Add the arugula to a large bowl and season with the salt and pepper. If your melon halves don't sit straight, slice a little off the bottom to make them flat. Divide the greens evenly between the melon halves and add half a sliced avocado to each.

3 For the vinaigrette, whisk together the vinegar, syrup, garlic, salt, and pepper in a bowl. Stir in the olive oil while continuing to whisk. Pour over the salad. Add the crispy prosciutto on top.

melon-avocado-arugula salad with crispy prosciutto & maple-balsamic vinaigrette

SERVES 2 · TIME: 20 minutes

¼ pound prosciutto, thinly sliced

6 cups arugula

¼ teaspoon salt

¼ teaspoon freshly ground black pepper

1 cantaloupe, washed, halved, and seeded

1 avocado, pitted, peeled, and sliced

VINAIGRETTE

2 tablespoons balsamic vinegar

1 tablespoon maple syrup

1 garlic clove, minced

¼ teaspoon salt

¼ teaspoon freshly ground black pepper

⅓ cup extra-virgin olive oil

spinach, tomato & fresh green bean salad with seared sliced beef tenderloin

SERVES 2 · TIME: 30 minutes

FILLET

1 (6-ounce) beef tenderloin

¼ teaspoon salt

¼ teaspoon freshly ground black pepper

1 tablespoon canola oil

SALAD

6 cups fresh spinach

¼ teaspoon salt

¼ teaspoon freshly ground black pepper

8 ounces fresh green beans

1 pint heirloom cherry tomatoes, quartered

2 ounces Parmigiano-Reggiano cheese, shaved

There is a local Italian restaurant that my parents have been going to for nearly 25 years. It has a semi-fancy dining room but there is also a classy not-so-bar-like bar that serves pizza and appetizers and my all-time favorite "boring" salad.

A traditional salad. A house salad.

While the salad is anything but boring, it is incredibly regular for my liking. If you haven't, you know, picked up on my fascination for oddly paired things yet.

The thing that this salad has that others do not? Fresh green beans. Yep. It sold me. The vegetables actually sold me!

The beans add this unexpected fresh crunch to the salad. In addition to that, I had to go and throw some beef tenderloin on the darn thing because, well, it's me.

1 For the fillet, season the beef tenderloin with the salt and pepper. Heat a large skillet over high heat and add the canola oil. Add the beef tenderloin to the skillet and sear until it is deeply browned on both sides, 3 to 4 minutes per side. If you prefer the beef more well-done, cover the skillet while searing. Remove the beef tenderloin and let it rest on a cutting board for 10 minutes before slicing.

2 For the salad, put the spinach in a large bowl and season with the salt and pepper. Toss with the green beans and tomatoes. Top with the beef tenderloin slices and the shaved cheese.

toasted
sesame broccoli

. . . .

SERVES 2 to 4 • TIME: 45 minutes

. . . .

4 cups broccoli florets

2 tablespoons toasted sesame oil

1 tablespoon extra-virgin olive oil

½ teaspoon flaked sea salt

½ teaspoon freshly ground black pepper

2 tablespoons sesame seeds, toasted (see page 27)

Yep. I'm going there.

This is a way I've learned to eat "The Broccoli." I feel like it needs a formal title because it's just so . . . ominous. My taste buds have always felt threatened by these little trees. Measures must be taken.

Instead of plain old olive oil, I use toasted sesame oil. That flavor is unreal.

And instead of stopping there, or stopping after a shake of salt and pepper, I add a bunch of toasted sesame seeds on top for some extra crunch. It is ALL about the texture, people. I can say it until I'm blue in the face, but the crunchiness . . . it will get you.

Every time.

 Preheat the oven to 400°F. Add the broccoli to a bowl and toss it with the sesame oil, olive oil, salt, and pepper.

 Spread the broccoli on a baking sheet in a single layer. Roast it for 20 minutes, then toss the broccoli, then roast for 15 minutes more. Remove the pan from the oven and cover the broccoli with the sesame seeds.

NOTE: Try this flavor combination with asparagus or even kale chips. Rub them down with the sesame oil, roast until crispy, then top with the seeds. So good.

Updated creamy dressings that contain a lot of protein and a little fat? Sign me up.

Just a word, though: You may not see me eating this on salads. Because sometimes my pizza accidentally falls into a vat of this ranch and I just can't help it.

1 Combine all of the ingredients in a food processor and blend until pureed and smooth. Taste the dressing and season additionally if desired.

greek yogurt parmesan ranch dressing

MAKES about ¾ cup • TIME: 10 minutes

⅓ cup full-fat or low-fat Greek yogurt

⅓ cup low-fat buttermilk

2 tablespoons mayonnaise

2 tablespoons freshly grated Parmesan cheese

2 tablespoons chopped fresh parsley

2 tablespoons chopped fresh dill

1 tablespoon chopped fresh chives

1 teaspoon honey

½ teaspoon Worcestershire sauce

½ teaspoon salt

½ teaspoon garlic powder

½ teaspoon onion powder

¼ teaspoon smoked paprika

¼ teaspoon freshly ground black pepper

I will never forget the day I tried Brussels.

Growing up, these things were abhorred. This was long before the day when bacon and brown sugar and maple syrup played a part and, well, sprouts everywhere should just thank those three ingredients.

To this day, my mom still can't believe that I eat them. She never prepared them when I was a kid, since I believe her only affiliation to these green things was when Mother Lovett boiled them or something. And I don't blame her. I remember walking over to my best childhood friend's house 20 years ago and she was eating a plate of Brussels—nothing else, green Brussels on a plate, and they were steamed. Maybe some salt and pepper, but no other seasonings or butters or oils. I was scarred for life.

The day I picked up a carton at my local Italian grocer, it was long after I had seen these new and improved, actually delicious-looking little green nuggets making their way around the internets. And I didn't expect to like them at all. But I was willing to try.

I pan-roasted them in bacon grease with shallots and, well, I was hooked. To this day, I still am. And I'm still in awe. Below is my simplest but favorite way to eat them without the bacon grease. You can still swap the coconut oil for the grease, though. You know . . . just in case you'd want to do something like that.

① Slice each Brussels sprout into 3 or 4 slices.

② Heat a large skillet over medium-high heat and add the coconut oil. Add the Brussels sprouts to the skillet, tossing them well to coat with the oil. Use a spatula or heatproof spoon to spread the sprouts into a single layer (the best you can) in the skillet. Let the sprouts cook until crispy on the bottom, 5 minutes. Flip the Brussels and cook until the other side is crispy, 5 minutes. Flip any remaining sprouts and cook until golden and crisp.

③ Remove the skillet from the heat and toss the salt and pepper with the Brussels. Top with shaved Parmesan and serve.

NOTE: Try the bacon grease. Just do it.

crispy salt & pepper brussels sprouts

SERVES 2 • TIME: 30 minutes

1 pound Brussels sprouts, stems trimmed

2 tablespoons coconut oil

1 teaspoon flaked sea salt

1 teaspoon freshly ground black pepper

1 ounce freshly shaved Parmesan cheese

addicting *grilled corn* with basil butter & smoked *paprika*

SERVES 2 to 4 • TIME: 30 minutes

6 ears corn, husked

8 tablespoons (1 stick) unsalted butter, at room temperature

1 teaspoon salt

1 teaspoon freshly ground black pepper

3 tablespoons chopped fresh basil

¼ teaspoon salt

1 to 2 teaspoons smoked paprika

There is something about grilled corn that makes me FREAK THE HECK OUT.

Sorry for the shouting.

It's just really insane.

This is how I do it.

1 Preheat the grill to medium-high heat. Rub each ear of corn with a teaspoon or so of the butter, then sprinkle the ears with the salt and pepper. Wrap each ear in a small sheet of aluminum foil—you only want to have two layers of foil around each ear.

2 Place the foil-wrapped ears directly on the grill and cook for 5 minutes. Continue to cook, rotating every 4 to 5 minutes, for 20 to 25 minutes. Remove an ear of corn and gently open the foil to inspect it. I like my corn kernels to be golden and caramelly, but as long as the corn is cooked for a few minutes per side, it will be good. Be careful when opening the foil, as the corn will be hot.

3 In a small bowl, stir together the remaining butter, basil, and salt. Spread the butter on the hot corn and add a sprinkle of smoked paprika on top.

NOTE: Once cooled, the corn can also be cut from the cob and used as a side dish, in salads, or in salsas.

Now this . . . this is how we do vegetables. Crunchy with dip. I like it.

Before I ever was able to order fried zucchini in a bar, my mom served it to me one summer. She makes the best fried zucchini rounds—coating them liberally in cheese and bread crumbs and then frying until a deep, golden brown.

Her version tastes better than any restaurant one I've tried, and better yet, doesn't taste like a deep fryer. Nothing worse than ordering some late-nite bar food only to have it come out tasting like everything else that was in the deep fryer that week.

She cooks them in less than a half-inch of oil, which I believe makes them healthy. Right? RIGHT?

Okay. We can bake them.

These make an awesome weeknight side dish and even . . . a perfect single-lady dinner. Just add wine.

1 Preheat the oven to 450°F. Line a baking sheet with aluminum foil and place a nonstick wire rack on top. Spray the rack with nonstick spray.

2 In one bowl, lightly beat the eggs. In a second bowl, mix together the bread crumbs, flour, cheese, salt, black pepper, paprika, garlic powder, and cayenne.

3 Dip each zucchini "nugget" into the egg and coat it evenly, then press it into the bread crumb mixture. Press gently on the zucchini so the crumbs adhere. Set each nugget on the wire rack. Lightly spritz each nugget with a coating of canola oil to moisten the crumbs. This helps to crisp them up.

4 Bake the zucchini for 30 to 35 minutes, gently tossing once during the cooking time. Remove the sheet from the oven and let the zucchini cool slightly on the wire rack before serving.

5 For the honey-chipotle ketchup, whisk all of the ingredients together in a small bowl. Serve on the side.

spicy zucchini nuggets with honey-chipotle ketchup

SERVES 2 • TIME: 45 minutes

2 large eggs, lightly beaten

1 cup panko bread crumbs

1 cup fine bread crumbs

¼ cup all-purpose or whole wheat flour

2 tablespoons freshly grated Parmesan cheese

1 teaspoon salt

1 teaspoon freshly ground black pepper

½ teaspoon smoked paprika

½ teaspoon garlic powder

¼ teaspoon cayenne pepper

1 zucchini, cut into 1-inch cubes

Canola oil, for spritzing

HONEY-CHIPOTLE KETCHUP

¼ cup your favorite ketchup

1 chipotle chile pepper in adobo sauce, diced

2 teaspoons adobo sauce from the can of chipotle chile peppers

1 teaspoon honey

double-herb
kale pesto

MAKES about 1 cup • TIME: 15 minutes

¼ cup pine nuts, toasted

2 garlic cloves, minced

2 cups green curly kale

⅓ cup torn fresh basil

¼ cup torn fresh parsley

2 tablespoons freshly grated Parmesan cheese

5 to 6 tablespoons extra-virgin olive oil

¼ teaspoon salt

¼ teaspoon freshly ground black pepper

Speaking of green stuff: Holy cow. If you are looking for a way to really trick someone into eating kale? Whip it in a food processor with some herbs and call it pesto.
Add lots of cheese.
Smother warm noodles with it. Add more cheese.
Done and done.

1 Add the pine nuts and garlic to a food processor and pulse until crumbly. Add the kale, basil, and parsley to the processor and puree until combined and only tiny bits of green appear. Add the cheese, pulsing once more, and then with the processor on, stream in the olive oil until the pesto comes together. Scrape down the sides of the food processor when necessary. Add the salt and pepper and pulse once more. Taste and season additionally if desired.

2 Store the pesto in a sealed container or jar in the fridge for up to 1 week.

While I've ventured out into the world of Brussels sprouts and beets, Eddie's favorite vegetable side dish continues to be classic green beans. It's my mom's, too, so it must have something going for it.

We love to eat this side dish crisp and fresh, but did you know you can roast the heck out of the beans and sort of eat them like French fries? Yes. You can.

 Preheat the oven to 425°F.

2 Add the green beans and the garlic slices to a large bowl and toss with the olive oil, salt, and pepper. Spread the beans and the garlic in a single layer on a nonstick baking sheet. Bake for 15 minutes, flip the beans with a spatula, then bake for 15 to 20 minutes more. Top with the shaved cheese.

crispy roasted garlic green beans with shaved pecorino

SERVES 2 • TIME: 30 minutes

1 pound fresh green beans

4 garlic cloves, thinly sliced

2 tablespoons extra-virgin olive oil

½ teaspoon salt

½ teaspoon freshly ground black pepper

2 ounces Pecorino Romano cheese, shaved

Never did I ever think I'd be the gal who ate mushrooms from a baking dish for dinner when her husband was out of town.

Guess there's a first time for everything.

These mushrooms are packed with flavor and work on fillets or chicken, as a baked potato topping, as a simple side dish, or layered over grilled garlic toast. Really, there is no end in sight to the outrageous amount of things you can do with them.

If you're overwhelmed, just eat them straight from the baking dish. I think they solve some life problems too. Probably.

① Preheat the oven to 350°F. Add the mushrooms to a baking dish. Cover the mushrooms with the olive oil, syrup, and vinegar and toss them well to coat. Roast the mushrooms for 30 minutes, tossing once or twice during the cooking time.

② As the mushrooms are roasting, heat a small skillet over medium heat. Add the chopped bacon and cook until it is crispy and the fat is rendered, 5 minutes. Remove the bacon from the skillet with a slotted spoon and place on a paper towel.

③ Once the mushrooms are softened, juicy, and finished roasting, remove from the oven. Sprinkle them with the parsley, thyme, salt, and pepper, then add the crumbled bacon on top.

roasted *maple-balsamic* mushrooms with *bacon*

SERVES 2 to 4 • TIME: 40 minutes

1 pound baby portobello mushrooms

2 tablespoons extra-virgin olive oil

2 tablespoons maple syrup

2 tablespoons balsamic vinegar

2 slices thick-cut bacon, chopped

2 tablespoons chopped fresh parsley

2 tablespoons chopped fresh thyme

1/4 teaspoon salt

1/4 teaspoon freshly ground black pepper

baked
baby artichokes

SERVES 3 to 6 • TIME: 45 minutes

6 baby artichokes

2 tablespoons extra-virgin olive oil

1 shallot, diced

1/2 red bell pepper, diced

2 garlic cloves, minced

1/4 teaspoon salt

1/4 teaspoon freshly ground black pepper

1/3 cup panko bread crumbs

1/3 cup freshly grated Parmesan cheese

I didn't eat a whole baked artichoke until I was in my early twenties, and it was only because I was dating a guy whose family ate them on Easter.

I was instantly hooked. I didn't want to break up with him because of the artichokes. They had a hold on me.

Only one answer: learn to make them myself. Mission accomplished.

Large artichokes can be a pain to prepare, simply because they are so big. Stuffing three or four into a giant stockpot to parboil and having to do so a couple times before the stuffing and baking process—I just don't always have the patience for it. So I started stuffing the baby versions, and not only is it much easier, but they are also quite possibly the cutest things ever.

Little food. Can hardly stand it.

1 Bring a large pot of water to a boil.

2 Take each artichoke and slice off the bottom stem so it can sit up straight. Lay the artichoke down on its side and slice 1/2 to 1 inch off the top. Using kitchen shears, snip off the prickly tip of each leaf. Add the artichokes to the boiling water and cook until parboiled, 5 to 6 minutes. Try to keep the top of the artichokes submerged while boiling. Remove the artichokes and let drain upside down on a plate.

3 Preheat the oven to 375°F.

4 Heat a medium skillet over medium heat and add the olive oil. Add the shallots, bell pepper, garlic, salt, and pepper and toss to coat. Cook until the mixture is softened, 5 minutes. Turn off the heat and stir in the bread crumbs and Parmesan.

5 Place the artichokes in a small dish or pie plate, preferably something where they are close enough to touch so they can stand up. Pull apart the leaves of each artichoke and spoon a few tablespoons of the filling inside. Bake the artichokes for 20 minutes. Remove the dish from the oven and let the artichokes cool in the dish for 10 to 15 minutes before serving.

NOTES: You can use this recipe to stuff larger artichokes too—just double or triple the ingredients. Oh, and whip up a quick hollandaise to dip these in. You will not be sorry.

creamy *blue* **cheese– avocado** dressing

I was late to the blue cheese party, but when I arrived, I arrived strong.

Much like the stinky cheese itself.

I fell hard for all things moldy cheese–related, but perhaps did the biggest face-plant for this creamy avocado dressing.

Two of my favorite things combined!

PS: It also makes a killer chip dip.

1 Add the avocado, garlic, lemon juice, buttermilk, mayonnaise, yogurt, salt, and pepper to a food processor. Blend until the mixture is pureed and creamy, scraping down the sides if needed. Once the dressing is smooth, scoop it into a large bowl and stir in the crumbled blue cheese. Store the dressing in a sealed container in the refrigerator to prevent the avocado from browning.

MAKES about ¾ cup • TIME: 10 minutes

1 very ripe avocado, pitted and peeled

1 garlic clove, minced

Juice of ½ lemon

6 tablespoons low-fat buttermilk

1 tablespoon mayonnaise

1 tablespoon plain full-fat or low-fat Greek yogurt

¼ teaspoon salt

¼ teaspoon freshly ground black pepper

6 ounces blue cheese, crumbled

To make life more complicated than it already is, I separate biscuits into different categories. I am a woman, after all.

We have the biscuits you can eat for breakfast. You know, buttermilk, maybe even chocolate chip—any flavor will do the trick, but they are often warm, topped with a square of butter or eggs, and taste best at 7AM.

We have the biscuits that are best suited for snack time. Ones that are neither strictly sweet nor savory and that work best with a slathering of almond butter or jam or something extra to hold you over.

Then we have the biscuits you can eat with lunch or dinner—particularly corn bread biscuits, sometimes stuffed with cheddar and bacon, sometimes stuffed with jalapeños and beer, but best when dipped in hearty chili on a chilly night. Stuck on the side of a salad, passed in a basket for your soup.

That's exactly what these are. Just too cute for words.

1 Preheat the oven to 425°F.

2 In a large bowl, whisk together the flours, cheese, baking powder, basil, parsley, rosemary, salt, and garlic powder. Add the cold butter and, with a fork or your fingers (my preference), combine the butter into the dough until coarse crumbs remain. I like to rub the butter and ingredients through my fingers for 1 to 2 minutes.

3 Pour in the milk and stir until the dough comes together. Add some flour to your hands and your counter and place the dough down on the counter. Knead the dough 4 or 5 times and then pat it into a circle that is slightly less than 1 inch thick. Use a small biscuit cutter 1 to 1½ inches in diameter (or heck, even the lid to one of your spices) to cut rounds out of the dough. Place the rounds 1 inch apart on a nonstick baking sheet. Bake until the tops are golden, 7 to 9 minutes.

mini parmesan-herb biscuit puffs

MAKES 30 to 35 puffs · TIME: 25 minutes

1 cup whole wheat pastry flour

1 cup all-purpose flour, plus extra for dusting

2/3 cup freshly grated Parmesan cheese

2½ teaspoons baking powder

2 tablespoons chopped fresh basil

2 tablespoons chopped fresh parsley

1 tablespoon chopped fresh rosemary

1 teaspoon salt

½ teaspoon garlic powder

4 tablespoons (½ stick) cold unsalted butter, cut into pieces

3/4 cup whole or 2% milk

parmesan-*pistachio* kale chips

SERVES 2 · TIME: 40 minutes

⅓ cup roasted salted pistachios

2 tablespoons freshly grated
   Parmesan cheese

1 very large head kale, stems removed

2 tablespoons extra-virgin olive oil

Kale chips are the number-one reason that I began eating vegetables (happily) on a somewhat consistent basis. It sounds absolutely nuts, considering kale gets a bad rap for its chewy texture and bitter flavor. BUT.

In chip form? It's a complete winner. When kale chips came on the scene a few years ago, I was hesitant. After deciding that I absolutely loved them, I went hog wild and consumed them nearly every single day for two years. In my constant search for new flavor combinations, this became my favorite. Completely addicting, I promise.

1 Preheat the oven to 350°F. Line a baking sheet (or two) with aluminum foil or parchment paper and set aside.

2 Add the pistachios to a food processor and pulse until the nuts are in fine crumbs. It is okay if there are a few slightly larger pieces. Pour the ground pistachios into a bowl. Stir in the Parmesan cheese.

3 Add the kale pieces to a very large bowl. Pour the olive oil over the top and, using your hands, toss the kale and massage the oil into the leaves. Once the oil has been evenly dispersed, spread the kale out on the baking sheet. Sprinkle the pistachio and cheese mixture evenly over the top of the kale. If needed, press gently so the crumbs adhere to the leaves. Bake the kale for 15 minutes. Gently toss the leaves and bake them for 12 to 15 more minutes, until they are crispy but not brown.

5

tex-mex, burgers, pizza & everything else (some fancy, some not)

That title basically *sums up my life.*

It's where I come from, where I start from, where I always want to be going. I can turn anything into a taco, a burger, or a pizza. I draw the most inspiration from tacos, burgers, and pizzas and often eat a taco somewhere, then come home and put the ingredients on a pizza. Or eat a pizza and the next weekend, make an identical burger.

Sometimes I make healthy ones. Sometimes I create ***indulgent*** versions. It depends on how I'm feeling, what's in my fridge, and whether I am in need of eating my emotions that day.

It happens. You know it.

I find that these three types of dishes can ***please everyone*** in one way or another. The only thing they might be lacking is a strand of spaghetti.

While I focus on these three delicious staples, there is still an abundance of other recipes here in this little chapter. I share a few of my favorite seafood dishes, my method for roasting a chicken, some pasta recipes because if they aren't a staple then I don't know what the heck is, and a whole hodgepodge of ideas that I hope can make it into your kitchen.

When I was a kid, dinners were pretty standard in our house. Every Thursday night was pasta night, and I can't even tell you the tantrums I would throw about this. I know. Such a brat. Mondays were usually tacos or chicken Marsala, Wednesdays might be pork chops. We grilled a lot of flank steak and chicken, with my dad eventually graduating to salmon fillets, which thrilled me. Occasionally my mom would throw a wrench into the plans and make city chicken (which isn't even chicken…it's pork) or ***breakfast for dinner,*** and it was all so, so good.

Even though the options didn't differ much, we never noticed because her food was so delish. She knows her classics and she does them well.

These days, things are different but not entirely so. This chapter serves as a perfect example, because while we may not eat the same things day in and day out, we sure as heck eat a lot of pizza, burgers, and tacos. It's where the standard begins and grows from. It's my ***comfort level,*** but I enjoy being tossed out of it too.

On days when I feel like challenging myself, I'll cook a dish from a cuisine that I don't have much experience with or, my personal favorite, prep a meatless meal and see if I can manage to get Eddie to consume it without asking where the beef is.

As I've said all along, the keys to these meals are time and ease. I prefer things to be done simply and quickly, but there are just a ***handful of staples*** that may take a little longer; however, I could not resist sharing. They are for the times when you have a little extra time to be in the kitchen, when you want to enjoy the cooking process with happy results. This chapter is ME. This is about what cooking means to me and how I often share my food with loved ones.

Annnnnd about how I convince them to do the dishes.

It's true.

our favorite pizza crust

I first developed this pizza crust back in 2011, and it is our absolute favorite dough.

The crust is a bit on the puffier side. With this dough, if you use a pizza stone or a cast-iron skillet (my preferred ways of making pizza), it might even remind you of a wood-fired grill pizza.

It works like a charm, and I've got an all-purpose and a whole wheat version for you. Have some extra fun by throwing spices or dried herbs into the flour before stirring the dough. Such a treat.

MAKES enough for 1 pizza • TIME: 2 hours

1⅛ cups warm water

3 teaspoons active dry yeast

1 tablespoon honey

1 tablespoon extra-virgin olive oil, plus extra for oiling the bowl

3 cups all-purpose flour, plus extra for dusting

1 teaspoon salt

1 In a large bowl, combine the water, yeast, honey, and olive oil. Mix it together with a spoon, then let it sit until foamy, 10 to 15 minutes. Add 2½ cups of the flour and the salt, and stir with a spoon until the dough comes together but is still sticky. Using your hands, form the dough into a ball and work the additional ½ cup flour (you don't need to use all if it is not needed) into the dough, kneading it on a floured surface for a few minutes.

2 Rub the same bowl with a few drops of olive oil and place the dough inside, turning it over to coat. Cover the bowl with a towel and place in a warm place to rise for about 1½ hours.

3 Once the dough has risen, punch it down and remove it from the bowl. Place on a floured counter and, if it is sticky, knead a few tablespoons of flour into it until it is silky and smooth.

1. In a large bowl, combine the water, yeast, honey, and olive oil. Mix it together with a spoon, then let it sit until foamy, 10 to 15 minutes. Add 2 cups of the flour and the salt, and stir with a spoon until the dough comes together but is still sticky. Using your hands, form the dough into a ball and work an additional ⅓ cup of the flour into the dough, kneading it on a floured surface for a few minutes. Add the remaining ⅓ cup if the dough is still very sticky.

2. Rub the same bowl with a few drops of olive oil and place the dough inside, turning it over to coat. Cover the bowl with a towel and place in a warm place to rise for about 1½ hours.

3. Once the dough has risen, punch it down and remove it from the bowl. Place on a floured counter and, if it is sticky, knead a few tablespoons of flour into it until it is silky and smooth.

the 100% whole wheat version

MAKES enough for 1 pizza · **TIME:** 2 hours

1⅛ cups warm water

3 teaspoons active dry yeast

1 tablespoon honey

1 tablespoon extra-virgin olive oil, plus extra for oiling the bowl

2⅔ cups 100% whole wheat flour, plus extra for dusting

1 teaspoon salt

jalapeño-pineapple pizza with a bourbon BBQ drizzle

In weird combinations, this might win a medal. But don't run away just yet.

It's sweet and spicy. It's cheesy. Thinking of getting yourself out of your comfort zone? This will do it.

It's superb as dinner with a side salad and glass of wine. It's awesome made into a flatbread and served as an appetizer for party guests. It's meatless but won't mind if you add some chicken, pepperoni, or even bacon to the party. It's versatile. It will make you a believer.

1 Preheat the oven to 375°F if you are using a baking sheet for your pizza. If you are using a pizza stone, follow the heating instructions according to your stone.

2 Heat a small skillet over low heat and add 1 tablespoon of the olive oil. Add the shallots with the salt and stir. Cook the shallots for 5 to 6 minutes, stirring occasionally, until they begin to soften and turn golden. Stir in the brown sugar and cook for 2 to 3 more minutes, then add the garlic. Cook for 30 seconds. Turn off the heat.

3 Roll or pat the pizza dough into a 15-inch circle.

4 Brush the pizza dough with the remaining tablespoon of olive oil and cover it with the shallots and garlic. Add the mozzarella cheese and place the pineapple rings and jalapeño slices over the top. Add the crumbled goat cheese and drizzle the BBQ sauce over the pizza. Bake the pizza until the cheese is golden and bubbly, 30 to 35 minutes. Let cool slightly.

SERVES 2 • TIME: 50 minutes

2 tablespoons extra-virgin olive oil

2 shallots, sliced

1/4 teaspoon salt

1 tablespoon light brown sugar

2 garlic cloves, minced

1 batch pizza dough (see page 172)

4 ounces mozzarella cheese, freshly grated

4 fresh pineapple rings

2 jalapeño chile peppers, seeded and sliced

6 ounces goat cheese, crumbled

2 tablespoons Homemade Vanilla-Bourbon BBQ Sauce (page 204), or store-bought BBQ sauce

BBQ chicken & sweet corn pizza

SERVES 2 to 4 • TIME: 45 minutes

1 tablespoon extra-virgin olive oil

1 red onion, sliced

¼ teaspoon salt

¼ teaspoon freshly ground black pepper

2 garlic cloves, minced

1½ cups cooked and shredded chicken

1½ cups BBQ sauce

1 batch pizza dough (see page 172)

6 ounces sharp cheddar cheese, freshly grated

1 cup fresh or thawed frozen sweet corn kernels

4 ounces Gouda cheese, freshly grated

¼ cup torn fresh cilantro

So by now it's clear that not only do I really like pizza, but I also really love corn. And BBQ sauce. Accept it. It's going to get worse.

When it comes to things like BBQ chicken, I find a sprinkling of sweet corn to be incredibly refreshing. BBQ chicken pizza is probably the first nontraditional pizza I tried—meaning, no tomato sauce, mozzarella, or pepperoni—and I was hooked. It practically spoiled me, because after? I never wanted regular pizza again.

Or at least not for a day or two.

There is a time and a place for pizza like this. I firmly believe that if you have a true pizza craving, the only thing that will fix it is a classic pie with sauce and cheese. This is for the nights when you're not sure what sounds good, when you don't want to have a delivery guy showing up at your door, and when you just want something . . . different.

And if you're in the boat of reheated pizza being one of the best things ever (which, um, hello—I am), then you'll even enjoy this reheated the next day for lunch.

Summer on a pizza.

1 Preheat the oven to 375°F if you are using a baking sheet for your pizza. If you are using a pizza stone, follow the heating instructions according to your stone.

2 Heat a medium skillet over medium heat and add the olive oil. Add the onions, salt, and pepper and cook, stirring, until the onions soften, about 5 minutes. Stir in the garlic, shredded chicken, and ½ cup of the BBQ sauce and turn off the heat.

3 Roll or pat the pizza dough into a 15-inch circle.

4 Spread the remaining BBQ sauce all over the prepared pizza dough. Add the cheddar cheese on top and then evenly spread out the chicken mixture. Sprinkle the corn all over the pizza and cover it with the Gouda cheese. Bake the pizza until the cheese is golden and bubbly, 30 to 35 minutes. Remove the pizza from the oven and immediately cover it with the cilantro. Let cool for 10 to 15 minutes before slicing.

Eggs on pizza freak people out, and I'm not ashamed to admit that I maaaaybe used to be one of those people. I didn't know if I could do it.

As it turns out, though? It's fantastic. I like to put eggs on all things, that's for sure. And, you know, because of the eggs, this definitely qualifies as breakfast. Breakfast pizza can be a thing. Maybe just not with beer?

Pizza and beer for breakfast? Let me check. I'll get back to you on that.

1 Preheat the oven to 375°F if you are using a baking sheet for your pizza. If you are using a pizza stone, follow the heating instructions according to your stone.

2 Heat a large skillet over medium heat and add 2 tablespoons of the olive oil. Add the leeks, Brussels, salt, and pepper, stirring to coat. Cook, stirring occasionally, until the vegetables soften, 5 to 6 minutes. Stir in the garlic and cook for 30 seconds. Add the mushrooms, toss to coat, cover, and cook for 5 minutes. Turn off the heat.

3 Roll or pat the pizza dough into a 15-inch circle. Brush the pizza dough with the remaining ½ tablespoon olive oil. Add the provolone cheese to the dough and cover the cheese with the leek, mushroom, and Brussels mixture. Add half of the Fontina cheese on top. One at a time, gently crack each egg into a dish and slowly pour the egg onto the pizza. Cover the pizza with the remaining Fontina cheese.

4 Bake the pizza until the cheese is golden and bubbly, 30 to 35 minutes. Keep an eye on the eggs and cook for more or less time, depending on your desired doneness. Remove the pizza from the oven and let cool for 10 to 15 minutes before slicing.

mushroom, leek & brussels pizza with fried eggs

SERVES 2 to 4 • TIME: 45 minutes

2½ tablespoons extra-virgin olive oil

2 leeks, cleaned, trimmed, and sliced

8 ounces Brussels sprouts, stems removed and chopped

¼ teaspoon salt

¼ teaspoon freshly ground black pepper

2 garlic cloves, minced

12 ounces cremini mushrooms, chopped

1 batch pizza dough (see page 172)

6 ounces provolone cheese, freshly grated

4 ounces Fontina cheese, freshly grated

4 large eggs

crispy black bean tacos with mango pico de gallo

SERVES 4 • TIME: 30 minutes

1 mango, peeled, pitted, and diced

1 jalapeño chile pepper, seeded and diced

½ sweet yellow onion, diced

½ pint grape tomatoes, quartered

Juice of 1 lime

¼ teaspoon salt

¼ teaspoon freshly ground black pepper

1½ cups canned black beans, rinsed and drained

4 ounces queso fresco, crumbled, plus extra for serving

2 tablespoons chopped fresh cilantro

2 tablespoons canola oil

12 (4-inch) corn tortillas

We had an awesome little taco shop in Pittsburgh for a hot five minutes or so before it shut down. I made everyone I know dine there in four of those minutes, and we ate queso like there was no tomorrow. And I'm glad we did because apparently there wasn't a tomorrow. It was a sad day.

My cousin Lacy always ordered the crispy black bean tacos, and it was a treat we both missed once they closed. We were absolutely adamant on re-creating the dish because it was a change from your regular taco. Plus, the whole texture thing was going on and, well, you know I can't pass that up.

These tacos get crispy in two ways: First, you crisp up the black beans by giving them a coarse mash in a hot hot hot skillet. An electric skillet or griddle works best, but make do with what you've got. After those beans are slightly crisp, stuff them inside tortillas with a little cheese, fold 'em, and crisp up both sides of the taco.

There is nothing like a warm, crunchy taco.

Oh, except for a warm crunchy taco covered in mango pico de gallo. New best friends.

1 In a bowl, combine the mango, jalapeño, onion, and tomatoes and mix. Add the lime juice, salt, and pepper and toss to coat. Place the bowl in the fridge until you're ready to serve.

2 Place the black beans on a paper towel and pat completely dry. Heat a large nonstick skillet or electric griddle over medium-high heat. Add the beans to the hot surface and use a spatula to coarsely mash them. Turn the mixture over with a spatula every minute or so. After about 5 minutes, the beans will become a bit crispy. Remove them with a spatula and place them in a bowl. Toss the queso fresco and cilantro with the black beans.

3 Using the same skillet or griddle, brush the surface with a tablespoon of the canola oil. Add a tortilla to the skillet and cook for 30 seconds. Add a spoonful of the crispy black beans to one side of the tortilla and fold the other side over to create a taco. Continue to cook until the tortilla is golden, a bit bubbly, and crisp, 2 to 3 minutes. Gently flip (being careful not to lose the beans) and crisp up the other side. Repeat with the remaining tortillas, adding more oil as needed to crisp the tacos.

4 Serve immediately with a garnish of the mango pico and extra queso fresco.

We've already established that I am wild about tacos, so let's discuss this slaw.

Traditional coleslaw has never been my thing, and it wasn't until I started eating obnoxious amounts of tacos that I would consume slaw at all. There is something about crunchy slaw on top of warm tacos and melted cheese that just gets me. Completes me. All comes back to the texture. And the flavor . . . duh.

An old friend introduced me to the idea of Gorgonzola slaw, and I've never looked back. It was all his idea, and I totally jacked it. It's now a taco staple and tastes even better on pork and beef versions. Just try it.

1 Preheat the oven to 325°F. Arrange the chicken breasts in a baking dish and rub with the olive oil, including the skin. In a small bowl, combine the cumin, paprika, onion powder, chili powder, salt, and pepper. Rub the spices all over the chicken, making sure to rub underneath the skin as well. Roast the chicken for 45 minutes. Increase the oven temperature to 425°F and roast for 30 minutes more.

2 Remove the chicken breasts and allow them to cool until you can handle them. Use your hands and a fork to shred the chicken, and discard the skin and bones.

3 For the slaw, add the shredded cabbage to a large bowl. In a smaller bowl, whisk together the yogurt, Gorgonzola, lime juice, salt, and pepper. Pour it over the shredded cabbage and use your hands to thoroughly distribute and mix.

4 Assemble the tacos by adding the roasted chicken to the tortillas. Top them with the slaw, some torn fresh cilantro, and extra Gorgonzola.

slow-roasted chicken tacos with gorgonzola slaw

SERVES 4 · TIME: 2 hours

2 pounds bone-in, skin-on chicken breasts

3 tablespoons extra-virgin olive oil

1½ teaspoons ground cumin

1½ teaspoons smoked paprika

1 teaspoon onion powder

½ teaspoon chili powder

½ teaspoon salt

½ teaspoon freshly ground black pepper

GORGONZOLA SLAW

½ green cabbage, shredded

3 tablespoons plain full-fat or low-fat Greek yogurt

4 ounces Gorgonzola cheese, crumbled, plus extra for serving

Juice of 1 lime

⅛ teaspoon salt

⅛ teaspoon freshly ground black pepper

FOR SERVING

12 (4-inch) flour tortillas, warmed

¼ cup chopped fresh cilantro

chipotle-lime shrimp tacos with strawberry-jalapeño salsa

. . . .

SERVES 4 · TIME: 45 minutes

. . . .

SALSA

8 ounces fresh strawberries, hulled
   and chopped

1/2 red onion, diced

2 jalapeño chile peppers, seeded
   and diced

1/4 cup chopped fresh cilantro

Juice of 1 lime

Pinch of salt

Pinch of freshly ground black pepper

SHRIMP

1 pound peeled and deveined shrimp

Juice of 2 limes

2 garlic cloves, minced

3 tablespoons extra-virgin olive oil

1 tablespoon adobo sauce from a can of
   chipotle chile peppers in adobo sauce

1 teaspoon freshly grated lime zest

1/2 teaspoon salt

1/2 teaspoon freshly ground black pepper

FOR SERVING

8 (4-inch) corn tortillas, warmed

1 cup shredded cabbage

4 ounces queso fresco, crumbled

1 lime, cut into wedges

It is true. I will put almost anything inside a tortilla and call it a taco.
   Is that a problem?
   More fruit salsa. This is life.

1 Make the salsa first so the flavors have time to marry. In a bowl, combine the strawberries, red onion, jalapeño peppers, and cilantro and toss. Add the lime juice, salt, and pepper and toss to coat. Place the bowl in the fridge until ready to serve.

2 For the shrimp, place the shrimp in a baking dish or resealable plastic bag. In a small bowl, whisk together the lime juice, garlic, 2 tablespoons of the olive oil, adobo sauce, lime zest, salt, and pepper. Pour over the top of the shrimp and toss to coat. Marinate in the refrigerator for 30 minutes.

3 Heat a large skillet over medium-high heat and add the remaining 1 tablespoon olive oil. Remove the shrimp from the dish or plastic bag and discard the marinade. Add the shrimp in a single layer to the skillet and cook just until the shrimp turn pink and opaque, 1 to 2 minutes. Flip the shrimp and cook for 1 to 2 minutes more. Transfer the shrimp to a plate for serving.

4 Serve the tortillas with the shrimp, salsa, cabbage, and the crumbled queso fresco for topping. Garnish with a lime wedge on the side.

For my non-meat-eating friends? This is for you.

It's also for me. Because I'm selfish.

I learned way back when that tacos were another excellent vehicle for me to consume vegetables. As long as a little cheese and maybe something crunchy was involved, I could handle it and most of the time, craved it.

Plus, I felt really good knowing that I could still eat the things I loved by making a few tiny sacrifices. It's all about the give and take, my friends.

On another note, let's discuss grilled corn. Freaking nuts over it. The best grilled corn I ever had was on Nantucket, at Corazon del Mar, but I frequently make it at home on our grill. Heck, sometimes I even roast it in the oven or shove it under the broiler if it's raining cats and dogs outside.

Since we have zucchini AND corn here, I like to think of these tacos as veggie powerhouses. I know, you are probably laughing so hard at me right now. But this IS a veggie powerhouse for me!

Please still be my friend?

1 Heat a large skillet over medium-low heat and add the olive oil. Add the shallots and garlic and, stirring, cook until softened, 2 to 3 minutes. Add the cubed zucchini, salt, and pepper and stir. Cook, stirring, until the zucchini becomes slightly tender, 5 to 6 minutes. Remove the skillet from the heat and set aside.

2 For the corn salsa, combine the corn, jalapeño peppers, cilantro, lime juice, salt, and pepper in a bowl and toss it together.

3 For the crema, whisk together the yogurt, adobo sauce, lime juice, salt, and pepper.

4 To assemble the tacos, add some of the zucchini mixture to each warm tortilla and cover it with corn salsa. Drizzle the crema on top.

zucchini tacos
with grilled corn salsa

SERVES 2 to 4 • TIME: 30 minutes

2 tablespoons extra-virgin olive oil

2 shallots, diced

2 garlic cloves, minced

2 cups cubed zucchini

1/2 teaspoon salt

1/2 teaspoon freshly ground black pepper

CORN SALSA

2 ears grilled corn (see page 158), kernels cut from cob

1 jalapeño chile pepper, seeded and diced

2 tablespoons chopped fresh cilantro

Juice of 1 lime

1/4 teaspoon salt

1/4 teaspoon freshly ground black pepper

CHIPOTLE CREMA

3 tablespoons plain full-fat or low-fat Greek yogurt

2 teaspoons adobo sauce from a can of chipotle chile peppers in adobo sauce

Juice of 1 lime

Pinch of salt

Pinch of freshly ground black pepper

FOR SERVING

8 (4-inch) flour tortillas, warmed

roasted pork & pineapple baked taquitos

SERVES 2 to 4 • TIME: 2 hours to overnight prep time; 1 hour cook time

· ·

1 (2-pound) pork butt

1 teaspoon salt

1 teaspoon freshly ground black pepper

2 cups cubed fresh pineapple

¼ cup pineapple juice

¼ red onion, chopped

½ jalapeño chile pepper, seeded and diced

1 teaspoon adobo sauce from a can of chipotle chile peppers in adobo sauce

10 (4-inch) corn tortillas

Now, if you REALLY want something different for dinner? I have just the ticket.

By the way, every time I say that, it reminds me of Patrick Dempsey in the movie *Sweet Home Alabama* and all of his fabulous hair. Not a bad correlation to make. I would just like to run my hands through that hair and eat some roasted pineapple pork.

I am hesitant to say that this is similar to al pastor (a traditional dish combining pork and pineapple), but it's my little rip-off of that. Pulled pork and caramelly pineapple, all combined into a crispy little tortilla that is baked, not fried.

If this sounds strange, please take a bite. It's all I can do to not eat every single taquito off the baking sheet when I make them. It's certainly a fun food. Oh, and a heads-up? You can obviously eat this pork however your little heart desires. No tortillas required.

1 Take the pork butt and trim any excess fat from it. Using a sharp knife, cut the pork into 1-inch cubes, removing any bones as you go. Season the pork with the salt and pepper.

2 Add 1 cup of the pineapple, pineapple juice, onion, jalapeño, and adobo sauce to a food processor and blend until pureed. Place the pork cubes in a bowl or resealable plastic bag and cover them with the pureed pineapple mixture. Refrigerate the pork while it marinates, for anywhere from 2 hours to overnight.

3 Preheat the oven to 425°F. Add the pork to a baking dish along with the remaining 1 cup pineapple. Roast the pork for 30 to 35 minutes. Remove the dish from the oven and let the pork cool slightly, just until it's cool enough to work with.

4 Warm the tortillas two at a time in either the microwave or the oven, just for a few minutes so they are easier to work with. Fill each tortilla with a tablespoon or two of the roasted pork mixture and gently roll it up, placing it on a baking sheet seam side down. Repeat with the remaining tortillas. Spray the tortillas with a mist of canola, olive, or coconut oil or nonstick spray and bake them until crispy, 10 to 12 minutes.

5 Serve the taquitos immediately with your choice of toppings, such as salsa, guacamole, and fresh cilantro.

green chili turkey & white bean enchiladas

SERVES 4 · **TIME: 50 minutes**

1 tablespoon extra-virgin olive oil

1/2 sweet yellow onion, diced

1/2 red bell pepper, diced

1/2 green bell pepper, diced

1/2 teaspoon plus a pinch of salt

2 garlic cloves, minced

1 (4-ounce) can diced green chiles

1 pound lean ground turkey

1 1/2 teaspoons ground cumin

1 teaspoon smoked paprika

1/2 teaspoon chili powder

1/2 teaspoon garlic powder

1/2 teaspoon freshly ground black pepper

1/4 cup low-sodium chicken stock

1 cup canned white beans, rinsed and drained

2 1/2 cups enchilada sauce

6 ounces Monterey Jack cheese, freshly grated

8 whole wheat tortillas

2 tablespoons chopped chives (optional)

Good old chicken enchiladas can't be beat, and in my opinion, neither can the cheese version. But if you eat them as often as we do—say, like, at least twice a month—sometimes you want a little change.

For years, I was stuck on the belief that ground turkey was always dry and flavorless and just . . . blah. Always. No exceptions to the rule.

Not so, my friends . . . not so.

Not only are these enchiladas jam-packed with protein and fiber, which makes them extra filling, but they also taste enough like traditional enchiladas that you curb your craving. They're slightly different, so your taste buds aren't bored. What? I know.

Don't your taste buds get bored? Just mine?

We like to serve them with salads.

Who am I kidding? I mean chips and a margarita.

1 Preheat the oven to 350°F.

2 Heat a large skillet over medium heat and add the olive oil. Add the onions and peppers with the pinch of salt and toss to coat. Cook, stirring, for 5 minutes. Add the garlic and green chiles. Stir and cook for 30 seconds.

3 Push the vegetables to the side of the skillet and add the ground turkey. Break it apart with a wooden spoon and cook it until the turkey is browned, 5 to 6 minutes. Add the cumin, paprika, chili powder, garlic powder, remaining 1/2 teaspoon salt, pepper, and chicken stock to the skillet. Stir well to mix the turkey and vegetables together and reduce the heat to low. Add in the white beans. Cook for another 1 to 2 minutes. Add 1/2 cup of the enchilada sauce to the skillet along with 2 ounces of the cheese and stir it together. Turn off the heat.

4 Pour ½ cup of the enchilada sauce into the bottom of a 9x13-inch baking dish and use a spoon to spread it evenly over the surface. Spoon about one-quarter of the turkey filling into each tortilla and roll them up tightly. Place them in the baking dish, seam side down. Once all of the tortillas have been filled and rolled, pour the remaining enchilada sauce over the top and brush it to cover every portion of the tortillas. Sprinkle the remaining cheese on top. Bake the enchiladas until the cheese is golden and the sauce is bubbling, 30 to 35 minutes. Top with freshly chopped chives if desired.

NOTE: I find that tortilla sizes can differ in the package, and occasionally I will end up with extra turkey filling. I save this to make a taco for lunch later in the week or to scoop it up with tortilla chips.

mini crab cakes with sweet corn & blueberry salsa

SERVES 2 to 4 • **TIME: 30 minutes**

SALSA

1 pint fresh blueberries, coarsely chopped

$^2/_3$ cup fresh or thawed frozen sweet corn kernels

$^1/_4$ red onion, finely diced

2 tablespoons chopped fresh cilantro

Juice of 1 lime

$^1/_4$ teaspoon salt

$^1/_8$ teaspoon pepper

CRAB CAKES

1 pound lump crabmeat

2 tablespoons diced red bell pepper

2 tablespoons diced green bell pepper

2 tablespoons diced red onion

1 garlic clove, minced

8 multigrain crackers, crushed

1 large egg, lightly beaten

1 tablespoon Dijon mustard

1 tablespoon plain full-fat or low-fat Greek yogurt

$^1/_4$ teaspoon salt

$^1/_4$ teaspoon freshly ground black pepper

$^1/_8$ teaspoon cayenne pepper

1 tablespoon extra-virgin olive oil

My Grandma Lois made the BEST crab cakes. The recipe was ridiculously simple: It contained only six or so ingredients, and she actually counted out the saltines before crushing them, then cooked the suckers in butter. They were so delicious, and while my mom makes a mean re-creation, Grandma's were the best. My brother Will still can't get over them.

But as I'm sure you can agree, crab cakes are funny little things. They can be either outrageously impressive or disappointing when you order them in a restaurant, and I've never quite understood the places that serve crab cake sandwiches when their actual crab cake is a mess of bread crumbs to begin with. It's like eating a bread crumb sandwich. With a side of shells.

Here's what I do with crab cakes: Sometimes I make big ones. Giant crab cakes, eaten as a main dish with some coleslaw on the side and perhaps a few fries. Other times, I make itty-bitty ones, perfect for throwing on a salad or serving as an appetizer with an aioli. But I almost always make a fruit salsa to go on top. It's super-refreshing and light. It adds a new element of flavor and . . . it's pretty. You know I like pretty.

1 For the salsa, combine the blueberries, corn, onion, and cilantro in a bowl. Mix it together well. Add the lime juice, salt, and pepper and stir to toss the ingredients together. Place the salsa in the fridge until you're ready to use it.

2 For the crab cakes, in a large bowl, combine the crabmeat, peppers, onions, garlic, and crackers and mix them together well. In a small bowl, whisk together the egg, mustard, and yogurt. Add the egg mixture to the crab and mix well to combine. Stir in the salt, black pepper, and cayenne.

3 Use your hands to form the crab mixture into 8 to 10 patties. Heat a large skillet over medium heat and add the olive oil. Add the crab cakes to the skillet and cook until golden on each side, 5 to 6 minutes per side. Top the crab cakes with the salsa.

NOTE: You can definitely sandwich these guys between two buns. I prefer sliders. So cute!

accidental
white wine baked scallops

SERVES 4 · TIME: 45 minutes

4 tablespoons (1/2 stick) unsalted butter

1/2 small sweet yellow onion, finely diced

2 garlic cloves, minced

1 pound fresh bay scallops

1/4 teaspoon salt

1/4 teaspoon freshly ground black pepper

1 (750 ml) bottle dry white wine

1 lemon, halved

3/4 cup panko bread crumbs

This is a recipe that's been gracing our table since 1985. And it's from my dad.

Every summer my mom's side of the family has vacationed at the Jersey shore. Like, we are talking nearly 35 years. It is one week when my mom and aunt barely cook a thing—most of our dinners are taken care of by "the dads" and are often giant seafood feasts. The girls may prepare a salad, but other than that, everything is off-limits.

I wish you could sit down with my dad right now so he could tell you the story about these scallops. It's insanely entertaining.

If you listen to how he tells it? It goes a little something like this: Back in the late '80s, while on vacation, my mom decided that she just wasn't cooking. And can you blame her? Three kids under the age of five—break needed. So that left the men to quickly prepare dinner and, well, they kind of screwed themselves. It was so delicious that it's happened ever since. Now we all just expect it. Now on vacation, THEY want the break.

We don't let them get it.

My dad doesn't measure a thing these days when he preps this recipe, and it's essentially perfected by tasting. It's been 30 years in the making and while it rarely tastes different, it always tastes incredible. Every time we've served it to new guests, whether it be significant others or new friends, they beg for the recipe. I actually didn't think he would give it to me since it's a little bit of a secret . . . but he did it for you.

Thanks, Dad.

1 Preheat the oven to 250°F.

2 Heat a large skillet over medium-low heat and add the butter. Once it's melted, add the onion and stir to coat. Cook, stirring, until the onion begins to soften, 2 to 3 minutes. Add the garlic and stir for 30 seconds, then add the scallops. Cook the scallops just until the edges begin to firm up, 30 to 60 seconds. Sprinkle the mixture with the salt and pepper.

3 Remove the skillet from the heat and spoon all the ingredients into an 8x8-inch baking dish. Pour in 1½ cups of the white wine and squeeze the juice from half of the lemon over the top. Sprinkle ½ cup of the bread crumbs over the top. Cover the dish and place it in the oven.

4 Bake the scallops for 15 minutes. Remove the lid of the dish and add another glug of white wine and another squeeze of lemon. Bake the scallops for 15 minutes more, then repeat with the wine and lemon juice and add the rest of the bread crumbs over the top. Reduce the oven temperature to 225°F to keep the scallops warm until you're ready to serve.

NOTES FROM MY DAD: This baking time and temperature was discovered by accident due to the extended time needed to prepare other varied meal courses for a large group of vacationing family members; courses like fried flounder, wild rice, hot dogs in croissants, grilled cheese sandwiches, fresh tossed salad, steamed clams, and crab or lobster claws. The repeated addition of wine and lemon keeps the scallops moist during the extended baking time and the addition of the bread crumbs helps to thicken the delicious wine-flavored sauce that envelops the scallops. Many who have enjoyed these scallops are known to have soaked up the wine sauce with fresh bread.

By having this little thing called a food blog, I've learned something. People have really strong feelings about fish. A ton of people just really hate it. Like . . . a ton. Others are allergic. Sad face. Many haven't experienced it "outside the box."

If you know of someone who is trying to eat more fish but doesn't particularly love it, I personally think tilapia is the way to go. It's affordable and flaky, and not fishy or offensive in the slightest. Who wants fishy fish?

While I often sub it for other white fish inside of tacos (surprise, surprise—it just flakes beautifully), I love crusting it with bread crumbs, crushed nuts, or even coconut. The crunchy outside gives you just a little reminder of how good fried fish tastes. This is barely even remotely close, but you've got the crunch and you've got the fish, so can we call it even?

My all-time favorite fried fish is at the BRI in Boyne City, Michigan. It doesn't get much fresher than that. Whenever I'm craving it but don't want to drag out the deep fryer or oil, I coat some tilapia and bake it until crunchy. It sort of handles the craving—and is a lot quicker than driving the ten hours to get to Boyne City.

 Preheat the oven to 425°F. Line a baking sheet with aluminum foil and cover the baking sheet with a nonstick wire rack. Spray the rack with nonstick spray.

2 Add the egg whites to one bowl. In another bowl, whisk together the almond meal, lemon zest, salt, and pepper. Dip each tilapia fillet into the egg white and then dredge it through the almond meal mixture. Press gently to adhere the coating and cover the entire fillet. Set each piece of fish on the wire rack. Give each fillet a spritz of extra-virgin olive oil or canola oil to moisten the almond meal. This will help the breading become crisp.

3 Bake the fish for 15 minutes, and then gently flip the tilapia and bake for 15 minutes more.

4 As soon as the fish goes into the oven, prepare the rice. Add the rice, coconut milk, water, and salt to a saucepan and bring to a boil. Reduce the heat to low and cover the pan, cooking until the liquid is absorbed, 30 to 40 minutes. Double-check your rice for directions on the cook time and adjust accordingly. Once the liquid is absorbed, stir in the coconut oil and flaked coconut.

 Serve each tilapia fillet with a sprinkle of fresh herbs, the rice, and lemon wedges.

lemon-almond tilapia with coconut macaroon rice

SERVES 2 to 4 • TIME: 35 minutes

3 large egg whites, lightly beaten

1 cup almond meal

1 tablespoon freshly grated lemon zest

1/2 teaspoon salt

1/2 teaspoon freshly ground black pepper

4 (4-ounce) tilapia fillets

Olive or canola oil, for spritzing

1 1/2 cups jasmine rice

1 1/2 cups canned light coconut milk

1 1/2 cups water

1/4 teaspoon salt

1 tablespoon coconut oil

2 tablespoons unsweetened flaked coconut, toasted (see page 27)

2 tablespoons chopped fresh herbs of your choice

1 lemon, sliced into wedges

garlic butter roasted chicken

SERVES 4 to 6 • TIME: 2 hours

1 (5-pound) whole chicken

4 tablespoons (½ stick) unsalted butter, at room temperature

4 garlic cloves, minced

1 teaspoon salt

1 teaspoon freshly ground black pepper

1 head garlic, top sliced off

2 tablespoons extra-virgin olive oil

My life changed when I learned how to roast a chicken.

I was scared for years—a bit skeeved out at the thought of touching all of the parts and just dealing with the whole thing . . . raw. I was dubious.

And I'm not even being dramatic in the slightest (for real) when I say this changed my life. The day I pulled up Ina Garten's roasted chicken recipe on my computer screen, stuff changed. It got better. Not only did I feel like I was cooking for my own personal Jeffrey (which, duh, I was), but the fear disappeared.

After you roast a chicken a few times, the thought is **not daunting** anymore. In fact, it's so easy that I do it once a week. Preferably on Sundays or Mondays so that we have chicken for the rest of the week. And even though I do this as a preemptive strike—to save my soul when it comes to dinnertime on weeknights (which I will forever refer to as "school nights")—I personally find that the best moments of chicken roasting come about 10 minutes after the bird is finished.

The skin. It's so dang crispy. I have been known to stand there and pull all the crispy chicken skin off the bird and eat it while standing over the stove, hoping my husband doesn't hear what I'm doing because there is no way I want to share.

Now THAT'S my favorite part. Don't miss out.

1 Preheat the oven to 425°F. Remove any loose parts (giblets) from the chicken and discard. Trim any excess fat or feathers (yes!) from the bird. Pat the chicken completely dry with paper towels.

2 In a small bowl, mix together the softened butter with the minced garlic, ½ teaspoon of the salt, and ½ teaspoon of the pepper. Take the butter mixture and stuff it under the skin of the chicken, focusing on the breast and the legs. All of the butter should be under the skin, not on top of it. Stuff the head of garlic into the cavity of the chicken.

3 Rub the entire bird with the olive oil and cover it with the remaining salt and pepper. Use kitchen twine to tie the legs together and tuck the wings underneath the chicken's body. Place the chicken in a roasting pan or baking dish. I prefer to roast my chickens breast side down so all of the juices flow into the meat.

4 Roast the chicken until the juices run clear when sliced, 80 to 85 minutes. Remove the chicken from the oven and let it rest for 10 to 15 minutes before carving.

make-ahead mini freezer meatballs

I am married to a meat man and that is the understatement of the century. He is a meat fah-reak. You can tell him all the benefits you want about going meatless and he will listen intently and then go home and prepare a steak and two chicken breasts.

Needless to say, I've made a LOT of meatballs since 2008. A lot.

Eventually, I figured out that I could make a big batch at once and freeze some. Not only am I sharing that method with you, but this is also a recipe we love that combines both ground beef and ground turkey. Reduces the saturated fat a little bit but keeps all the flavor. Big-time meat-lover pleaser. Big time-saver. Big smile maker.

Forgive the cheesiness.

MAKES about 60 mini meatballs
TIME: 45 minutes

1 pound lean ground beef
1 pound lean ground turkey
1 large egg, lightly beaten
1/3 cup panko bread crumbs
1/3 cup freshly grated romano cheese
3 garlic cloves, minced
1 1/2 teaspoons dried basil
1 teaspoon dried oregano
1 teaspoon onion powder
1 teaspoon smoked paprika
1/2 teaspoon salt
1/2 teaspoon freshly ground black pepper

1 Line two baking sheets with aluminum foil, waxed paper, or parchment paper.

2 Add the beef and turkey to a large bowl and gently mix with your hands to combine. Add the egg, bread crumbs, cheese, garlic, basil, oregano, onion powder, smoked paprika, salt, and pepper. Use your hands to mix the meat together, and try to distribute the ingredients evenly without over-mixing.

3 Take 1 to 2 tablespoons of the meatball mix and roll it into a ball. Place on one of the baking sheets, and repeat this process until all of the meat has been used, utilizing the second baking sheet if necessary. Once finished, place the baking sheets in the freezer, uncovered. Freeze the meatballs until just firm and frozen, 1 to 2 hours. Remove the baking sheets from the freezer and place the meatballs in a large resealable plastic freezer bag. Squeeze all of the air out of the bag and seal tightly. Freeze for up to 3 months.

4 When you are ready to use the meatballs, remove the bag from the freezer. You can place them directly in a slow-cooked sauce, stew, or soup and give them about 4 hours to cook. You can also place them in a baking dish and cover them with tomato sauce. At 350°F, they should take about 1½ hours to cook through. Otherwise, allow the meatballs to defrost completely and cook them as you normally would. I like to quickly panfry them and cover them with tomato sauce for meatball subs.

crunchy baked chicken fingers with chive-honey mustard

If Eddie could choose one meal to eat for the rest of his life, I believe it would come down to three things: burgers, pizza, or chicken fingers.

He may be on to something. Or he may just be secretly four years old inside.

We have made these chicken fingers for so many years now that I can truly say I prefer them over any fast-food or restaurant version. They are so crispy and crunchy, and the chicken stays tender. The breading stays put, and they are perfect for a trio of dipping sauces, like honey mustard, barbecue, and buffalo.

It was awesome when I realized I could make something taste so good—something that was healthy and just as delicious as the not-so-healthy version—at home and in the comfort of my own kitchen. This is one of those recipes that opened up the floodgates of flavor for me. I have seasoned chicken fingers with homemade ranch spices, Asiago cheese, pesto and Parmesan, and my own barbecue spice rub. They can even be made a few hours in advance if necessary and you can make one giant batch at once, especially if you have two baking sheets with wire racks.

That's the thing: The wire rack is the key here. It allows the heat to surround each chicken finger and crisp up all sides . . . whereas if it's lying flat on a baking sheet? That side can get a little soggy. If you don't own a wire rack and desperately need these fingers in your life today, the baking sheet will work just fine. Just get one of those racks for next time. It makes all the difference. In a really good way.

Says the most dramatic cook ever.

SERVES 2 to 4

TIME: 2 hours to overnight prep time;
45 minutes cook time

- 1½ pounds boneless, skinless chicken tenders
- 4 cups low-fat buttermilk
- 2 cups panko bread crumbs
- ½ cup fine bread crumbs
- ¼ cup all-purpose or whole wheat flour
- 1 teaspoon salt
- 1 teaspoon freshly ground black pepper
- ½ teaspoon onion powder
- Canola oil, for spritzing

1 Add the chicken to a 9x13-inch baking dish and pour the buttermilk on top. All the chicken pieces should be submerged in the milk. Refrigerate for at least 2 hours or preferably overnight.

2 Preheat the oven to 450°F. Line a baking sheet with aluminum foil and place a nonstick wire rack on top. Spray the rack with nonstick spray.

3 In a large bowl, combine the bread crumbs, flour, salt, pepper, and onion powder and mix well. Remove each piece of chicken from the dish—it should be covered in a thick coat of buttermilk—and dredge it through the bread crumbs. Press lightly so the bread crumbs adhere and cover all the meat. Lay each chicken tender on the wire rack. Give each piece a spritz of canola oil to moisten the crumbs.

4 Bake the chicken for 15 minutes, then gently flip each piece with kitchen tongs. Bake it for 15 minutes more. Remove the chicken and let cool slightly on the rack before serving.

5 For the honey mustard, add the mustard, honey, and chives to a bowl and mix to combine. This sauce will stay fresh in a sealed container in the fridge for up to 1 week.

CHIVE-HONEY MUSTARD

⅓ cup Dijon mustard

¼ cup honey

2 tablespoons chopped fresh chives

chili-garlic roasted salmon

SERVES 4 • TIME: 30 minutes

1½ pounds salmon fillet, about 1 inch thick

1½ tablespoons extra-virgin olive oil

4 garlic cloves, minced

2 teaspoons light brown sugar

1 teaspoon crushed red pepper flakes

½ teaspoon salt

½ teaspoon freshly ground black pepper

With the prolific amount of people who either don't care for seafood or are allergic, I feel blessed to not only love it, but also be able to consume it without issue.

I freaking adore it.

I am sure that one of the reasons I favor it so much stems from spending summers in northern Michigan, where my dad and brothers (and sometimes me, when I wasn't afraid to bait my own hook) would fish for a few hours and then later, fry up what they caught.

They never caught enough fish to feed the family—it was not the intent, as they really only were fishing for fun. But it was still a tradition that my dad would keep one or two (throwing the rest back) and beer-batter it, and fry it in his favorite pancake-making skillet, and we'd all get a bite or two. It was super fun. And I've loved fish ever since.

One bite takes me back there.

I'm grateful that I married a guy who likes it too, and salmon has become a weeknight staple at our dinner table. I find that the toppings and flavors that mesh with salmon can be endless, and it just makes for the best salad topping ever. I think it's the flakiness. It flakes into your salad and then you can almost make a chopped salad. Which are my favorite salads. Little bits of everything!

Most times when I'm preparing salmon, you'll find me rubbing it down with some spices and placing it under the broiler. Not only is it a superfast way to prepare the fish, but it also gets slightly crispy on top. Doesn't get much better than that . . . unless it's coming right out of the lake.

1 Preheat oven to 400°F.

2 Place the salmon in a large baking dish or on a rimmed baking sheet. In a small bowl, whisk together the olive oil, garlic, brown sugar, red pepper flakes, salt, and pepper. Use your hands to rub the mixture all over the top of the salmon fillet. Place the baking dish or sheet in the oven. Roast the salmon until it is opaque and flakes easily with a fork, 20 to 25 minutes. Remove the salmon from the oven and let cool for 5 minutes.

NOTE: This method works with skinless or skin-on salmon fillets. I prefer to not remove the skin before roasting since it can be time-consuming, and I also prefer to not flip the salmon while roasting, because it can be messy and fall apart. If your salmon has the skin, roast it skin side down. When you go to serve the fish, it should slide right off the skin when slicing.

If I have anything to hope for, it's that you don't get sick of quinoa by the end of this book. Puh-lease.

Quinoa patties remind me of crab cakes in a way: super-adaptable and can be used in many recipes. These can serve as your main dish but also work on a salad or a sandwich. They can be served hot or eaten cold if you're in a hurry, and they just have this CRUNCH. You have to know by now how I feel about that.

Crunch essentially runs my life.

① In a large bowl, combine the quinoa, eggs, shallot, garlic, cheese, rosemary, salt, and pepper, stirring well. You want all of the quinoa to be wet. Add the flour and bread crumbs and stir again to combine. Use your hands to form 10 to 12 small quinoa patties, 1½ to 2 inches in diameter.

② Heat a large skillet over medium heat and add the olive oil. Add the quinoa patties to the skillet and cook until crispy and golden, 5 to 6 minutes per side. Remove the patties and set them on a paper towel, allowing them to drain and cool for 1 to 2 minutes.

crispy
rosemary &
parmesan
quinoa
patties

MAKES 10 to 12 patties • TIME: 30 minutes

2 cups cooked quinoa

2 large eggs plus 1 egg white, lightly beaten

1 shallot, diced

2 garlic cloves, minced

½ cup freshly grated Parmesan cheese

3 tablespoons chopped fresh rosemary

½ teaspoon salt

½ teaspoon freshly ground black pepper

¼ cup whole wheat pastry flour

2 tablespoons panko bread crumbs

2 tablespoons extra-virgin olive oil

homemade
vanilla–bourbon BBQ sauce

MAKES about 1 cup • TIME: 45 minutes

1 cup ketchup

¹/₂ cup bourbon

¹/₂ cup honey

3 garlic cloves, minced

2 tablespoons apple cider vinegar

2 tablespoons Dijon mustard

1 teaspoon Worcestershire sauce

1 teaspoon vanilla extract

¹/₂ teaspoon onion powder

¹/₂ teaspoon smoked paprika

¹/₄ teaspoon freshly ground black pepper

1 vanilla bean, seeds scraped

Being the first condiment I ever made from scratch so many moons ago, barbecue sauce finally won my heart. I grew up with two brothers who slathered it on everything—even perfect beef fillets—and in the words of Carrie Bradshaw, I so many times wanted to cry, "Stop! You're ruining it!"

But then I made my own. I guess I chose the perfect recipe to try that day, because I was sold and immediately started using it on everything. My favorite throwback? Microwaved tortilla chips with freshly grated cheese and a big, fat barbecue sauce drizzle. Sound weird and terrible and just so 1989? Judge not.

Since I can't leave well and good alone, bourbon and vanilla somehow managed to figure out their way to into the sauce, and I've never looked back. It just does . . . SOMETHING to the sauce. So fantastic.

Use it on, well, everything.

 In a medium saucepan, whisk together the ketchup, bourbon, honey, garlic, vinegar, mustard, and Worcestershire sauce. Add the vanilla extract, onion powder, smoked paprika, pepper, scraped vanilla seeds, and vanilla bean pod and stir. Heat over medium heat and bring the mixture to a boil, then reduce the heat to low and cook, stirring occasionally, for 30 minutes. Remove the sauce from the heat and discard the vanilla bean pod. Let sit at room temperature until it cools and thickens, about 1 hour.

2 Store in a jar or sealed container in the fridge for up to 2 weeks.

I can always smell spring when it arrives, and it's one of my favorite times—blooming flowers, green grass, fresh air. Is that annoying? It's real life.

I love it.

True, you will hear me say that about all the seasons: how much I love them. After all, it's one of the reasons why I don't think I could ever fully leave Pennsylvania—I'd miss the changing leaves and dusting of snow and humid summers way too much. And I just love as each season approaches while the other ends. Maybe it's that nostalgia in me, but whatever. They are beautiful times.

Spring is like one giant cool breeze that whisks in new life. Some of my favorite foods come into their own—fresh peas, citrus, artichokes. This is also about the time when I will start sneezing like a maniac because anything remotely floral-scented makes my allergies go into a tailspin. Worth it, though.

And while this world has made it possible for us to get all sorts of out-of-season produce all year-round, there is nothing like asparagus in the spring. It's superthin and flavorful, and I take almost any chance I get to throw it into a tart, under eggs with breakfast, or in this case, in pasta. Add in that little burst of lemon and, well, this is spring in a dish. It really freaking is.

1 Bring a large pot of salted water to a boil and prepare the linguine according to the package directions. Reserve ½ cup of the starchy cooking liquid. Drain the pasta.

2 While the pasta is cooking, heat a large skillet over low heat and add the olive oil. Stir in the shallots and cook for 5 minutes. Add the asparagus spears and garlic and cook for 5 minutes more. Increase the heat to medium and add the starchy pasta water, mascarpone cheese, 2 tablespoons of the Parmesan cheese, the lemon zest and juice, salt, and pepper. Stir and cook until a bit of a sauce begins to come together, 2 to 3 minutes. Add the peas and cooked linguine, tossing well to coat. Cover with the remaining Parmesan cheese, the scallions, and the bread crumbs.

lemon, garlic & asparagus spring pasta skillet

SERVES 4 • TIME: 35 minutes

8 ounces whole wheat linguine

2 tablespoons extra-virgin olive oil

1 shallot, diced

10 asparagus spears, woody stems removed and chopped into thirds

4 garlic cloves, minced

4 ounces mascarpone cheese

¼ cup freshly grated Parmesan cheese

Zest and juice of ½ lemon

½ teaspoon salt

½ teaspoon freshly ground black pepper

⅔ cup fresh peas

2 scallions, sliced

2 tablespoons panko bread crumbs

honey-glazed pork tenderloin with roasted grapes

SERVES 4 • TIME: 1½ hours

1 (1½-pound) pork tenderloin, extra fat trimmed

1 teaspoon salt

1 teaspoon freshly ground black pepper

2 tablespoons grapeseed oil

1 red onion, sliced

3 cups seedless red grapes

½ cup dry red wine

½ cup low-sodium chicken stock

2 tablespoons honey

2 tablespoons toasted sesame oil

There are not many things worse in life than when you eat a dry cut of pork.

Except for paying for, preparing, and cooking that dry cut of pork yourself. Oh, and maybe the worst? Serving it to friends.

My mom makes a killer pork tenderloin that is always incredibly moist. Oh, I'm sorry, does that word make you cringe? Let's take a look in the thesaurus and come up with something better: clammy? Damp? Soggy? Which would you prefer?

I think we'll stick with moist. And tender. It's unfortunate, but it's life.

Anyway, one of the keys to a perfect pork tenderloin? Patience. That's why moms are so good at it. My mom has more patience than anyone I know. I have no idea why I inherited none of it.

Roasted grapes may sound a little crazy, but don't knock 'em till you try 'em. I'm well aware that I can get a little wacky in the fruit department, but it's all with good intent. If you really don't want to do the grape, stick your favorite veggie next to it instead.

I think I can forgive you. Maybe.

1. Preheat the oven to 400°F. Season the pork with the salt and pepper.

2. Heat a large cast-iron or oven-proof skillet over high heat. Add the oil and, once it's hot, add the pork and sear it on all sides until golden, 1 to 2 minutes per side. Turn off the heat and add the onions, grapes, wine, and stock to the skillet. Whisk together the honey and sesame oil and brush it all over the pork.

3. Transfer the skillet to the oven and roast the meat until the pork reaches 170°F, 45 to 60 minutes. Let the pork rest for 10 minutes before slicing and serving with the roasted grapes.

homemade chicken pitas with jalapeño whipped feta & quick tzatziki

SERVES 4 • TIME: 2 hours to overnight prep time; 35 minutes cook time

I'm not sure that there has been a more frequently made meal in my kitchen in the past few years than this one. These homemade chicken pitas were not my idea, nor my recipe. I swiped it.

See, I don't have a sister. My cousin Lacy doesn't have a sister either, and the two of us along with my brothers and her brother were sort of raised like siblings. In the words of Meredith Grey, she is my person.

The thing about Lacy is that she knows her food. She knows way more about food than I do; she inspired at least half of this book. She knows all the best restaurants; she has the best taste. She just gets it.

So one night, she made these. And I ate them.

I showed up to her house when she was grilling chicken and warming pitas and scooping tzatziki into a bowl. When I took my first bite of this seemingly simple sandwich, I could not believe the flavor. It looked fairly simple but makes for such a delicious dinner. Tons of flavor. Leftovers are easy and crave-worthy. Warming the hummus is a suggested surprise. The jalapeño whipped feta is a play on a popular feta dip from my blog and is not overly spicy at all. All of the flavors just WORK.

The ingredient list may seem long, but all it takes for this delicious meal is a bit of prepping ahead. If you can marinate the chicken the night before and prep the tzatziki and feta, the meal can be made within 30 minutes the next day.

If it doesn't soon become a heavily requested meal in your house, just invite me over. Please.

CHICKEN

1½ pounds boneless, skinless chicken breasts

¼ cup extra-virgin olive oil

Zest and juice of 2 lemons

2 garlic cloves, minced

2 tablespoons chopped fresh dill

1 tablespoon red wine vinegar

1 tablespoon honey

1 teaspoon salt

1 teaspoon freshly ground black pepper

1 For the chicken, add the chicken to a large baking dish or resealable plastic bag. Whisk together 3 tablespoons of the olive oil, the lemon zest and juice, garlic, dill, vinegar, honey, salt, and pepper. Pour it over the chicken and toss it to coat. Place the dish or bag in the refrigerator and marinate for at least 2 hours or overnight.

2 While the chicken is marinating, prep the tzatziki. Combine all of the ingredients together in a large bowl and mix them together until combined. Store the dip in the fridge until ready to use.

3 For the whipped feta, preheat the broiler in your oven on high and move an oven rack directly below it. Place the jalapeño peppers on a baking sheet. Once the broiler is hot, set the baking sheet underneath to roast the peppers. As soon as the skin begins to char and bubble, pull the baking sheet out and rotate the peppers to roast all sides. This should take about 5 minutes. Immediately remove the peppers and place them in a resealable plastic bag for 20 minutes. The bag will steam up.

4 After 20 minutes, remove the peppers from the bag and gently push and peel the charred skin on the peppers to remove it. Slice the tops of the peppers off and cut them in half. Remove the seeds and cut the peppers into pieces.

5 Add the feta cheese and cream cheese to a food processor. Puree until the cheeses are completely blended and smooth, then add the chopped jalapeño peppers, the roasted garlic cloves, the lemon zest and juice, and the salt and pepper. Blend again until all of the ingredients are combined. If you are serving the dish within the next 2 hours, the feta can sit at room temperature. Otherwise, store it in a sealed container in the fridge and set it out an hour before serving.

6 For the pitas, remove the chicken from the marinade and discard the juices. You can cook the chicken any way you like—I find the quickest method to be heating a large skillet over medium heat and adding the remaining 1 tablespoon of olive oil. Put the chicken in the skillet and cook it until golden and brown on both sides, 10 minutes per side. Remove the chicken from the skillet and let it rest for 1 to 2 minutes. Cut it into pieces or shred it.

7 Assemble the pitas by heating the pitas in the oven or microwave for a minute or two. Spread the feta dip on the pitas, then top with chicken, lettuce, tomatoes, cucumbers, red onion, hummus, and tzatziki.

NOTE: The tzatziki and feta spread can be made a day ahead of time—the flavors only get better.

TZATZIKI

1 cup plain full-fat or low-fat Greek yogurt
1 seedless cucumber, diced
1 garlic clove, minced
Juice of $1/2$ lemon
1 tablespoon extra-virgin olive oil
1 tablespoon chopped fresh dill
$1/2$ teaspoon honey
$1/4$ teaspoon salt
$1/4$ teaspoon freshly ground black pepper

JALAPEÑO WHIPPED FETA

2 jalapeño chile peppers
8 ounces feta cheese, crumbled
2 tablespoons whipped cream cheese
1 head roasted garlic (see page 29)
Zest and juice of $1/2$ lemon
$1/4$ teaspoon salt
$1/4$ teaspoon freshly ground black pepper

FOR SERVING

4 whole wheat pita breads
2 cups chopped butter lettuce
1 tomato, chopped
$1/2$ cucumber, thinly sliced
$1/2$ red onion, sliced
$1/2$ cup hummus

butternut squash
whole wheat lasagna

. . . .

SERVES 4 to 6 • TIME: 1½ hours

. . . .

1 tablespoon coconut oil

8 fresh sage leaves, chopped

2 garlic cloves, minced

1 shallot, diced

1 medium butternut squash, peeled and cubed (6 cups)

½ teaspoon salt

½ teaspoon freshly ground black pepper

¼ teaspoon ground nutmeg

2 tablespoons unsalted butter, browned (see page 26)

MASCARPONE BÉCHAMEL SAUCE

1 tablespoon unsalted butter

1 tablespoon all-purpose or whole wheat flour

1 cup whole milk

4 ounces mascarpone cheese

2 tablespoons freshly grated Parmesan cheese

¼ teaspoon salt

¼ teaspoon freshly ground black pepper

Pinch of ground nutmeg

So. I don't think I've told you yet, but . . . I'm not a giant fan of tomato sauce.

I know. Please don't harm me, Italian friends. I still like your bread. And your wine.

Obviously, I have eaten some very delicious meals with tomato sauce. However, it's just not my sauce of choice. It never has been.

I've talked about how Thursday nights were pasta nights in our house when I was growing up. Otherwise known as: the nights I would starve. I was such a little jerk. For a few years, I'd have a breakdown on Thursdays because I just really did not like tomato sauce and did not want to eat pasta. Then I learned to eat cereal, and soon enough, learned to coat my noodles in tons of melted butter, garlic salt, and Parmesan cheese. That was a good day. All was right in the world.

But because of this, lasagna wasn't something I went after. There isn't one ounce of Italian blood in my family (all right, maybe there is SOMEWHERE way way back), so that should at least explain this whole not-liking-sauce mess.

I've always loved the idea of lasagna, though: the layers, the noodles, the cheese upon cheese upon cheese. If only it could be something other than red-sauced and meaty.

So now it is.

1 Preheat the oven to 350°F.

2 Heat a large skillet over low to medium heat and add the coconut oil. When melted, add the sage, garlic, and shallots and cook for 1 to 2 minutes, then add the butternut squash. Add the salt, pepper, and nutmeg and toss to coat. Cover and cook until the squash is soft and golden brown, 10 to 12 minutes. Toss the squash once or twice while cooking.

3 Remove the skillet from the heat and add the squash mixture to a large bowl. Add the browned butter and use a fork or potato masher to coarsely mash the squash until it's somewhat smooth and resembles mashed potatoes. Set aside.

4 For the béchamel, heat a saucepan over medium heat and add the butter. Once it is sizzling, whisk in the flour and stir to create a roux. Cook for 1 to 2 minutes, until it is golden brown and a nutty scent develops. Pour in the milk and whisk constantly until it has thickened slightly. Reduce the heat to low and add the mascarpone, Parmesan, salt, pepper, and nutmeg. Stir continuously until the cheese melts, about 5 more minutes.

5 To assemble the lasagna, spray an 8x8-inch baking dish with nonstick spray. Layer 4 noodles on the bottom of the dish. Spread one-third of the squash mixture over the noodles evenly and sprinkle with 2 ounces of the Fontina cheese. Pour about ⅓ cup of the béchamel sauce over the top. Cover with 4 more lasagna noodles. Repeat the process, adding half of the remaining squash, 2 ounces of the cheese, and ⅓ cup béchamel. Add 4 more noodles. Repeat the process one more time, finishing with the remaining 4 noodles. Add the remaining Fontina on top and pour the remaining sauce all over. Cover the top with the sage leaves.

6 Bake the lasagna until the cheese on top is golden and bubbly and the sage leaves appear crispy, 45 to 60 minutes. Let the lasagna sit for 15 to 20 minutes before slicing.

LASAGNA

16 whole wheat lasagna noodles, cooked or no-boil

8 ounces Fontina cheese, freshly grated

10 fresh sage leaves, for topping

grilled
flank steak
with feta & sriracha *crema*

SERVES 4 · TIME: 2 to 24 hours prep
time; 30 minutes cook time

SRIRACHA CREMA

½ cup plain full-fat or low-fat Greek
  yogurt

3 tablespoons low-fat buttermilk

2 teaspoons sriracha or your favorite
  hot chili sauce

1½ pounds flank steak, about 1 inch
  thick

⅓ cup low-sodium soy sauce

¼ cup dry sherry

2 tablespoons extra-virgin olive oil

2 tablespoons light brown sugar

3 garlic cloves, minced

1 teaspoon grated fresh ginger

1 teaspoon salt

1 teaspoon freshly ground black
  pepper

4 ounces crumbled feta

1 pint grape tomatoes, quartered

4 scallions, sliced

Sundays were made for flank steak. At least in my house.
Back in the '90s. The good old days!

Nearly every Sunday night, when it wasn't snowing and was warm
enough out to use the grill, my mom would marinate a flank steak all day,
then my dad would grill it. I can still see him slice it perfectly against
the grain, which honestly isn't that tough to remember since I just watched
him do so last week.

Old habits die hard.

We'd eat it with baked potato wedges, some green beans that my
mom would cover in almonds toasted in butter, and a side of applesauce.
I'd cover my applesauce in cinnamon sugar because my mom let us.

That meal tastes like home.

Today, we still eat a lot of flank steak. I find that I prefer my steak best
when grilled, but broiling it indoors is a quick way you can get it done if
the weather doesn't permit or if you don't own a grill. Leftovers work on
sandwiches too.

And I've totally eaten it cold, directly from its foil-wrapped packet in
the fridge. That's how you know something is good.

1 For the crema, whisk together the yogurt, buttermilk, and
sriracha. Taste and add more hot sauce or seasoning if desired.
Refrigerate until ready to serve.

2 Add the steak to a 9x13-inch baking dish or resealable plastic
bag. Whisk together the soy sauce, sherry, olive oil, brown
sugar, garlic, and ginger. Pour the marinade over the steak and turn
it to coat with the marinade. Stick the dish in the refrigerator and
marinate for 2 to 24 hours.

3 Preheat the grill to the highest heat setting. Remove the steak
from the marinade and discard the liquid. Cover the steak with
the salt and pepper. We prefer our flank steak medium to medium-
rare and grill it for 3 to 4 minutes per side to reach that doneness.

4 Once the steak has reached your desired doneness, remove it
from the heat and let it rest on a cutting board for 10 minutes.
Slice the steak against the grain; otherwise, it will be tough. Serve
it covered with a drizzle of the spicy crema, the crumbled feta,
tomatoes, and scallions.

loaded
havarti
portobello
sliders

SERVES 2 to 4 • TIME: 30 minutes

ARUGULA

2 cups arugula

1 teaspoon extra-virgin olive oil

Juice of $1/2$ lemon

$1/4$ teaspoon salt

$1/4$ teaspoon freshly ground black
    pepper

QUICK AIOLI

$1/4$ cup mayonnaise

2 tablespoons whole-grain Dijon
    mustard

1 garlic clove, minced

4 teaspoons freshly squeezed lemon
    juice

2 tablespoons extra-virgin olive oil

2 tablespoons extra-virgin olive oil

8 baby portobello mushrooms

2 tablespoons balsamic vinegar

$1/2$ teaspoon salt

$1/2$ teaspoon freshly ground black
    pepper

4 ounces Havarti cheese, cut into 8
    small squares

8 slider buns or small dinner rolls

My dad insists that I should not eat mushrooms because they are a fungus. I insist that, Dad, I HAVE to eat mushrooms because they are essentially considered a vegetable and it adds to the list of vegetables I will eat, therefore making me a healthier person.

This is how it works.

The truth is, I was on his side for many years. I had only experienced raw mushrooms with dirt from the ground still lodged inside the stems and mushy canned ones that are often dumped on delivery pizza.

Then Eddie went through a phase. He goes through a lot of them, by the way. He drank a few cans of diet Mountain Dew every day for years. Quit that, thankfully. And if you read the beginning of this book, then you know he survived on only plain ground turkey for about two solid years. Every night for dinner. Currently, as I write this, he has eaten oatmeal for about 734 days straight. Is this real life?

So while he was in this mushroom phase—it was a sautéed mushroom phase, might I add—I found myself putting them on everything for him. And then one day, I decided to taste them.

Never looked back. Have been in love ever since.

Oh, and then I got real brave. I started eating them smashed in between buns. I will never be the person to tell you that portobellos taste like steak or beef, but they sure do taste fantastic.

1 For the arugula, add the arugula to a bowl and toss it with the olive oil, lemon juice, salt, and pepper.

2 For the quick aioli, combine the mayonnaise, mustard, garlic, lemon juice, and olive oil in a bowl and whisk together.

3 Heat a large skillet over medium-low heat and add the olive oil. Add the mushrooms and cook until juicy and tender, about 5 minutes per side. Add the vinegar and cook for another 1 to 2 minutes, flipping the mushrooms once. Season them with the salt and pepper. Reduce the heat to low, add a square of Havarti to each mushroom, cover the skillet, and cook until the cheese is melted, 1 to 2 minutes.

4 Assemble the sliders by adding a mushroom to the bottom of each bun. Top the mushroom with the aioli, a handful of the arugula, and the top of the bun.

A *few years ago,* my friend Ashley served me my first savory stuffed sweet potato. I say it was my first because up until that point, I had only eaten sweet potatoes stuffed with brown sugar, butter, and marshmallows. Not that it was a problem.

Ashley made me a sweet potato stuffed with beans, Swiss cheese, and a fried egg. It was incredibly delicious and immediately I was riding the stuffed sweet potato train. Options are endless, oh yes they are.

This is one of my go-to stuffed potatoes, and I love it because it not only can work as a healthy meal, but it can be a side dish as well. Plus, it's sooooo good for you. I feel like I'm eating a plate full of vitamins.

creamy spinach & spiced chickpea-stuffed sweet potatoes

....

SERVES 2 · TIME: 65 minutes

....

2 medium sweet potatoes

2 tablespoons coconut oil

2 garlic cloves

10 ounces fresh spinach

$1/3$ cup canned coconut milk

1 cup canned chickpeas, rinsed and drained

$1/4$ teaspoon ground nutmeg

Pinch of ground cardamom

Pinch of cayenne pepper

$1/4$ teaspoon salt

$1/4$ teaspoon freshly ground black pepper

1 Preheat the oven to 400°F. Poke holes in the sweet potatoes with a fork and place them on a baking sheet. Bake until tender to the touch, 45 to 60 minutes. Remove the sweet potatoes from the oven and allow them to cool slightly on the baking sheet.

2 A few minutes before the sweet potatoes are finished cooking, heat a large skillet over medium-low heat. Add the coconut oil and the garlic and cook for 1 minute, then stir in the spinach. Cook until the spinach wilts, tossing occasionally, about 5 minutes. Increase the heat to medium and add the coconut milk. Bring the mixture to a simmer and cook for 1 to 2 minutes. Reduce the heat to low.

3 In a bowl, combine the chickpeas with the nutmeg, cardamom, and cayenne. Add the chickpeas to the spinach, cooking until the mixture is warmed through. Season with the salt and pepper and stir.

4 Slice the sweet potatoes open through the center. Use a fork to scrape some of the sweet potato flesh loose, just so it's easier to eat. Stuff each potato with the creamy spinach and chickpea mixture.

I make a lot of bean burgers because, frankly, I love burgers. I don't make vegetarian options for vegetarians or vegans, or even because we are trying to eat less meat, though that's a bonus: I make them because I genuinely love the flavor and like trying new things. It's a whole new world.

On top of that, beans rank up there as one of my favorite foods. They sit on a pedestal with bacon and avocado, and are just so versatile because they can constitute an entire meal.

I guess so can bacon, but . . . you know.

With bean burgers, you can test out a lot more flavors and they stand out more than they do with beef, chicken, or turkey and actually taste better. Love.

On top of just loving bean burgers in general, I find that covering them in a sauce or spread ranks way up there too. This avocado cream not only works as a topping but also can double as a dip for your chips or fries. Or even veggies. I guess. If you're into that kind of thing.

1 Heat a large skillet over medium-low heat and add the bacon. Cook it until crispy and the fat is rendered, then remove the bacon with a slotted spoon and let it drain on a paper towel. To the same skillet, add the spinach and garlic and stir to coat it in the bacon grease. Cook until the spinach is wilted, 5 minutes. Turn off the heat.

2 Add all of the contents of the spinach skillet to the bowl of a food processor. Add the beans, bacon, flour, eggs, cheese, scallions, salt, and pepper. Pulse until the mixture is coarsely chopped but not fully pureed.

3 Use a spatula to remove the bean mixture from the food processor. Use your hands to form 6 to 8 patties out of the bean mix, depending on the size of your buns.

4 Heat the same skillet over medium heat and add the olive oil. Add the bean burgers and cook until golden on both sides, 4 to 5 minutes per side.

5 While the burgers are cooking, make the avocado cream. Quickly wash or wipe out the food processor from the burgers. Add the yogurt, avocado, salt, and pepper and puree until smooth. This stays good in the fridge for 1 to 2 days if tightly covered or sealed.

6 Serve the burgers on the toasted buns with the avocado cream on top.

greens & beans
burgers

SERVES 4 to 6 • TIME: 35 minutes

2 slices thick-cut bacon

6 ounces fresh spinach

2 garlic cloves, minced

3 cups canned cannellini beans, rinsed and drained

1/4 cup all-purpose or whole wheat flour

2 large eggs, lightly beaten

2 tablespoons freshly grated Parmesan cheese

2 scallions, sliced

1/4 teaspoon salt

1/4 teaspoon freshly ground black pepper

2 tablespoons extra-virgin olive oil

AVOCADO CREAM

2/3 cup plain full-fat or low-fat Greek yogurt

1 avocado, pitted, peeled, and chopped

1/4 teaspoon salt

1/4 teaspoon freshly ground black pepper

6 to 8 whole-grain buns, toasted

6

stuff to sip on

(the happiest hour)

It should come as no surprise that as a self-proclaimed *girly girl,* I really love cocktails.

But I'm talking all kinds of cocktails. I don't discriminate when it comes to wine, beer, rum, vodka, tequila, or whiskey. I appreciate it all, even more so when paired with food.

I tend to combine equal parts *Sex and the* City and *Mad Men*, and go from there. If you need a visual description.

And while I consistently drink water on the reg, on **hot summer days** there is nothing more refreshing than an iced tea or lemonade. It's such a treat. Am I right?

So at the last minute, I decided I wanted to share a few of my favorite cocktails and **mocktails** with you. I love mixing up a few drinks and sitting on the deck on a summer evening or in front of the fire on an chilly autumn night. Nothing beats it.

Except when you add snacks.

cantaloupe-basil agua fresca

SERVES 4 • TIME: 10 minutes

1 cantaloupe, peeled, seeded, and cut into cubes

1 big handful fresh basil leaves, plus extra for garnish (optional)

1½ cups water

Juice of 3 limes

2 tablespoons granulated sugar

Fresh mint, for garnish (optional)

If you crave variety in your life, then agua fresca should be your new best friend. It's fresh fruit water (and yes, this can be the base for a little splash of vodka or tequila . . . gah, I cannot stop) that is delicious with herbs like mint and basil and just awesome with a splash of fresh lime.

The best part is that nearly any fruit can become an agua fresca. Er, well, maybe not bananas. I wish.

But almost anything else. It just requires a little puree and strain. It's easy, too, which means you can make a few different flavors for a party and everyone will be so impressed. It's like the most stunning beverage ever.

1 Add cantaloupe and half of the basil leaves to a blender and blend until completely pureed. Hold a fine-mesh strainer over a large bowl and pour the puree through, using a spoon to press all the juice out of the pulp at the end. Combine the cantaloupe juice, remaining basil leaves, water, lime juice, and sugar in a large pitcher. Stir well to combine. Taste and add more sugar if desired. Store the agua fresca in the fridge for an hour or so before serving.

2 Pour over ice and garnish with extra basil or fresh mint if you like.

I've always been grateful ***that I'm a water drinker because I love food so*** much. I can't imagine how I'd manage if I enjoyed drinking my calories as much as eating them. Know what I'm saying?

With that being said, there is nothing more lovely than a glass of fresh, icy citrus juice on a hot summer day. Since I can never let things just be, I'll swap limeade for lemonade any day for a summery change of pace. Maybe because it reminds me of margaritas?

And blueberries!? Can we say antioxidants?

1 Add ¾ cup of the water and the sugar to a small saucepan. Use a vegetable peeler and shave a few slices of the rind off of the lime and add it to the saucepan. Slice the lime in half and add the juice of half of it to the saucepan. Heat over medium heat, whisking constantly, until the mixture boils and the sugar dissolves. Reduce the heat to a simmer and cook for 1 to 2 minutes. Remove from the heat and let the simple syrup cool for 15 minutes. Discard the lime rind shavings.

2 Add the lime juice, remaining 2 cups water, blueberries, and simple syrup to a blender. Puree the mixture until blended and then taste it, as the sweetness of the blueberries and tartness of the lime juice can differ. Add more sweetener if desired. Pour over ice, or blend with ice to make a frozen version.

blueberry
limeade

SERVES 4 to 6 • TIME: 25 minutes

2³⁄₄ cups water
³⁄₄ cup granulated sugar
1 lime
2²⁄₃ cups freshly squeezed lime juice
1 pint fresh blueberries

strawberry **soda** (floats!)

SERVES 2 to 4 • TIME: 15 minutes

1 pound fresh strawberries, hulled

1½ cups water

12 ounces club soda or seltzer water

Granulated sugar, if needed to sweeten

Vanilla ice cream, for floats

I am very weird and do not totally love carbonated drinks. The fizz and bubbles tickle my throat, my nose, my esophagus, and everything. With that being said, there are a few times when soda (okay, okay, I call it pop) is necessary: in a movie theater with popcorn, with a greasy cheeseburger, and with ice cream scooped into it.

I first created my own "soda" a few years ago for the blog and fell in love. You get to determine the flavor and the sweetness and every ingredient that goes inside. It's perfect.

Oh, and you get to determine the ice cream too. Best job ever.

1 Add the strawberries and water to a blender and blend until pureed. Strain the mixture through a fine-mesh sieve or strainer over a bowl to remove the strawberry seeds. In a bowl or pitcher, stir together the strawberry juice and club soda until combined. Taste and add sugar if desired.

2 Fill a glass with ice cream and pour strawberry soda over the top.

prosecco-**cider** spiced punch

SERVES 4 to 6 • TIME: 30 minutes

1 (750 ml) bottle prosecco

2 cups apple cider

2 oranges, sliced

4 cinnamon sticks

¼ teaspoon ground cardamom

Behold my ideal winter drink.

Well, after a cup of spiked hot chocolate, of course.

There are few flavors that bring back memories quite like apple cider does. It just tastes like fall. It tastes like pumpkins and haystacks and cornstalk mazes that I used to get lost in at a local farm. It tastes like my birthday (I'm a Scorpio, a true one) and like Halloween and like all the excitement you anticipate before Christmas.

This prosecco-spiked cider is perfect for hayrides and bonfires. It works for autumn parties or weddings. It works for nights in with yourself and five *Friends* reruns. It just works.

1 Add all of the ingredients to a large bowl or pitcher and stir. Refrigerate the punch until it's cold, at least 30 minutes.

As I am the girliest of girly girls, this drink was made for me.

1 For the simple syrup, add the raspberries and ½ cup of the water to a blender or food processor and puree until smooth. Strain the mixture through a fine-mesh sieve over a bowl to remove the seeds. Add the raspberry juice, sugar, and remaining water to a small saucepan and heat over medium heat. Whisk constantly until the sugar dissolves and, once it comes to a boil, reduce the heat to medium-low. Cook for 5 minutes, then remove the pan from the heat and let cool to room temperature.

2 For the sparklers, fill two glasses with ice. Combine 4 ounces of the raspberry simple syrup, the vodka, and rose water in a cocktail shaker and shake for 30 seconds. Pour over the ice in the glasses and top off with the club soda. Stir and garnish with a rose petal or two, if desired.

raspberry-rose sparklers

SERVES 2 • TIME: 10 minutes

RASPBERRY SIMPLE SYRUP

1 cup fresh raspberries

½ cup plus ⅓ cup water

⅓ cup granulated sugar

SPARKLERS

4 ounces vodka

1 ounce rose water

4 ounces club soda

Fresh rose petals, for garnish (optional; make sure they are unsprayed)

My grandpa has always been a gin drinker, and for years, I would sniff the bottle when he was making a drink. I couldn't do it. Sure, I got the whole pine needle scent but it was like . . . pine needles and lighter fluid combined. I was convinced that gin and I would never, ever, ever be getting together. Like ever. Taylor Swift–style.

But then I had my first gin fizz and shortly after that, a gin float! Crazy things are happening with gin these days. I've fallen victim to the gin train. I'm on it. Enjoying the ride.

1 Add the kiwifruit to a food processor and blend until pureed. Add the pureed kiwi, gin, and lime juice to a cocktail shaker and shake for 30 seconds. Pour the mixture into glasses over ice and top each off with the club soda. Pop in a few cucumber slices and serve.

cucumber kiwi gin fizz

SERVES 2 • TIME: 10 minutes

2 kiwifruits, peeled and sliced

4 ounces gin

2 ounces freshly squeezed lime juice

4 ounces club soda

1 seedless cucumber, sliced

Cantaloupe-Basil Agua Fresca (page 220)

Blueberry Limeade (page 221)

Strawberry Soda (Floats!) (page 222)

Prosecco-Cider Spiced Punch (page 222)

Raspberry-Rose Sparkler (page 223)

Cucumber Kiwi Gin Fizz (page 223)

Grapefruit Mimosas (page 226)

Watermelon-Mint Margaritas (page 227)

grapefruit
mimosas

· · · · · · · · · · · · · · · · · · ·

SERVES 6 · TIME: 10 minutes

· · · · · · · · · · · · · · · · · · ·

2 tablespoons honey
¼ cup white sanding sugar
1½ cups grapefruit juice
1 (750 ml) bottle Champagne

Here we go: my typical spin on a traditional breakfast cocktail. Is there anything more perfect in the brunch world than a mimosa? Maybe a Bellini, but who's comparing when you can have both?

I adore mimosas. Fact: I used to adore mimosas a lot more back in college. I'm sure you can figure out why. Too much of a good thing. Hence the flavor switch.

One thing I've always loved (and never had too much of, cough cough) is grapefruit. It's totally weird—I've been eating grapefruit since I was a kid, probably after I watched my dad eat one almost every day. But most other kids hated grapefruit. In fact, sometimes I felt like eating grapefruit made me downright elderly. Does anyone under the age of 75 even enjoy grapefruit?

Yes. I do.

In addition to the actual fruit, I love the juice and all things grapefruit scented. I'm a marketer's dream because they sure are playing to my gullible senses, what with all these grapefruit disinfectants, grapefruit lip balms, grapefruit hand soaps. My entire life smells like pink citrus.

Grapefruit mimosas aren't for the faint of heart. Make sure to serve them to friends who actually enjoy grapefruit, since, you know . . . we are few and far between. In addition to that, grapefruit has the tendency to be a little . . . tart. So if you're juicing your own? You may want to use an extra-sweet Champagne or even a drop of agave nectar if necessary.

Trash up your mimosa! It's fun.

1 Use your fingers to rub the honey along the rim of six champagne flutes. Add the sanding sugar to a plate and dip the honey rim in the sugar, pressing gently so the sugar adheres.

2 Fill the bottom of each champagne flute with 2 ounces of grapefruit juice. Fill the glass with Champagne and serve immediately.

NOTE: These days, with all the fresh fruit juices out there, and especially if you have your own juicer, the mimosa flavor opportunities are endless. Try strawberry, raspberry, or heck, even watermelon.

A *margarita was my first* legal alcoholic beverage. I'm not sure if it had to do with the oodles of chips and salsa constantly surrounding them, the salt on the rim, or the pretty light green color, but I was smitten. They were instantly and have remained my all-time favorite cocktail.

Because of that, I've become a pretty big marg snob. Don't even come near me with a powdered sour mix. I much prefer a higher-end tequila, a hint of orange, tons of lime, and lots of simple syrup. There hasn't been a margarita flavor I've yet to turn down, and watermelon? They take the cake.

watermelon-*mint* margaritas

SERVES 2 • TIME: 10 minutes

WATERMELON SIMPLE SYRUP
1 cup water
1 cup granulated sugar
1 bunch fresh mint
1½ cups cubed watermelon, seeds removed

MARGS
1 lime, cut into wedges
2 tablespoons coarse sea salt
1 bunch fresh mint leaves
4 ounces Grand Marnier
4 ounces freshly squeezed lime juice
3 ounces silver tequila

 For the simple syrup, combine the water, sugar, and mint in a small saucepan over medium heat. Whisk it constantly until the sugar dissolves and bring the liquid to a boil. Reduce the heat to a simmer. Cook for 5 minutes, then remove from the heat and allow the syrup to cool slightly, about 15 minutes.

2 Remove the mint from the syrup and discard. Add the watermelon and simple syrup to a blender and puree until combined.

3 For the margaritas, rub the glass rims with a lime wedge. Place the salt on a plate and dip the rim of the glasses in the salt, pressing gently so it adheres. Fill the glasses with ice, the fresh mint leaves, and the remaining lime wedges.

4 In a cocktail shaker, combine 5 ounces of the watermelon simple syrup, the Grand Marnier, lime juice, and tequila. Shake for 30 seconds and then pour over the ice in the glasses.

spicy
strawberry
margaritas

. . . .

SERVES 2 • TIME: 10 minutes

. . . .

STRAWBERRY SIMPLE SYRUP

1 cup water

1 cup granulated sugar

1 bunch fresh mint

1½ cups sliced fresh strawberries

MARGS

1 lime, cut into wedges

2 tablespoons coarse sea salt

1 teaspoon granulated sugar

¼ teaspoon cayenne pepper

1 bunch fresh mint leaves

**1 jalapeño chile pepper, sliced and
    seeded**

4 ounces Grand Marnier

4 ounces freshly squeezed lime juice

3 ounces silver tequila

Since I'm not a huge fan of super-spicy food, I was hesitant when it came to tasting cocktails with a kick.

I haven't looked back, though. The perfect spicy cocktail gives you a hint of peppery burn at the end. It's not overwhelming and, when paired with the right flavors, is actually refreshing.

I can't believe I now support it . . . but put anything in a margarita and I'll probably slurp it down.

 For the simple syrup, combine the water, sugar, and mint in a small saucepan over medium heat. Whisk constantly until the sugar dissolves and bring the liquid to a boil. Reduce the heat to a simmer. Cook the liquid for 5 minutes, then remove it from the heat and allow it to cool slightly, 15 minutes.

2 Remove the mint from the syrup and discard. Add the strawberries and simple syrup to a blender and puree until combined.

3 For the margaritas, rub the glass rims with a lime wedge. Place the salt, sugar, and cayenne pepper on a plate and dip the rim of the glasses in the salt mixture, pressing gently to adhere. Fill the glasses with ice, the fresh mint leaves, and the remaining lime wedges. Add the jalapeño pepper slices.

4 Combine 5 ounces of the strawberry simple syrup, the Grand Marnier, lime juice, and tequila in a cocktail shaker. Shake for 30 seconds and then pour over the ice in the glasses.

NOTE: You can also make a homemade jalapeño tequila by slicing the peppers and adding them to a jar. Pour tequila over the top and soak for a few days. Drain and use!

Please don't look at me that way.

It's true, I am putting bacon in your cocktail, but I swear it's all in good fun.

Manhattans are my family's signature drink. They order them wherever we go and only crack once or twice every few months for a beer or a margarita.

This is my version. Some are not down with it. I am! More for me.

1 Fill two glasses with ice. Add 3 ounces of the whiskey, and ½ ounce of the vermouth, and a dash of bitters to each glass and stir. Add the cherries and lay a bacon slice across each glass.

bacon
manhattans

· ·

SERVES 2 · TIME: 10 minutes

· ·

6 ounces bourbon or rye whiskey

1 ounce sweet vermouth

2 dashes angostura bitters

4 maraschino cherries

2 slices Cinnamon Sugared Bacon
(page 266)

vanilla-ginger mojitos

SERVES 2 • TIME: 15 minutes

VANILLA-GINGER SYRUP

½ cup water

½ cup granulated sugar

1 vanilla bean, seeds scraped

½ teaspoon vanilla extract

1 teaspoon-size piece fresh ginger

MOJITOS

⅔ cup fresh mint leaves

4 ounces vanilla rum

2 ounces club soda

2 ounces ginger ale

2 ounces freshly squeezed lime juice

Lime wedges, for garnish

Right after margaritas comes my love for mojitos. See? Told you I was the girliest of the girly girls.

I draw the line at pink Zinfandel. But don't worry. Boone's Farm and Arbor Mist are acceptable.

One of the reasons I enjoy mojitos is because Eddie loves them too. He isn't a margarita fan due to one too many tequila shots in college (been there?), but rum? He can do. And he likes it too.

These mojitos are spectacular—no artificial flavor needed. They are pure and simple and perfectly refreshing.

1 For the syrup, combine the water, sugar, scraped vanilla seeds, vanilla bean pod, vanilla extract, and ginger in a saucepan. Bring the mixture to a boil while whisking to dissolve the sugar. Reduce the heat to a simmer and cook for 1 to 2 minutes. Remove the pan from the heat and let it sit at room temperature for 15 minutes. Remove the vanilla bean pod and ginger before using.

2 For the mojitos, take two glasses and fill each with about ⅓ cup fresh mint leaves. Add 2 ounces of the vanilla rum to each glass and muddle the mint in the bottom of the glass. Fill each glass with ice and then add 2 ounces of the syrup and 1 ounce of the club soda, the ginger ale, and the lime juice to each glass. Stir well. Add a lime wedge to each glass to garnish.

One of the only times you will see me drink a vegetable. Live it up.

1 For the simple syrup, combine the water and sugar in a small saucepan and heat over medium heat. Whisk constantly until the sugar dissolves and the liquid comes to a boil. Reduce the heat to medium-low. Cook for 1 to 2 minutes, then remove the pan from the heat and let cool to room temperature.

2 For the mojitos, slice the cucumber in half. Peel and chop one half and slice the other half into rounds. Add the chopped cucumber to a blender or food processor and blend until completely pureed.

3 Fill two glasses with ice, the mint leaves, the lime wedges, and the cucumber rounds. Add 5 ounces of the simple syrup, the rum, lime juice, and cucumber puree in a cocktail shaker for 30 seconds. Pour over the ice in the glasses. Top each drink off with the club soda and stir.

With such a ridiculous amount of delicious fruit in this icy beverage, it practically has to be considered a healthy, hydrating snack. Wink wink.

1 Combine the coconut milk, pineapple, mango, rum, and ice in a blender and puree until combined. Pour into halved coconuts or frosty glasses and garnish with a cherry or two.

cucumber
mojitos

SERVES 2 • TIME: 15 minutes

SIMPLE SYRUP

1/2 **cup water**

1/2 **cup granulated sugar**

MOJITOS

1 seedless, peeled cucumber

10 fresh mint leaves

6 lime wedges

4 ounces rum

Juice of 2 limes

4 ounces club soda

frosty
mango
piña
coladas

SERVES 4 • TIME: 15 minutes

1 cup canned full-fat coconut milk

1 cup cubed fresh pineapple

1/2 **cup cubed fresh mango**

4 ounces coconut rum

1 1/2 **cups ice**

Maraschino cherries, for garnish

7
lighten up
(just not too much)

This is a *fine line* to walk.

Lightened-up treats probably mean different things to you than they do to me. Let's jump in.

I'm not a giant proponent of fruit for dessert. I mean, you know I love fruit. But if I'm going to have fruit after dinner, it's fruit. It's not dessert.

Fruit IN desserts is a ***different story.*** And we have plenty of them here.

I've reached the point in my life where I am done eating gross dessert just because I want something sweet. If I want something decadent, I will eat it. Sometimes I want something light—and that's perfect. Other days I want either or and have nothing to show for it—but I always have some high-quality chocolate, and an ounce or two of that may do the trick.

I view **lightened-up desserts** just like I do things such as whole wheat cinnamon rolls and sweet potato fries. They still may not be the healthiest option. They may not fit into your Weight Watchers points or your allotted calories for the day if you are on a diet. But they are going to satisfy your craving. They are going to be legit dessert.

My versions of lightened-up treats lean more toward the camp of using whole wheat flour in place of all-purpose (many times), coconut oil in place of butter (sometimes), or fruit as the base but with something delicious on top (hello, crisps and crumbles).

Because ***the truth is*** that if I want a slice of cheesecake and eat an apple instead? An hour later, I still really want that cheesecake. The curse of the sweet teeth.

Working on this chapter was therapeutic and exciting. It was full of discoveries, and I actually came across tons of what I can now call well-loved desserts that don't break the caloric bank. Or my jeans buttons.

The no-bake banana split Greek cheesecake ***makes me go wild.*** It doesn't have the exact same texture as full-fat, creamy cheesecake . . . but it's so darn good. The tart frozen yogurt is something I almost never wish I made—only because now I feel compelled to hoard every topping imaginable.

And the cashew butter crispy treats? So old-school and so addictive. I just can't stop.

I'm fairly certain you'll be able to find something here that you love too. Maybe just not as much as my over-dramatic self.

homemade
tart frozen yogurt

. . . .

Makes about 1 quart
TIME: at least 6 hours, or overnight

. . . .

24 ounces plain full-fat or low-fat
   Greek yogurt

1 cup low-fat milk

⅓ cup powdered sugar

2 teaspoons vanilla extract

There's a reason I love frozen yogurt, and it has absolutely nothing to do with the frozen yogurt. It's those toppings.

It's like complete sensory overload. It's like the Vegas of dessert. You mean, I can put WHAT on my yogurt? Brownie pieces? Cheesecake chunks? Kiwi? Little bubbles that burst in my mouth? Marshmallow cream? RAINBOW SPRINKLES?!

My bowls of fro yo are notoriously expensive and obnoxious. But it's yogurt. So it's healthy, right?

1 Whisk all of the ingredients together in a large bowl until no lumps remain. Set the bowl in the fridge and refrigerate until cold, at least 30 minutes.

2 Pour the mixture into your ice cream maker and churn according to directions. Freeze for 6 to 8 hours, or overnight. When the yogurt is frozen, serve with an array of fresh fruit and any toppings you would like.

NOTE: This isn't soft serve yogurt like the trendy cafes serve, but it's delicious nonetheless. Sometimes I'll have a bowl drizzled with honey, or even make a semi-savory version with basil and fresh mango.

If you haven't had your head stuck in a hole since 2010, you may have heard of this little thing called Pinterest. I know. How pinteresting.

The thing is that after a hot five minutes, Pinterest started stressing me out. I wanted to do, eat, see, and live All The Things. After browsing for a recipe, I'd lose two hours of my evening and not only that: I'd immediately need to paint my nails mint and white chevron, spend a good 35 minutes searching online for an ombré skirt I fell in love with only to discover it was from four years ago, be instantly ticked off that my summer vacation would not include a large house with a swing that swung me into a shark-free blue ocean, and need to plan the perfect first birthday party for a child I didn't even conceive yet. Really. It's all just a bit much.

In addition to all that, stuffed strawberries started popping up everywhere, and were literally, stuffed with everything. Cheesecake, Jell-O, fresh herbs, tuna—trust me, I've seen it all.

So that's how we got here. A strawberry stuffed with marshmallow crème before being dipped. Marshmallow crème is one of my guilty pleasures, I must admit. And I've always had a little love affair with chocolate-covered strawberries since my mom and I accidentally-on-purpose stole one from a candy counter in Horne's when I was, like, six years old.

Ah. Memories.

1 Take each hulled strawberry and gently cut out more of a hollow into the center. Fill the centers of the strawberries with marshmallow crème—I find it is easiest to do this with a piping tip and a pastry or plastic bag.

2 Melt the chocolate chips in a bowl in the microwave. Stir in the coconut oil until it is melted. Fill a small bowl with the graham crumbs. Line a baking sheet with parchment or waxed paper. Dip each strawberry into the chocolate, leaving the top quarter exposed, then lightly into the graham cracker crumbs. Place on the baking sheet to set.

3 If desired, before serving you can toast the top of the marshmallow crème with a kitchen torch. I love storing these in the fridge and eating one for a sweet snack.

NOTE: The coconut oil helps the chocolate firm up. If you're not a fan, leave it out.

s'mores-
stuffed
strawberries

SERVES 4 • TIME: 30 minutes

12 large fresh strawberries, hulled
2/3 cup marshmallow crème
1 cup milk chocolate chips
1 tablespoon coconut oil
1/3 cup graham cracker crumbs

I rarely condone a whole wheat cookie. I mean, if you want a cookie, just have a cookie. A real cookie.

But these . . . barely taste like whole wheat cookies. You may not even know what's going on inside these cookies, but the fact is: It's some good stuff. If you can make the real stuff taste just as good . . . why not do it? That's my story and I'm sticking to it.

1 Preheat the oven to 350°F. In a bowl, whisk together the flours, baking soda, and salt. Set aside.

2 In the bowl of your electric mixer, beat the butter on medium speed until smooth and creamy. Add both sugars and beat on high speed until fluffy, 3 to 4 minutes. Add the egg, egg yolk, and vanilla extract and beat until combined, another 2 to 3 minutes. Make sure to scrape down the sides of the bowl if needed.

3 With the mixer on low speed, slowly add the dry ingredients. Mix until just combined. Use a large spoon to stir in the chocolate chips.

4 Scoop out about 2 tablespoons of the dough and roll it into a ball. Place the dough balls on nonstick baking sheets 2 inches apart. Bake until cookies are set around the edges and slightly golden, 10 to 12 minutes. Allow the cookies to cool on the sheets for 5 minutes, then remove them with a spatula and place on a cooling rack.

NOTE: This recipe yields a slightly thin, somewhat crisp cookie. For a puffier cookie, you can refrigerate your dough for 2 to 4 hours before baking.

whole wheat chocolate chip cookies

Makes 24 cookies • TIME: 35 minutes

1 cup whole wheat pastry flour

1/3 cup white whole wheat flour

1/3 cup oat flour

1 teaspoon baking soda

1/4 teaspoon salt

8 tablespoons (1 stick) unsalted butter, at room temperature

1/2 cup loosely packed light brown sugar

1/3 cup granulated sugar

1 large egg plus 1 large egg yolk

2 teaspoons vanilla extract

1 cup dark chocolate chips

banana split no-bake greek yogurt cheesecake

SERVES 4 • TIME: 20 minutes
+ overnight to set

¼ cup coconut oil, melted

1 cup graham cracker crumbs

1½ cups plain full-fat or low-fat Greek
yogurt

8 ounces cream cheese, at room
temperature

⅓ cup sweetened condensed milk

1 teaspoon vanilla extract

¼ teaspoon salt

If I ever had to answer one of the big questions—you know, the really big questions—like what would your ultimate last meal be or what is your all-time favorite dessert, my response would not be cookies or chocolate or brownies or ice cream.

It would be cheesecake.

I have always, always, always been a cheesecake fanatic, since my very first bite. It's no surprise, because it takes a lot to satisfy these sweet teeth. And the truth is that thick and creamy, often too-rich cheesecake fits the bill every single time.

And it's not like I even discriminate in flavor. I'll never forget eating at the Cheesecake Factory for the first time with my grandma and her horror at the array of choices—she claimed that nothing was better than a slice of New York–style cheesecake with strawberries. Nothing? Really? Nothing?

I dunno. I can come up with a few things. I love every and all kind of cheesecake. And my life improved tenfold when I discovered no-bake cheesecakes. Because let's be real: Baking cheesecake is a royal pain in the ass. It's super high maintenance, often requires a water bath (whatever that is), then after you've poured all your tears into one springform pan, the darn thing cracks down the center and looks like the biggest geographic fault on Earth. It's stressful.

Greek yogurt cheesecake is my solution to eating cheesecake weekly. The banana split topping is simply that: a topping. The cheesecake is a plain, traditional base that can be served however you'd like. And while we're on that topic, my favorite way to serve no-bakes are in little mason jars or cute shot glasses so everyone gets their own portion. It's perfect for this, too, since the Greek yogurt yields a softer, not-quite-as-forgiving cake.

Also: sprinkles for life.

1 In a bowl, mix together the coconut oil and graham crumbs until moistened. Press them into the bottom of an 8-inch springform pan and set it in the fridge.

2 Add the Greek yogurt and cream cheese to the bowl of an electric mixer. Beat on medium speed until smooth and creamy, 5 minutes. With the mixer on low speed, slowly pour in the sweetened condensed milk. Mix until combined. Add the vanilla extract and salt, beating for another 1 to 2 minutes. Remove the pan from the fridge and pour the batter on top of the crust, spreading the top evenly with a spatula. Refrigerate for at least 12 hours or overnight.

3 When you're ready to serve the cheesecake, set up a toppings bar with the bananas, strawberries, cherries, almonds, and sprinkles in small bowls and a jar of chocolate syrup. Remove the cheesecake from the fridge and use a sharp knife to immediately cut it into servings. Top the cheesecake with whatever toppings you wish.

FOR SERVING

3 bananas, sliced

1 cup fresh strawberries, hulled and sliced

½ cup maraschino cherries

¼ cup sliced almonds

¼ cup rainbow sprinkles

Chocolate syrup, for drizzling

NOTE: If serving these in a jar, you don't need to refrigerate as long. Only 4 hours.

vanilla‑ coconut hot cocoa

SERVES 2 • TIME: 15 minutes

1 vanilla bean
1 (14-ounce) can light coconut milk
¼ cup unsweetened almond milk
4 ounces dark chocolate, chopped
Pinch of salt

Here we have a culmination of three of my favorite flavors: vanilla, coconut, and chocolate.

Can we make this into a candle? How about a body lotion? A lip balm? A dish soap?

I'm reaching. I know.

There is nothing like whipped cream melting into a warm mug of homemade hot chocolate. Seriously. I just don't even know how to cope with the deliciousness.

Deliciousness? Are we using that word now? Are you one of those people who instantly cringes when someone attaches "ness" to the end of all words?

Hmm. And I thought we were friends.

1 Slit open the vanilla bean lengthwise with a sharp knife. Scrape the seeds from the inside of the pod. Discard the pod and reserve the seeds.

2 Add the vanilla seeds and the remaining ingredients to a saucepan and heat over low heat. Stir constantly until the chocolate melts, then pour the mixture into mugs.

For the love of all things holy, please drop a scoop of this sorbet into your Champagne.

Yes, that means there will be extra wine in your Champagne. Is that wrong?

1 Combine all of the ingredients in a saucepan over medium heat. Stir constantly until the sugar dissolves, then remove from the heat and pour into a bowl. Refrigerate the bowl until cold, at least 30 to 60 minutes.

2 Pour the mixture into your ice cream maker and churn according to directions. Freeze for at least 6 hours before serving.

pomegranate-
pinot
sorbet

MAKES about 1 quart
TIME: at least 6 hours, or overnight

3 cups pomegranate juice
1/2 cup Pinot Noir
1/4 cup granulated sugar

pumpkin-banilla bread

MAKES one 5x9-inch loaf
TIME: 1½ hours

1²/₃ cups whole wheat pastry flour

1 teaspoon baking soda

½ teaspoon pumpkin pie spice

½ teaspoon salt

2 large eggs

²/₃ cup loosely packed light brown
    sugar

1½ cups pumpkin puree

2 very ripe bananas, mashed

¹/₃ cup canned light coconut milk

4 tablespoons (½ stick) unsalted
    butter, melted and slightly cooled

2 tablespoons molasses

2 tablespoons vanilla bean paste

Yes, banilla. Banana and vanilla.

This bread is like if my two favorite breads had a baby. Birthed a loaf, if you will.

Too much?

It's simple, really. I love banana bread. I love pumpkin bread. Both banana and pumpkin are incredible at creating soft and tender baked goods. Both have loads of flavor. I really like vanilla too. In everything. All flavors are inside this bread. It is good. The end.

1 Preheat the oven to 350°F. Spray a 5x9-inch loaf pan with nonstick spray. In a small bowl, whisk together the flour, baking soda, pumpkin pie spice, and salt. Set aside.

2 In a large bowl, whisk together the eggs and brown sugar until smooth. Stir in the pumpkin puree and bananas and mix until combined. Stir in the coconut milk, butter, molasses, and vanilla bean paste. Mix until the ingredients come together.

3 Add the flour mixture to the wet ingredients and mix until just combined. Pour the batter into the loaf pan. Bake until the top of the bread is golden brown and set, 85 to 90 minutes.

4 Remove the bread from the oven and let cool for 1 hour. Gently remove it from the loaf pan and allow it to cool on a cutting board before slicing.

You know who loves Bundt cakes? My mom. Perhaps it's because she is a baby boomer or perhaps it's just because she is really good at making them, but you can almost always count on a Bundt cake being in her kitchen.

And as a reminder, she is also the kind of woman who can bake a cake, then let it sit on her counter all week in a pretty dome while she savors one slice a day. ONE SLICE, PEOPLE.

Now isn't that the kind of woman we all aspire to be? I have the best example ever.

 Preheat the oven to 350°F. Liberally spray a 6-cup Bundt pan with nonstick spray.

2 In a small bowl, whisk together the flour, baking powder, baking soda, and salt.

3 Add the eggs and brown sugar to the bowl of your electric mixer. Beat on medium speed until fluffy, 3 to 4 minutes. Add the grapeseed oil and beat for 1 to 2 minutes on low speed. Scrape down the sides of the bowl if needed. Add half of the yogurt and the vanilla extract and beat until combined. With the mixer on low speed, add the dry ingredients. Add the remaining yogurt and beat until just combined.

4 Toss the blueberries with the flour and add them to the batter. Fold them into the batter with a spatula, then pour the batter into the Bundt pan. Bake until the top of the cake is golden brown, 45 minutes. Remove the cake from the oven and let cool in the pan for 15 minutes.

5 For the blueberry glaze, add the blueberries to a food processor and blend until pureed. Add the powdered sugar, vanilla extract, and milk. Blend until creamy and combined.

6 Gently invert the pan on a cake plate to remove the cake. As soon as you remove the cake from the Bundt pan, pour the glaze over the top.

NOTE: Glazes can be tricky. If your blueberries are juicy, the glaze may need a bit more sugar. If the glaze is too thick, add more milk, 1 tablespoon at a time until it's pourable.

whole wheat blueberry bundt cake

SERVES 6 to 8 · TIME: 1½ hours

2 cups whole wheat pastry flour

2 teaspoons baking powder

1 teaspoon baking soda

¼ teaspoon salt

3 large eggs

⅔ cup loosely packed light brown sugar

½ cup grapeseed oil

1 cup plain full-fat or low-fat Greek yogurt

2 teaspoons vanilla extract

1 pint fresh blueberries

1 tablespoon whole wheat pastry flour

BLUEBERRY GLAZE

½ cup fresh blueberries

1½ cup powdered sugar

½ teaspoon vanilla extract

2 tablespoons milk

oatmeal–
apple butter
squares

MAKES 9 to 12 squares
TIME: 45 minutes

1 cup old-fashioned rolled oats

1 cup whole wheat pastry flour

1 teaspoon baking soda

¼ teaspoon salt

¾ cup creamy peanut butter, melted

½ cup loosely packed light brown sugar

1 teaspoon vanilla extract

½ cup low-fat cow's or almond milk

1 cup apple butter

CRUMBLE

⅓ cup old-fashioned rolled oats

⅓ cup loosely packed light brown sugar

2 tablespoons whole wheat pastry flour

2 tablespoons unsalted butter, at room temperature

1 teaspoon vanilla extract

Fruit butter. For someone who loves butters and someone who loves fruits, they are priceless.

This is one of those treats that not only works as dessert but also as a snack. Double trouble!

Is it just me or do you find excuses to put granola or jelly into things just so they can be snack-worthy?

I thought so.

1 Preheat the oven to 350°F. Spray an 8x8-inch baking dish with nonstick spray. In a small bowl, combine the oats, flour, baking soda, and salt. Set aside.

2 In the bowl of your electric mixer, add the peanut butter and brown sugar. Beat on medium speed until fluffy, 2 to 3 minutes. Add the vanilla extract and beat the mixture until combined.

3 With the mixer on low speed, slowly add the dry ingredients. Slowly add the milk and continue to mix until a dough forms. Remove the dough from the bowl and press it into the baking dish. Spread the apple butter over the top of the dough.

4 For the crumble, combine the oats, brown sugar, and flour in a bowl. Add the butter and vanilla extract and crumble it together with your fingers until the butter is distributed. Sprinkle the mixture over the apple butter.

5 Bake for 25 to 30 minutes. Remove the pan from the oven and let the bars cool completely in the dish before cutting into 9 or 12 squares.

frozen bananas with peanut butter & bacon

SERVES 4 · TIME: 10 minutes
+ at least 1 hour freezing time

4 firm bananas

4 wooden craft sticks for baking

1/3 cup creamy peanut butter, melted

2 tablespoons coconut oil, melted

2 slices bacon, cooked and crumbled

Can I call these Elvis pops?

While frozen bananas seem like a cop-out, these frozen bananas are anything but. If you have cooked bacon on hand (which, hello, since we are friends, you probably do), these will take you merely an instant to prepare. And then maybe an instant to eat. Oops.

1 Cover a baking sheet with a piece of parchment paper.

2 Peel each banana and stick a wooden stick into one end. Stir together the melted peanut butter and coconut oil. Dip the banana in the peanut butter and lay it down on the parchment. Sprinkle the crumbled bacon on top.

3 Freeze for at least 1 hour before serving.

The whole homemade ice pop thing was a welcomed fad. At least by me.

I'll never forget watching *Full House* when I was a tween—it was the episode where DJ thinks she needs to lose weight and goes on a crazy diet by making an ice pop. Read: a wooden stick shoved inside an ice cube.

For some reason, that just sparked something inside of me and I realized that, dude, I could make my own Popsicles. I LOVED Popsicles. This was huge!

More than Popsicles, I loved things like Creamsicles and Fudgsicles and cheesecake pops. They were richer and tasted so much more dessert-like. Right up my alley.

I'm not even going to bother telling you about the 1995 version. Let's stick with this new millennium one. So much better.

1 Whisk together the coconut milk, chocolate, almond butter, and salt in a large bowl until smooth. Pour the mixture into ice pop molds and freeze for at least 4 hours. Right before serving, place the chopped almonds on a plate. Remove the pops from their molds and roll them in the almonds, pressing gently to adhere.

chocolate– almond butter popsicles with a smoky almond crunch

SERVES 6 to 8 • TIME: at least 4 hours

1 (14-ounce) can full-fat coconut milk

3 ounces 70% dark chocolate, melted

2 tablespoons creamy almond butter, melted

Pinch of salt

1/4 cup chopped smoked almonds

It took me a long while to get on board with lemon and other citrus desserts. I've always been such a chocolate person that, lemon? Ew. I never thought it would cut it. And honestly, I felt like lemon desserts were something that only older people liked. Not kids! Not me! Not I who is still so young!

Ha. Not really.

I hate to prove my own theory, but my lemon dessert craving grew with age. Perhaps it's because I just began to appreciate it more. Perhaps it's because after 25 years of binging on chocolate, I was ready to try something new. Perhaps it's because lemon desserts tend to just be so . . . aesthetically appealing.

I don't know. All I do know is that my Grandma Lois used to make a mean lemon bar, and now that she is gone? I miss it and am having a tough time re-creating it.

So I made cake instead.

I like cakes in skillets. Heck, I like everything in skillets. The cakes are just so easy, though. The skillets are heavy, too, which makes me feel better since it's like I'm getting an arm workout while baking with sugar.

Can I describe this cake in two words? RE. FRESHING.

So light. So bright and delicious with a touch of whipped cream.

Oh, and the actual lemons? Don't freak out. Meyer lemons are sweet and when sliced superthin and caramelized? Delicious. You will die. I've even put them on pizza before. Totally a thing. Trust me.

① Preheat the oven to 375°F. In a small bowl, whisk together the flour, baking powder, baking soda, and salt.

② In a large bowl, whisk together the eggs and granulated sugar until combined. Add the lemon zest and olive oil and mix until combined. Add the dry ingredients to the wet and stir to mix. Add the milk and mix until the batter comes together.

③ Pour the batter into a 12-inch cast-iron skillet. Bake until the cake is golden and set on top, 25 to 30 minutes. When finished, remove the skillet from the oven and let the cake cool for 30 minutes.

④ For the Meyer lemons, heat a skillet over low heat and add the olive oil. Add the lemons and salt and toss to coat. Cover and cook for 10 minutes, stirring once or twice during the cooking time to ensure the lemons don't burn. Remove the lid and stir in the brown sugar. Cover and cook for 5 to 10 more minutes. Add the lemons to the top of the cake for garnish and serve with the whipped cream.

olive oil & lemon skillet cake with caramelized meyer lemons

SERVES 6 · TIME: 1 hour

2 cups whole wheat pastry flour

2 teaspoons baking powder

1/2 teaspoon baking soda

1/4 teaspoon salt

2 large eggs

1 cup granulated sugar

Zest of 4 lemons

3/4 cup extra-virgin olive oil

1/3 cup milk

CARAMELIZED MEYER LEMONS

1 tablespoon extra-virgin olive oil

2 Meyer lemons, thinly sliced

1/4 teaspoon salt

2 tablespoons light brown sugar

Whipped cream, for serving

white cheddar apple crisp

SERVES 4 · TIME: 45 minutes

4 medium Gala apples, cored and cut into 1-inch chunks

2 tablespoons light brown sugar

1 1/2 teaspoons whole wheat pastry flour

1/2 teaspoon ground cinnamon

1/4 teaspoon salt

CRISP TOPPING

2/3 cup old-fashioned rolled oats

1/2 cup loosely packed light brown sugar

1/4 cup whole wheat pastry flour

1/4 teaspoon ground cinnamon

4 tablespoons (1/2 stick) unsalted butter, at room temperature

1 teaspoon vanilla extract

6 ounces white cheddar cheese, cut into 1/2-inch cubes

I know that apple pies with slices of cheddar or cheesy crusts have been around for ages, but the whole thing freaked me out for a while. I'd eat fruit and I'd eat cheese and I'd even eat cheese (Brie) topped with fruit (cranberries) . . . but cheese on my sweets?

Not so sure.

How about baking the cheese INTO the sweet so nobody gets a choice? So demanding I am.

This apple crisp is made with whole wheat flour, oats, and a little butter, but it's jam-packed with cinnamon-coated apple cubes and white cheddar chunks.

It's totally a thing.

 Preheat the oven to 375°F.

Add the apples to an 8x8-inch baking dish and toss them with the brown sugar, flour, cinnamon, and salt. Set aside.

For the topping, in a bowl, combine the oats, brown sugar, flour, and cinnamon and mix well. Add the butter and vanilla extract and use your fingers to disperse the butter throughout the oats, creating a crumbly topping.

Toss the cheese cubes with the apples in the baking dish. Sprinkle the crisp topping over the apples and cheese. Bake until the crisp is golden and the apples are softened, 25 to 30 minutes. Top with vanilla ice cream, if you like.

layered chocolate-raspberry pavlova

SERVES 4 to 6 · TIME: 4 hours

1 cup granulated sugar

1 tablespoon cornstarch

8 egg whites, at room temperature

1 teaspoon cream of tartar

¼ teaspoon salt

1½ teaspoons vanilla extract

Who would have thought that something so pretty was so simple?

I had my first run-in with meringue-like desserts after Mother Lovett passed away and I baked (and ate) my emotions through her old recipe index. Those things were called sin city cookies (I never understood the correlation either) and looked like cute little clouds.

I was late to the game with pavlovas, but it's only because I didn't know what all could be done with them. Add a few flavors, a few layers, and you've accelerated this to a high-class dessert.

It's also like you're basically eating whipped egg whites and air, so . . . lots of room left for chocolate. Lots.

1 Preheat the oven to 275°F. Line two baking sheets with parchment paper.

2 Add the granulated sugar and cornstarch to a food processor and blend until combined and the sugar is finely ground, 1 to 2 minutes. Pour into a bowl and set aside.

3 Add the egg whites, cream of tartar, and salt to the bowl of your electric mixer fitted with a whisk attachment. Start beating the mixture on low speed and gradually increase to high speed, beating until thick and soft peaks form, 2 minutes. With the mixer on high speed, slowly add the sugar, 1 to 2 tablespoons at a time. Once the sugar is all mixed in, add the vanilla extract. Beat until the egg whites are glossy and stiff peaks form, 5 to 6 minutes.

4 Spoon the mixture into three piles (two of them will be on one baking sheet) and gently press with a spoon to make them into 5- or 6-inch rounds. Use the spoon to make an indentation in the center. Bake until the rounds are firm and crispy on the outside but still white, 45 minutes. Turn off the oven and let the pavlovas sit inside until completely cooled.

5 Add 2 cups of the raspberries to a small saucepan with the water and heat over medium heat. Cook until the raspberries break down and become liquidy, 3 to 4 minutes. Set aside to cool.

6 Add the mascarpone cheese to a clean bowl of the electric mixer and beat until creamy. Add the powdered sugar and beat on high speed until the sugar is incorporated, 1 to 2 minutes. Remove the cheese from the bowl and set aside.

Add the cold whipping cream to a clean bowl of the electric mixer and beat on low speed, gradually increasing to high speed, until the cream is whipped and stiff peaks form. Gently fold the mascarpone cheese into the whipped cream.

I find that it works best to assemble the pavlova right before serving. Spread about ½ cup of the whipped cream mixture on the first and second meringue and gently place one on top of the other. Set the third meringue on top and add the remaining whipped cream mixture. Pile it high with the remaining fresh raspberries and pour the raspberry "sauce" over the edges. Sprinkle the top with the chocolate and serve.

FOR SERVING

4 cups fresh raspberries

¼ cup water

4 ounces mascarpone cheese, at room temperature

3 tablespoons powdered sugar

2 cups cold heavy whipping cream

2 ounces dark chocolate, shaved or grated

NOTE: Humidity affects the result of a pavlova, and if you live in a humid climate, the outside may not be crisp to the touch.

Peanut butter will always be my first true love. I've tried to go the almond butter route, whipped up my own pecan butter (with vanilla—so good), eaten spoonfuls of macadamia nut butter, and even attempted pistachio butter. I always go back to peanut butter as my standby, my favorite.

That was, until I found cashew butter. Now, let me clarify: I don't love cashew butter the way I love peanut butter. For instance, a spoonful doesn't do the trick like it does with good old PB. But inside of treats like cookies, or even spread on toast, topped with chocolate chips, this stuff is freaking good. It almost tastes batter-like, sort of like it's been stuffed with vanilla beans when it really hasn't been.

Oh, and there's a whole other side to this story, which includes me telling you how Eddie is so obsessed with Rice Krispies treats that I don't even get my mixture to treat stage. I make it right in the pot and we eat it. Straight, with a spoon.

I guess that was a story, right?

1 Spray a 9x13-inch baking dish with nonstick spray.

2 Heat a large pot over medium heat and add the butter. Whisk continuously until the butter begins to brown and brown bits appear on the bottom of the pot. Reduce the heat to low and add the cashew butter and marshmallows. Stir with a heatproof spoon until the cashew butter and marshmallows have melted.

3 Turn off the heat and fold in the cereal. Stir until all of the cereal is coated, and then press the mixture into the baking dish. Let cool for 30 minutes before cutting into squares and serving.

brown rice krispies treats with cashew butter

MAKES one 9x13-inch pan
TIME: 15 minutes

4 tablespoons (½ stick) unsalted butter
¼ cup cashew butter
4 cups mini marshmallows
8 cups brown rice cereal

grilled plums with toasted thyme crumble

. . . .

SERVES 4 · TIME: 30 minutes

. . . .

4 plums, sliced in half and pitted

1 tablespoon extra-virgin olive oil

Pinch of salt

2 tablespoons unsalted butter

½ cup old-fashioned rolled oats

2 tablespoons light brown sugar

2 teaspoons chopped fresh thyme

This recipe qualifies me as the biggest hypocrite to ever live, since it's basically just . . . fruit. I know, I know! I whine all about how fruit isn't an appropriate dessert, wah wah wah. Then I want to tell you about a recipe.

Does it count when it's grilled? Sprinkled with crunchy crumble? When it's topped with ice cream?

Do you suppose we can let this one slide?

 Preheat the grill to high. Brush the cut side of each plum with the olive oil and sprinkle with the salt. Place them on a grill pan and cook until slightly caramelly, 2 to 3 minutes.

 Heat a medium skillet over medium-high heat. Add the butter, oats, and brown sugar and stir to coat. Cook for 5 minutes, tossing occasionally, until the oats begin to toast. Stir in the thyme and turn off the heat.

3 Arrange the plums cut side up on a plate and spoon the crumble into the center of the plums.

8

celebrations

(for times when calories don't count)

There's a reason you save the ***best for last.***

Even though I strive to provide a healthy balance of recipes on my blog, the ones that follow are what I'm most known for. I can share four baconless, fresh, high-protein, low-starch, low-fat, pescatarian recipes in a row and then one crazy cake, and boom. It's all people remember. THE CAKE.

I sort of love it.

This is entertaining food. This is the ***food you share.*** This is the food you make in times of comfort and celebrations. This is the food that I find tastes best with no substitutions. No yogurt for sour cream. No whole wheat flour for all-purpose. No applesauce for butter. These are what they are.

This is the food that is memorable.

These are recipes that remind me of both of those grandmothers that I was able to spend so much wonderful time with. These are recipes that remind me of every day of my ***childhood,*** spending time with those I love. These are the recipes that remind me of those first (super-challenging) five years of marriage, the recipes that remind me of today, and the recipes that I'm sure I'll be cooking in the next 20 years to come, if I am so fortunate.

The dishes I share here are my favorite versions of things. My favorite mac and cheese. My favorite cheeseburger. My favorite brownie. Desserts that get talked about for ages. It's safe to say that coming up with what exactly I would share here was my favorite part of this entire book. Keeping it to only ***20 recipes*** was by far the most difficult thing ever. It was also the most rewarding in terms of recipe development, and also the most . . . um . . . indulgent. It is what it is, and I hope you love it.

And seriously! You know calories don't count with friends (or on weekends). Yes yes.

I love a good burger. I think everyone loves a good burger.

This burger isn't super-special or unique—after all, bacon and blue cheese is a common combo these days. But with fresh arugula and jalapeño jam? Ugh. So delish.

This quick jalapeño jam takes just a few minutes but makes every flavor pop. I was inspired to attempt such a recipe after having a soft pretzel dipped in sweet jalapeño jam at a Ritz-Carlton bar one night with my husband. We literally fought over the last bite.

While apart these flavors may seem simple, together they create an explosion in your mouth. I don't even care how overused the expression is. It's so true.

1 For the jam, combine the jalapeño peppers, water, brown sugar, vinegar, and honey in a small saucepan over medium heat and stir. Bring the mixture to a boil, then reduce the heat to a simmer and cook until it becomes slightly syrupy and reduces by one-quarter, 8 to 10 minutes. Remove the pan from the heat and set aside to cool completely.

2 For the burgers, combine the beef, 1 tablespoon of the olive oil, salt, and pepper in a large bowl. Mix gently with your hands and form it into 4 equal patties. Let the burgers sit at room temperature for about 20 minutes.

3 Heat a large skillet over low to medium heat. Add the bacon slices and fry until crispy and the fat is rendered, about 5 minutes per side. Remove the bacon and place on a paper towel to drain. Pour all but 2 tablespoons of the bacon grease out of the skillet.

4 Heat the same skillet over medium-high heat and add the burger patties. Cook until browned on each side and your desired doneness is reached. For burgers done medium-well, I usually cook them for about 6 minutes per side.

5 About 1 minute before the burgers are finished, add the blue cheese on top and cover the skillet. Cook until the cheese just begins to melt, 1 to 2 minutes. Toss the arugula with the remaining 1½ teaspoons olive oil.

6 Spread the jalapeño jam on the bottom of each bun. Add the burger and place the bacon and arugula on top, followed by the top of the bun.

bacon-blue burgers
with arugula & quick jalapeño jam

SERVES 4 · TIME: 40 minutes

QUICK JALAPEÑO JAM

4 jalapeño chile peppers, seeded and finely diced

⅓ cup water

⅓ cup light brown sugar

1½ teaspoons apple cider vinegar

1 teaspoon honey

BURGERS

1 pound lean ground beef

1½ tablespoons extra-virgin olive oil

1 teaspoon salt

1 teaspoon freshly ground black pepper

FOR SERVING

8 slices thick-cut bacon

8 ounces blue cheese, sliced or crumbled

2 cups arugula

4 whole-grain buns, toasted

cinnamon sugared bacon

SERVES 4 · TIME: 45 minutes

1/4 cup loosely packed light brown sugar

1 teaspoon ground cinnamon

8 slices thick-cut bacon

Here we are, seven chapters later and back at the whole "Should bacon be sweet or savory?" debate. You know where I stand, so let's just talk about what you can do with these little slices of magic.

Obviously, serve them for breakfast. They make a surprising treat. Haven't you ever accidentally on purpose dipped your bacon in the maple syrup from your pancakes? It's similar.

Use them on a BLT with butter toasted brioche. Takes savory to a whole new level. I promise.

Toss them into your sweets: the cookies, the cupcakes, the brownies. The works.

Crush them and dump into a bowl of popcorn. Now we're talking.

Or just eat them. Plain. In your kitchen. While you rock out to some Taylor Dayne.

1 Preheat the oven to 375°F. Line a baking sheet with aluminum foil and place a nonstick wire rack on top. Spray the rack with nonstick spray.

2 Combine the brown sugar and cinnamon on a plate and stir to combine. Dredge each slice of bacon through the sugar and press gently so the sugar sticks. Lay the bacon slices on the wire rack. Bake the bacon for 30 to 35 minutes, flipping it once during the cooking time.

3 Remove the pan from the oven and place the bacon on a plate. Let cool slightly before serving.

This soup has one purpose: It's a vehicle for bread dipping. Crusty, golden, buttered bread dipping. It's practically like eating delicious gravy.

In a good way. I swear.

This soup is so decadent that it makes for an excellent appetizer or starter to a big salad. It's also super-cute served as shooters for a party.

Or for yourself. Made when you need some lovin'. You're worth it.

1 Heat the butter and olive oil over medium heat in a large stockpot. Once hot, add the onions, thyme, salt, and pepper and stir. Cook, stirring, until the onions are softened, 10 minutes. Stir in the garlic and chopped mushrooms. Cook until the mushrooms are tender, another 10 minutes. Stir in the flour and cook for 1 to 2 minutes. Add the wine and stock and bring the mixture to a boil, stirring as it cooks and slightly thickens. Reduce the heat to a simmer and cook for 10 minutes.

2 Stir in the cream and Parmesan and cook for 10 more minutes. Taste the soup and season it additionally with salt and pepper if desired. Serve topped with the chopped herbs and lots of bread on the side for dipping.

cream of mushroom soup

SERVES 4 to 6 • TIME: 45 minutes

4 tablespoons (½ stick) unsalted butter

2 tablespoons extra-virgin olive oil

1 sweet onion, diced

1 teaspoon dried thyme

½ teaspoon salt

½ teaspoon freshly ground black pepper

4 garlic cloves, minced

8 ounces portobello mushrooms, chopped

8 ounces shitake mushrooms, stems removed and chopped

2 tablespoons all-purpose flour

½ cup dry white wine

2½ cups low-sodium chicken or vegetable stock

2 cups heavy cream

2 tablespoons freshly grated Parmesan cheese

2 tablespoons chopped fresh herbs of your choice

obsessed-with-cheese mac & cheese

SERVES 4 to 6 • TIME: 75 minutes

1 pound elbow noodles

4 tablespoons (½ stick) unsalted butter

2 garlic cloves, minced

¼ cup all-purpose flour

2 cups whole milk

⅓ cup mascarpone cheese

8 ounces Gruyère cheese, freshly grated

8 ounces sharp cheddar cheese, freshly grated

8 ounces Fontina cheese, freshly grated

2 ounces Parmesan cheese, freshly grated

½ teaspoon freshly ground black pepper

¼ teaspoon salt

¼ teaspoon ground nutmeg

⅓ cup panko bread crumbs

2 slices thick-cut bacon, cooked and crumbled

Mother Lovett made THE BEST mac and cheese. Truly— the best.

It was consistently creamy. Her patience was astounding as she stood over the stove and stirred her cream sauce for close to 30 minutes. People think risotto is challenging? Ha! They never tried to make macaroni and cheese with Mother Lovett.

In true grandma fashion, she didn't measure a darn thing. You know, she also made the best pies ever and didn't measure a thing with those either.

I did not get the pie gene. I apologize.

Luckily, I did get the mac and cheese gene. Thank GOODNESS.

1 Preheat the oven to 375°F. Spray a 9x13-inch baking dish with nonstick spray.

2 Bring a large pot of salted water to a boil and prepare the pasta according to the directions, shaving 1 to 2 minutes off the cooking time. Drain the pasta once it's finished and set aside.

3 For the cheese sauce, heat the butter in a saucepan over medium heat. Once it is sizzling, add the garlic and cook for 15 seconds, then whisk in the flour to create a roux. Stir the roux until it is golden in color and fragrant, 1 to 2 minutes. Pour the milk in slowly and stir constantly until the liquid is slightly thickened, another 5 minutes. Reduce the heat to low and add the mascarpone, Gruyère, 6 ounces of the cheddar, 6 ounces of the Fontina, and the Parmesan cheese. Stir the sauce constantly with a heatproof spatula until the cheese is melted, then add the pepper, salt, and nutmeg. Stir to combine.

4 Add the pasta to the baking dish and pour the cheese sauce over the top. Mix to combine and disperse the sauce throughout the noodles. Cover the top with the remaining cheddar and Fontina cheeses, the bread crumbs, and bacon. Bake until golden and bubbly on top, 30 minutes.

chocolate & peanut butter lover's brownies

SERVES 10 to 12 · TIME: 1½ hours

BROWNIES

12 tablespoons (1½ sticks) unsalted butter, cut into pieces

3½ ounces semisweet chocolate, chopped

¾ cup all-purpose flour

⅔ cup unsweetened cocoa powder

1 teaspoon baking soda

½ teaspoon baking powder

½ teaspoon salt

1½ cups granulated sugar

2 large eggs plus 1 egg yolk, lightly beaten

2 teaspoons vanilla extract

⅔ cup chocolate chips

PEANUT BUTTER FILLING

1 cup creamy peanut butter, melted

½ cup powdered sugar

1 tablespoon coconut oil

I'm pretty sure we've been over this. Chocolate and peanut butter—is there any better combo?

I don't think so.

These are the brownies you make when your best friend breaks up with her boyfriend. When you don't get the job you want. When you studied your ass off for a test and it's finally over.

When you finish writing a book for your invisible Internet friends! You get it.

When it's Saturday. That's when you make these brownies.

1 Preheat the oven to 350°F. Spray a 9x13-inch baking dish with nonstick spray.

2 For the brownies, add the butter and chopped chocolate to a microwave-safe bowl and microwave until melted, 30 to 60 seconds. Once the chocolate is semi-melted, stir constantly to melt the rest. Set aside and allow the mixture to cool for 5 minutes.

3 In a small bowl, whisk together the flour, cocoa powder, baking soda, baking powder, and salt.

4 In a large bowl, whisk together the melted butter-chocolate mixture and granulated sugar. Whisk in the eggs, egg yolk, and vanilla extract, stirring until a smooth batter forms. With a large spoon, mix in the dry ingredients until combined. Stir in the chocolate chips. Add the batter to the baking dish. Bake until the brownies are set and no longer jiggly in the middle, 25 to 30 minutes. Remove from the oven and let them cool for 30 minutes.

5 For the peanut butter filling, stir together the melted peanut butter, powdered sugar, and coconut oil until smooth. The peanut butter will be warm and melt the coconut oil, so stir until melted. Pour the filling over the brownies, using a spatula to spread it around the top. Let cool completely and firm up, 20 minutes.

6 For the ganache, add the chocolate to a large bowl. Heat the cream in a small saucepan over medium heat just until it bubbles around the edges. Remove the cream from the heat and pour it over the chocolate. Let the mixture stand for 30 seconds, then stir continuously until the chocolate melts and a smooth ganache comes together, 1 to 2 minutes. Pour it all over the top of the brownies, then cover it with the chopped peanut butter cups. Let the brownies sit for 30 minutes before cutting.

7 The brownies will stay fresh for 2 to 3 days at room temperature if covered with a layer of plastic wrap and aluminum foil. I like to keep mine in the fridge—they keep a few days longer.

GANACHE TOPPING
8 ounces milk chocolate, chopped
1/2 cup heavy cream
1 1/2 cups chopped peanut butter cups

slow cooker short rib breakfast hash

SERVES 4 • TIME: 8 hours

SHORT RIBS

2¹⁄₂ pounds beef short ribs

1 teaspoon salt

1 teaspoon freshly ground black pepper

¹⁄₂ teaspoon onion powder

¹⁄₄ teaspoon garlic powder

1 tablespoon canola oil

1 cup low-sodium beef stock (or beer!)

HASH

4 slices bacon, chopped

1 sweet yellow onion, diced

¹⁄₂ green bell pepper, diced

2 garlic cloves, minced

4 Yukon gold potatoes, chopped

¹⁄₄ teaspoon salt

¹⁄₄ teaspoon freshly ground black pepper

4 to 8 large eggs

¹⁄₄ teaspoon crushed red pepper flakes

1 tablespoon chopped fresh herbs (basil, parsley, oregano, or your choice)

Gab. Hello, beautiful.

Okay, okay. Short ribs may be anything but beautiful. This breakfast, though? Off the hook.

It's another one of those recipes that was inspired by brunch at a local restaurant and oh, man . . . short ribs for breakfast are worth the hype. It's sort of crazy because I've always only desired them in tacos. On a whim I ordered the breakfast hash one morning and was completely sold. Within seconds.

This is quite possibly one of the richest, most decadent savory breakfasts I've ever had. The poached eggs combined with the pulled short ribs—I don't even have words.

I really don't.

1 For the ribs, season the ribs with the salt, pepper, onion powder, and garlic powder. Heat a large skillet over high heat and add the oil. Add the ribs to the skillet and sear until golden on all sides, 1 to 2 minutes per side. Remove the ribs from the skillet and add them to a 7-quart slow cooker. Add the stock and cook the ribs on low for 8 hours, turning once or twice if you can. Once the ribs are finished, remove from the slow cooker and place them on a plate. Allow them to cool to the touch, then shred the beef and discard the bones and fat.

2 For the hash, heat a large skillet over medium heat and add the bacon. Cook until it's crispy and the fat has rendered, then remove the bacon with a slotted spoon and allow it to drain on a paper towel. Add the onions and peppers to the same skillet and toss to coat. Cook, stirring, until the onions begin to soften, 5 minutes. Add the garlic, potatoes, salt, and pepper and stir. Cover the skillet and cook until the potatoes are tender and slightly crispy, 10 minutes, tossing once or twice while cooking. Once the potatoes are tender, add the bacon and beef to the skillet and toss to mix. Turn the heat down to low and cover.

3 Cook the eggs to your liking and sprinkle them with the crushed red pepper flakes. To serve the hash, spoon the beef and potatoes onto a plate and add an egg on top. Garnish with a bit of chopped herbs.

Do you think we all just go nuts over sliders because they are tiny and so darn cute?

It's either that or the fact that since they are tiny and so darn cute, we can easily eat more than one without a problem. Yeah. It's probably that. Everyone knows that mini foods mean you get to eat more! It's a life law or something.

I love adding a cool mango slaw to pork because it gives it such a refreshing touch. It makes the sandwich seem a bit less heavy and more summery. It gives them some color. It makes them even cuter than they already are.

1 For the pork, heat a large skillet over high heat and add the oil. Once hot, place the pork roast in the skillet and sear it on all sides until it is golden brown, 2 minutes per side. Turn off the heat and add the pork to a 7-quart slow cooker. Cover it with the cumin, paprika, onion powder, chili powder, salt, and pepper. Pour the beer over the top. Cook the pork on low for 8 to 10 hours.

2 After 8 to 10 hours, take kitchen tongs or forks and shred the pork inside the cooker. It should just fall apart. Discard any bones. Completely shred the pork and mix it with any of the liquid in the crock. Place the lid back on the slow cooker and cook on low for 15 minutes. The pork should absorb some of the liquid.

3 For the slaw, add the mango, red onion, and cabbage together in a large bowl. Toss it with the lime juice, vinegar, olive oil, salt, and pepper. Taste the slaw and season it additionally if needed.

4 Assemble the sliders by spooning the pork onto the toasted buns with the slaw on top.

slow cooker beer pulled pork sliders with mango slaw

SERVES 6 · TIME: 8 to 10 hours

PORK

2 tablespoons canola oil

1 (4-pound) pork shoulder roast

1½ teaspoons ground cumin

1½ teaspoons smoked paprika

1½ teaspoons onion powder

1 teaspoon chili powder

1 teaspoon salt

1 teaspoon freshly ground black pepper

12 ounces of your favorite beer

SLAW

1 mango, peeled, pitted, and sliced

1 red onion, sliced

½ head green cabbage, sliced

Juice of 1 lime

2 teaspoons red wine vinegar

1 teaspoon extra-virgin olive oil

¼ teaspoon salt

¼ teaspoon freshly ground black pepper

FOR SERVING

8 to 12 slider buns, toasted

roasted vegetable queso frittata

SERVES 4 to 6 • TIME: 1 hour

VEGETABLES

½ red onion, diced

½ green bell pepper, chopped

½ red bell pepper, chopped

1 cup fresh or thawed frozen sweet corn kernels

1 cup broccoli florets, chopped

2 tablespoons extra-virgin olive oil

½ teaspoon salt

½ teaspoon freshly ground black pepper

8 ounces mushrooms, chopped

QUESO

⅔ cup heavy cream

12 ounces white cheddar cheese, freshly grated

FRITTATA

8 large eggs

2 garlic cloves, minced

2 tablespoons heavy cream

½ teaspoon salt

½ teaspoon freshly ground black pepper

Soooo, this frittata is the frittata that made me like frittatas. What a mouthful. Literally.

This frittata is stuffed with lots of vegetables (health food!) and—get this—queso cheese sauce. Uh-huh. Like the stuff you dip your chips in? I KNOW.

It's one heck of a breakfast and an even better dinner.

1 For the vegetables, preheat the oven to 450°F. Add the onions, peppers, corn, and broccoli to a large bowl and toss them with 1½ tablespoons of the olive oil, the salt, and pepper. Add the mushrooms to another bowl and toss with the remaining olive oil. Add all of the vegetables to a nonstick baking sheet. Roast for 20 to 25 minutes, tossing once during the cooking time.

2 While the vegetables are roasting, make the queso. Heat the cream in a saucepan over medium heat until it bubbles along the edges. Add the cheese and stir constantly until it is all melted. Remove the pan from the heat and set aside. If the cheese firms up too much before you need to use it, simply warm it over low heat and stir until it becomes melty again.

3 For the frittata, add the eggs, garlic, cream, salt, and pepper to a large bowl and whisk. Add the vegetables to a 10-inch ovenproof skillet and mix them with a few spoonfuls of the queso sauce. Pour the eggs over the top of the vegetables and then spoon the remaining queso over the top. Bake the frittata until the eggs are set and the top is golden, 20 to 25 minutes. Let the frittata cool in the skillet for 10 minutes before slicing.

cheesy roasted cauliflower *dip*

SERVES 6 to 8 • TIME: 1½ hours

ROASTED CAULIFLOWER

1 head cauliflower, chopped into florets

2 tablespoons extra-virgin olive oil

1 teaspoon salt

1 teaspoon freshly ground black pepper

DIP

12 ounces cream cheese, at room temperature

8 ounces provolone cheese, freshly grated

8 ounces sharp cheddar cheese, freshly grated

¼ cup freshly grated Parmesan cheese

4 garlic cloves, minced

It was a fabulous day when I realized that roasting cauliflower made it edible. I mean, edible for me, of course.

I tried to do the mashed cauliflower. I really did.

I even tried the cauliflower pizza crust. I tried so hard.

The mashed cauliflower wasn't terrible, but the amount of cheese I threw in to enjoy it kind of . . . defeated the purpose. The cauliflower pizza crust just wasn't pizza crust.

I was so depressed.

So I did what every normal person does after realizing roasted cauliflower is enjoyable: Combined it with tons of cheese to make a delicious creamy dip.

See? I have totally branched out with vegetables. Things are good.

1 Preheat the oven to 400°F.

2 For the cauliflower, add the cauliflower to a nonstick baking sheet and toss it with the olive oil, salt, and pepper. Roast until the cauliflower is golden, about 30 minutes, tossing once during the cooking time. Remove and let the cauliflower slightly cool on the baking sheet.

3 While the cauliflower is roasting, in a large bowl, stir together the cream cheese, 6 ounces each of the provolone and cheddar, the Parmesan cheese, and the garlic. Fold the cauliflower into the cream cheese mixture. Scoop the dip into a round baking dish. Cover with the remaining provolone and cheddar cheeses.

4 Bake the dip until it's golden and bubbly on top, 30 to 35 minutes. Serve it with crackers, chips, or even veggies.

When it comes to me and s'mores, there is no love missing.

I am going to tell you something embarrassing. I think we all have an embarrassing snack or treat that we consume—a dessert that is sort of humiliating because of what it contains or what it takes to get there.

At one point in my life, I may have considered a spoonful of peanut butter dipped in a bag of chocolate chips semi-embarrassing, then I was like WHAT! Everyone does that. I'm so not alone.

But this—this snack I'm about to tell you about? Horrifying. I went through a period when I was so sincerely obsessed with s'mores that I would combine graham cracker crumbs and melted butter in a bowl. On top of that, I'd place some mini marshmallows or marshmallow Fluff— whatever I had on hand. Then on top of THAT would go some chocolate. Chocolate chips, chocolate bars, chocolate whatever.

Then I'd eat it with a spoon. Talk about desperation. Called it my white trash s'mores bowl.

I don't know what it is about s'mores, but I have been fanatical since childhood. I just love them so freaking much. I love every- and anything s'mores. I love all the recently trashed-up recipes with s'mores flavors. I live for them.

This is one. Helllllo, trashy shakes!

s'mores hot fudge shakes

SERVES 2 • TIME: 15 minutes

2 cups whole milk

2 cups vanilla ice cream

1/3 cup hot fudge

1/3 cup marshmallow crème

1/3 cup graham cracker crumbs, plus extra for garnish

Whipped cream, for serving

2 jumbo marshmallows

1 Add the milk, ice cream, hot fudge, marshmallow crème, and graham crumbs to a blender and puree until smooth. Pour the shake into two glasses and top with whipped cream. If desired, quickly toast the jumbo marshmallows under the broiler, over a burner on your gas stove, or with a kitchen torch. Place the marshmallows on top of the whipped cream and sprinkle the shakes with extra graham crumbs.

mocha-coconut *tiramisu*

SERVES 4 to 6 • TIME: 30 minutes
+ 8 hours refrigerating time

12 ounces mascarpone cheese, at room temperature

1/3 cup powdered sugar

1 teaspoon vanilla extract

1/2 teaspoon coconut extract

2 cans cold full-fat coconut milk (refrigerate them overnight)

1/3 cup cold espresso

1/4 cup coffee liqueur

1/4 cup coconut rum

1 (24-count) package ladyfingers

2 tablespoons unsweetened cocoa powder

1/2 cup unsweetened flaked coconut, toasted (see page 27)

2 ounces dark chocolate, shaved or grated

Oh my gosh.

I know, I know. You're most likely in one of two tiramisu camps. You either love it as a classic? Or you think it's overdone. SO '90s. So last year.

I'm changing that now.

Mocha and coconut is a flavor combo that I go nuts over. It started back in college when Starbucks first introduced a mocha-coconut Frappuccino, and I've never forgotten about it since.

This tiramisu is made with coconut rum and espresso, fresh coconut whipped cream, lots of chocolate, and tons of excitement. It gets better with age.

It's a crowd favorite. Promise.

1 Add the mascarpone cheese to the bowl of an electric mixer and beat on low speed until creamy. With the mixer on low speed, slowly add the powdered sugar and beat until combined. Add the vanilla and coconut extracts and mix until incorporated. Spoon the mascarpone into a bowl.

2 For the coconut whipped cream, remove the cans of coconut milk from the fridge and turn them upside down. Open the cans and drain out all of the liquid, setting it aside for another use. You will not need it for this recipe.

3 Scoop the thick coconut cream from the cans into the bowl of the electric mixer. Beat the cream on high speed until it is fluffy, thick, and stiff peaks form. It should be the consistency (or slightly thicker) of freshly whipped cream.

4 Slowly fold (do not stir) the mascarpone mixture into the coconut whipped cream until fully incorporated. This can take close to 5 minutes. Set the cream in the fridge for a few minutes until ready to use.

5 In a small bowl, combine the espresso, coffee liqueur, and coconut rum. Stir to combine.

6 Take a 9x9-inch baking dish and add the ladyfingers to the bottom in a single layer, covering the entire bottom. Use a pastry brush dipped in the coffee mixture to brush all sides of the ladyfingers until all are moist. Remove the whipped coconut cream from the fridge and spread a thick layer on top. Take as many ladyfingers as you used on the bottom and brush them with the coffee mixture, layering them one by one on the coconut whipped cream. Cover the ladyfingers with another thick layer of coconut cream. Cover the pan lightly with plastic wrap and refrigerate for at least 8 hours, or preferably overnight.

7. Before serving, remove the pan from the fridge. Sift the cocoa powder over the top of the cream. Add the toasted coconut and grated chocolate.

NOTE: You may have some extra whipped coconut cream depending on how thick you want your layers, and you'll most likely have extra ladyfingers. I always would like to have extra left over instead of running out while making the tiramisu, so with the leftovers, assemble single-portion tiramisu treats in small glasses. Or save the ladyfingers for something else and use the creamy mixture on ABSOLUTELY EVERYTHING for the next week.

pistachio cream cake with chocolate ganache

•••••••••••••••••••••••••••••

SERVES 8 • TIME: 1½ hours

•••••••••••••••••••••••••••••

CAKE

1⅓ cups unsalted pistachios

1⅓ cups cake flour

1⅓ cups all-purpose flour

3 teaspoons baking powder

½ teaspoon salt

1 cup (2 sticks) unsalted butter, at room temperature

1¼ cups granulated sugar

4 large eggs

2 teaspoons vanilla extract

1 cup whole milk

Because of my extreme lack of patience, layer cakes are not something I often bake. Instead of worrying about even layers and a frosting crumb coat, I'd rather just eat a darn cupcake and get it over with. Yes.

This is one exception.

I have an undying love for all things pistachio. Since you know most everything about me now, I will share a little secret: I really love the artificial pistachio flavors too. Like the cakes made with the pistachio pudding mix that turn a gorgeous color of minty green? Big heart.

This is my all-from-scratch version of that. It tastes incredibly . . . authentic. It is just to die for.

1 Preheat the oven to 350°F. Spray two 9-inch cake pans with nonstick spray. Cut a round sheet of parchment paper, place on the bottom of each pan, and spray once more with nonstick spray. Set them aside.

2 Add 1 cup of the pistachios to a food processor and pulse and blend until very small crumbs remain. Measure out ¼ cup of the crumbs and set them aside for the filling. Place the remaining crumbs in a bowl. In a large bowl, whisk together the flours, baking powder, and salt.

3 In the bowl of an electric mixer, beat the butter and sugar on high speed until fluffy, 3 to 4 minutes. Add the eggs one at a time, beating on medium speed after each addition. Add the vanilla extract and beat for 1 more minute. Add the pistachio crumbs, beating on medium speed until incorporated. With the mixer on low speed, gradually add in half of the dry ingredients. Add the milk, mixing until combined. Add the remaining dry ingredients and beat on medium speed until the batter comes together, scraping down the sides of the bowl if needed.

4 Scoop the batter equally into the greased and lined cake pans. Bake the cakes until the tops are golden brown and set, 25 to 30 minutes. Remove the pans from the oven and let the cakes cool for 20 minutes in the pans, then invert the pans and remove the cakes. Let them cool completely on a wire rack.

5 For the filling, beat the mascarpone and butter in the bowl of an electric mixer on high speed until creamy. Add the reserved crushed pistachios, beating until combined, then adjust the speed to low and gradually add the sugar. Add the milk and beat the filling for 1 to 2 minutes on high speed, scraping down the sides of the bowl if needed.

6 Place one of the cakes on a plate or stand. Spread the filling evenly over the top of the cake, then place the other cake on top of the filling.

7 For the ganache, add the chocolate to a large bowl. Heat the cream in a small saucepan over medium heat just until it bubbles around the edges. Remove the cream from the heat and pour it over the chocolate. Let the chocolate stand for 30 seconds, then stir continuously until the chocolate melts and a smooth ganache comes together, 1 to 2 minutes. Pour the ganache over the cake.

8 Chop the remaining ⅓ cup pistachios coarsely and sprinkle them over the cake.

9 This cake will stay fresh for 1 to 2 days if kept at room temperature and wrapped in plastic wrap or covered with a cake dome. I like to keep it in the fridge, where it will keep for an additional 2 to 3 days.

FILLING

⅔ cup mascarpone cheese, at room temperature

2 tablespoons unsalted butter

1½ cups granulated sugar

1½ teaspoons whole milk

GANACHE

8 ounces semisweet chocolate, chopped

½ cup heavy cream

fleur de sel caramel bourbon brownie milk shakes

A poem:
I like bourbon.
I like milk shakes.
I like bourbon milk shakes.
The end.

① Combine the milk, ice cream, bourbon, brownies, ½ cup of the caramel sauce, and salt in a blender and puree until smooth. Fill two glasses with ¼ cup of caramel each and pour the shakes into the glasses. Top the shakes with the whipped cream, an extra drizzle of caramel, and another pinch of salt. Crumble a brownie on top.

SERVES 2 · **TIME: 15 minutes**

2 cups whole milk

2 cups vanilla bean ice cream

½ cup bourbon

2 brownies, plus an extra for crumbling on top

1 cup caramel sauce, plus extra for drizzling

½ teaspoon fleur de sel (or flaked sea salt), plus extra for sprinkling

Whipped cream, for topping

buffalo chicken pizza

SERVES 2 to 4 • TIME: 1 hour

1 pound boneless, skinless chicken breasts, cut into cubes

1 teaspoon salt

1 teaspoon freshly ground black pepper

2 tablespoons extra-virgin olive oil

2 tablespoons unsalted butter

3/4 cup buffalo wing sauce, plus extra for drizzling

1 batch pizza dough (see page 172)

1/4 cup creamy blue cheese dressing

12 ounces Fontina cheese, freshly grated

8 ounces cheddar cheese, freshly grated

2 ounces blue cheese, crumbled

4 scallions, sliced

1/3 cup chopped fresh cilantro

1/4 cup chopped fresh chives

Eddie and I have a thing for anything done buffalo-style. I love things covered in wing sauce—actually, I love anything but wings covered in wing sauce. They can be too much work.

In early 2013, we went through a dual phase of buffalo chicken pizza love. I had made my own homemade version for years, but we found a local delivery pizza place and absolutely fell.in.love with their version. Oh my.

Buffalo chicken pizza at least once a week for six months. It happened. Delivery and homemade. We traded off.

After eating that delivery pizza we loved so much, I was able to improve it on my own. I find that this blend of cheeses, the herbs, the scallions, chives, and sauce are what make it. It is nowhere near as good if you try to lighten it up.

Oh, and as a side note, this pizza totally almost caught my house on fire when I photographed it. The entire thing fell onto the floor of my 450°F oven and I MANAGED TO SALVAGE IT.

Now that's dedication. Love.

1 Season the chicken with the salt and pepper. Heat a large skillet over medium-high heat and add the olive oil and butter. Add the chicken and cook until it's golden brown on all sides, 3 minutes per side. Add 1/4 cup of the buffalo wing sauce and stir. Turn off the heat and set the chicken aside.

2 Shape the pizza dough into a 15-inch round. Spread the blue cheese dressing on the pizza dough. Swirl on the remaining 1/2 cup wing sauce and cover the sauce with half of the Fontina cheese. Add the chicken mixture all over the top of the pizza. Cover the chicken with the remaining Fontina, the cheddar, and half of the blue cheese. Bake the pizza until the cheese is golden and bubbly, 30 to 35 minutes.

3 Once the pizza is finished baking, remove it from the oven and cover it with the remaining blue cheese. Drizzle extra wing sauce over the top and cover it with the scallions, cilantro, and chives. Let sit for 15 minutes before slicing.

grilled *gouda, bacon* & caramelized onion *grilled cheese* with a potato soup *dipper*

SERVES 2 • TIME: 1 hour

CARAMELIZED ONIONS

2 tablespoons extra-virgin olive oil

1 tablespoon unsalted butter

1 red onion, sliced

¼ teaspoon salt

1 tablespoon light brown sugar

Want to hear the best thing ever?

We have a local grilled cheese food truck. Yes, I said it. Grilled cheese truck, aka heaven.

Their stuff? Unreal.

They make a sandwich just like this. Since I've been a potato soup lover forever and ever, I had to do this at home. Now I always do this at home. Constantly.

Please try.

1 For the onions, heat a large skillet over low heat and add the olive oil and butter. Add the onions and salt and stir to coat. Cover and cook until the onions begin to caramelize, about 30 minutes, stirring every 5 minutes so they don't burn. Stir in the brown sugar and cook for another 10 minutes, stirring once or twice. Remove the onions from the heat.

2 While the onions are caramelizing, prepare the soup. Add the chopped potato to a microwave-safe bowl with a splash of water. Microwave until the cubes are tender, 2 to 3 minutes.

3 Heat a saucepan over medium heat and add the butter. Once it melts, add the flour and whisk constantly to create a roux. Cook the roux until it is slightly golden in color and bubbling, 2 to 3 minutes. Add the half-and-half and milk and stir continuously until the mixture thickens a bit, 5 to 6 minutes. Add the chopped potato and turn the heat down to low. Simmer until the potato breaks down, 10 to 15 minutes. Stir in the cheddar cheese. If the soup is too thick, add a few tablespoons of the chicken stock and stir. Season the soup with the salt and pepper and taste it. Season additionally if desired. Cover the soup and keep over low heat until the sandwiches are ready.

4 For the grilled cheese, heat a large skillet or griddle over medium-low heat. Spread the butter on the outsides of each of the bread slices. To assemble the sandwiches, add a handful of Gouda cheese on the first slice of bread, add half of the caramelized onions, 3 slices of bacon, and another handful of cheese. I always like to have cheese on both ends to act as "glue." Cook the sandwiches over medium-low heat until the bread is toasted and the cheese is melted, 5 minutes per side.

5 Garnish the potato soup with the scallions and use as a dip for the sandwiches.

SOUP DIPPER

1 medium russet potato, peeled and chopped

2 tablespoons unsalted butter

2 tablespoons all-purpose flour

1 cup half-and-half

1 cup whole milk

4 ounces white cheddar cheese, freshly grated

$\frac{1}{2}$ cup low-sodium chicken stock, or as needed

$\frac{1}{2}$ teaspoon salt

$\frac{1}{2}$ teaspoon freshly ground black pepper

2 tablespoons unsalted butter

4 slices bread of your choice

6 ounces Gouda cheese, freshly grated

6 slices cooked bacon

1 scallion, sliced

caramelized peach, dark chocolate & mascarpone grilled cheese

. . . .

SERVES 2 • TIME: 30 minutes

. . . .

4 tablespoons (½ stick) unsalted butter, at room temperature

2 peaches, sliced

¼ teaspoon salt

1 tablespoon light brown sugar

4 slices bread of your choice

⅓ cup mascarpone cheese

4 ounces 70% dark chocolate, broken into pieces

The only thing better than a traditional grilled cheese? A grilled cheese with chocolate. Obviously.

Is this dinner or dessert? I really have no idea. I want to say it's maybe even lunch—there is fruit and cheese, after all. And chocolate comes from a bean, right? Especially the bittersweet stuff. Like it's almost a vegetable.

Okay, it's official: It's dessert for dinner.

1 Heat a large skillet over medium-low heat and add 1 tablespoon of the butter. Add the peach slices and salt and stir to coat. Cook until the peaches begin to soften and turn golden, 5 to 6 minutes. Add the brown sugar to the peaches and stir. Cook until the peaches become caramelly, 2 to 3 minutes. Turn off the heat and spoon the peaches into a bowl.

2 Butter the outside of each of the bread slices with 2 tablespoons of the butter. Spread a little more than 1 tablespoon of mascarpone cheese on the inside of each slice of bread. Melt the remaining 1 tablespoon butter in the same skillet over medium heat. Assemble each grilled cheese by adding 2 ounces of the chocolate and half of the peaches on top of the mascarpone spread on 2 slices. Top with the remaining slices of bread. Cook the sandwiches until the bread is golden brown and the cheese is melty, 5 minutes per side.

coffee & doughnuts ice cream

. . . .

MAKES about 1 quart · TIME: 8 hours

. . . .

I'm about to tell you to go buy half a dozen doughnuts. And don't eat them.

Well, okay—maybe you can eat one.

But then? You're going to stuff the rest into ice cream.

Coffee ice cream, to be exact.

I have always had a giant coffee ice cream fetish. Even back in the day when I hated coffee. But now that I like coffee, coffee ice cream just seems so lonely without . . . doughnuts.

Is this allowed?

2¹/₂ cups heavy cream

1¹/₂ cups whole milk

²/₃ cup loosely packed light brown sugar

¹/₂ teaspoon salt

²/₃ cup freshly ground dark roast coffee

2 or 3 of your favorite cake doughnuts

1 Heat the cream, milk, brown sugar, and salt over medium heat in a large saucepan. Whisk constantly until the sugar dissolves and then cook until the edges begin to bubble and the milk is hot, 6 to 8 minutes. Remove the pan from the heat and stir in the ground coffee. Let the mixture sit at room temperature for 1 hour.

2 Strain the milk through cheesecloth or a very fine-mesh sieve into a bowl. Discard the coffee grinds and place the bowl in the fridge until it's cold, at least 30 minutes.

3 Once the mixture is cold, add it to your ice cream machine and churn according to the directions. In the last few minutes of churning, crumble in 1 or 2 of the doughnuts. Place the ice cream in a freezer-safe container and add pieces of another doughnut into the top of the ice cream, if desired. Freeze for at least 6 hours before serving.

confetti cupcakes

MAKES 12 cupcakes · TIME: 1½ hours

- 1½ cups cake flour
- 1 teaspoon baking powder
- ¼ teaspoon salt
- 8 tablespoons (1 stick) unsalted butter, at room temperature
- 1 cup granulated sugar
- 1 large egg plus 1 egg white
- 2 tablespoons vegetable oil
- 3 teaspoons vanilla extract
- ½ cup whole milk
- ⅓ cup assorted brightly colored sprinkles

I am not a hater of boxed cake mix. In fact, even Mother Lovett, the baker of the century, used a cake mix here and there. She "doctored them up," as my mom likes to say, but yes . . . she used them.

While I don't despise them, I also don't always use them. I like making my own. I like being in control. If you haven't figured it out already, I am one giant walking control freak. Huge.

There has always been one exception: confetti cupcakes. They always . . . ha-ha . . . take the cake. For real.

Oh and PS: I wish my daily life looked like this. All sprinkles, all the time.

1 Preheat the oven to 350°F. Line a cupcake tin with cupcake liners.

2 In a small bowl, whisk together the flour, baking powder, and salt.

3 Add the butter to the bowl of an electric mixer and beat it until creamy. Add the sugar and beat with the butter on high speed until fluffy, 2 to 3 minutes. Add the egg and egg white, mixing well on medium speed until combined. Scrape down the sides of the bowl if needed. Add the oil and vanilla extract, beating on medium speed for another minute. With the mixer on low speed, add half of the dry ingredients and blend. Pour in the milk and blend. Add the other half of the dry ingredients and mix on medium speed until the batter is combined. Use a large spatula to gently stir in the sprinkles.

4 Fill the cupcake liners two-thirds full. Bake until the tops are set, 18 to 20 minutes. Let cool completely before frosting.

VANILLA CREAM FROSTING

- 8 tablespoons (1 stick) unsalted butter, at room temperature
- 8 ounces cream cheese, at room temperature
- 2½ cups powdered sugar
- 1 tablespoon vanilla extract
- 1 tablespoon whole milk, or as needed
- ¼ cup assorted brightly colored sprinkles

 Add the butter and cream cheese to the bowl of an electric mixer and beat on high speed until creamy and combined. With the mixer on low speed, slowly add the powdered sugar. Beat until the sugar is incorporated, and then add the vanilla extract. Scrape down the sides of the bowl if needed. Beat the frosting on high speed for 2 to 3 minutes, until fluffy and creamy. If the frosting seems too thick, beat in the milk for 1 to 2 minutes, until combined. Frost the cupcakes and top them with the sprinkles.

This is straight outta my mom's kitchen.

It's all her.

If I had to pick a favorite chicken dish, other than the ever-so-predictable pizza and tacos, this would be it. This was one of the very first recipes I ever shared on my blog, and while I've made a few improvements, it's been a huge favorite.

This is a propose-to-me type of meal. I'm serious. It's happened.

1 Preheat the oven to 350°F. Season the chicken with the salt and pepper.

2 Set up an assembly line of three bowls. Add the flour, parsley, and garlic powder to one bowl. Add the eggs and milk to the next and beat them slightly. Add the cheese to the last bowl.

3 Heat a large ovenproof skillet over medium-high heat. Add the canola oil. Dredge a piece of chicken through the flour, coating it completely. Add it to the egg, coating it once more. Finally, add it to the cheese and press so the cheese adheres to the chicken. Add the chicken to the skillet, and repeat with remaining chicken breasts. Cook each breast until it is golden on each side, about 5 minutes per side. Be gentle when flipping the chicken so you don't lose the breading. Once the chicken is browned, add the wine to the skillet and turn off the heat. Add the chicken stock and the juice of 1 lemon. Cut the other lemon into wedges and place them in the skillet. Add the butter pieces to the skillet.

4 Cover the skillet and bake the chicken for 20 to 25 minutes. Remove the chicken from the oven and sprinkle on the chopped parsley. Let cool for 5 minutes before serving.

NOTE: This is commonly served with pasta, but we love it with salads, rice, or even potatoes. It's up to you!

lemon–
herb
chicken
romano

SERVES 2 to 4 • TIME: 1 hour

4 boneless, skinless chicken breasts

1 teaspoon salt

1 teaspoon freshly ground black pepper

1 cup all-purpose flour

2 teaspoons dried parsley

1 teaspoon garlic powder

4 large eggs

1 tablespoon whole milk

1 cup freshly grated romano cheese

2 tablespoons canola oil

1/2 cup dry white wine

1/3 cup light-sodium chicken stock

2 lemons

4 tablespoons (1/2 stick) unsalted butter, cut into pieces

1/4 cup chopped fresh parsley

cheesy polenta with garlic butter mushrooms

. . . .

SERVES 4 · TIME: 45 minutes

. . . .

4 cups low-sodium chicken stock, plus extra if needed

3/4 cup coarsely ground cornmeal

2 tablespoons unsalted butter

2 tablespoons mascarpone cheese

4 ounces Fontina cheese, freshly grated

4 ounces Pecorino Romano cheese, freshly grated, plus extra for topping (optional)

1/4 teaspoon salt

1/4 teaspoon freshly ground black pepper

MUSHROOMS

4 tablespoons (1/2 stick) unsalted butter

2 tablespoons extra-virgin olive oil

4 garlic cloves, minced

1 pound cremini mushrooms, sliced

1/4 teaspoon salt

1/4 teaspoon freshly ground black pepper

This is what I eat when my man is out of town and I feel like indulging. It is cheesy, buttery, garlicky, and insanely worth it.

1 Bring the chicken stock to a boil in a large saucepan. Once boiling, slowly pour in the cornmeal while constantly whisking. Turn the heat down to medium-low and continue to stir until the mixture thickens. Once the mixture has come together and the cornmeal is thoroughly combined, reduce the heat to low and cover. Cook the mixture until the polenta is creamy and resembles the consistency of oatmeal, stirring occasionally, for about 15 to 20 minutes. If at any time the polenta looks parched, dry, or too thick, add some extra chicken stock 1/4 cup at a time. After 30 minutes, stir in the butter, cheeses, salt, and pepper.

2 While the polenta is cooking, make the mushrooms. Heat a large skillet over low heat. Add the butter and olive oil and, once melted, add the garlic and mushrooms. Cover and cook until the mushrooms are softened and juicy, 15 to 20 minutes, stirring every few minutes. Turn off the heat, add the salt and pepper, cover the mushrooms again, and let them sit until ready to serve.

3 When ready to eat, spoon the polenta into bowls and cover liberally with the mushrooms. Add extra Parmesan on top if desired.

Index

Page numbers in *italics* indicate photos